Drug War Mexico

About the Authors

Peter Watt is Lecturer in Hispanic Studies at the University of Sheffield. His research field covers Latin American politics and history, with a particular focus on issues of human rights, political repression, narcotrafficking, freedom of expression and censorship in Mexico.

Roberto Zepeda holds a PhD in politics from the University of Sheffield and is currently working as a lecturer and academic researcher in Mexico. His research focuses primarily on neoliberalism, globalisation, trade unions, Mexican economic policies since 1982 and the political economy of narcotrafficking

Drug War Mexico

Politics, Neoliberalism and Violence
in the New Narcoeconomy

PETER WATT AND ROBERTO ZEPEDA

Zed Books
London & New York

Drug War Mexico: Politics, Neoliberalism and Violence in the New Narcoeconomy was first published in 2012 by Zed Books Ltd, 7 Cynthia Street, London N1 9JF, UK and Room 400, 175 Fifth Avenue, New York, NY 10010, USA

www.zedbooks.co.uk

Designed and set in Warnock Pro and Arial Black by Kate Kirkwood
Index by John Barker
Cover design: www.thisistransmission.com
Printed and bound by CPI Group (UK) Ltd, Croydon, CR0 4YY

Distributed in the USA exclusively by Palgrave Macmillan, a division of St Martin's Press, LLC, 175 Fifth Avenue, New York, NY 10010, USA

A catalogue record for this book is available from the British Library
Library of Congress Cataloging in Publication Data available

ISBN 978 1 84813 887 2 hb
ISBN 978 1 84813 886 5 pb

Contents

Figures and Tables

Abbreviations

AFI	Agencia Federal de Investigación (Federal Agency of Investigation)
ALBA	Alianza Bolivariana para los Pueblos de Nuestra América (Bolivarian Alliance for the Americas)
AMLO	Andrés Manuel López Obrador
ATF	Bureau of Alcohol, Tobacco, Firearms and Explosives
Banamex	Banco Nacional de México (National Bank of Mexico)
BBC	British Broadcasting Corporation
BP	British Petroleum
CANADOR	Combate Contra el Narcotráfico (Operación CANADOR later became Operation Condor)
CENCOS	El Centro Nacional de Comunicación Social AC
CEPAL	Comisión Económica para América Latina (Economic Commission for Latin America)
CIA	Central Intelligence Agency
CISEN	Centro de Investigación y Seguridad Nacional (National Security and Investigation Centre)
CNDH	Comisión Nacional de Derechos Humanos (National Human Rights Commission)
CNN	Cable News Network
CONAPO	Consejo Nacional de Población (Mexican National Population Council)
CONASUPO	La Compañía Nacional de Subsistencias Populares (National Company of Popular Subsistence)
CONEVAL	Consejo Nacional de Evaluación (National Evaluation Council)
DEA	Drug Enforcement Administration
DFS	Dirección Federal de Seguridad (National Security Directorate)

DIA	Defense Intelligence Agency
DIPS	Dirección de Investigaciones Políticas y Sociales (Office of Political and Social Investigations)
EAP	Economically Active Population
ENA	Encuesta Nacional de Adicciones (Survey of drug addicts carried out by the Mexican Department of Health)
ENIGH	Encuesta Nacional de Ingresos y Gastos de los Hogares (National Survey of Household Income and Expenditure)
EZLN	Ejército Zapatista de Liberación Nacional (Zapatista Army of National Liberation)
FAR	Fuerzas Armadas Revolucionarias (Revolutionary Armed Forces)
FARC	Fuerzas Armadas Revolucionarias de Colombia (Revolutionary Armed Forces of Colombia)
FBI	Federal Bureau of Investigation
FDI	foreign direct investment
FEADS	Fiscalía Especializada en Atención de Delitos contra la Salud (federal agency responsible for investigating organised crime organisations and corruption)
FMLN	Frente Farabundo Martí para la Liberación Nacional (Farabundo Martí National Liberation Front)
FOBAPROA	Fondo Bancario de Protección al Ahorro (Banking Fund for the Protection of Savings)
FSLN	Frente Sandinista de Liberación Nacional (Sandinista National Liberation Front)
GAFE	Grupo Aeromóvil de Fuerzas Especiales (Special Forces Airmobile Group)
GATT	General Agreement on Tariffs and Trade
GDP	gross domestic product
GIMSA	Grupo Industrial Maseca S.A.B.
HSBC	Hongkong Shanghai Banking Corporation
IACoHR	Inter-American Court of Human Rights
IDB	Inter-American Development Bank

IEPES	Instituto de Estudios Políticos, Económicos y Sociales (Institute of Political, Economic and Social Studies)
IFE	Instituto Federal Electoral (Federal Electoral Institute)
IMF	International Monetary Fund
INAH	National Institute of Archaeology and History
INEGI	Instituto Nacional de Estadística y Geografía (National Institute of Statistics and Geography)
INS	Immigration and Naturalisation Service
INSP	Instituto Nacional de Salud Pública (National Institute for Public Health)
ISI	import substitution industrialisation
LIMAC	Libertad de Información México AC (NGO for Freedom of Information)
LITEMPO	Code-name of secret CIA spy network in Mexico
Mercosur	Mercado Común del Sur (Common Market of the South)
NAFTA	North American Free Trade Agreement
NDIC	National Drug Intelligence Center
NGO	non-governmental organisation
NIDA	National Institute on Drug Abuse
OAS	Organization of American States
OECD	Organisation for Economic Co-operation and Development
PAN	Partido Acción Nacional (National Action Party)
PDLP	Partido de los Pobres (Party of the Poor)
PEMEX	Petróleos Mexicanos (Mexican state-owned petroleum company)
PFM	Policía Federal Ministerial (Federal Ministerial Police)
PFP	Policía Federal Preventiva (Federal Preventive Police)
PGR	Procuraduría General de la República (Attorney General's Office)
PJF	Policía Federal Judicial (Federal Judicial Police)
PLO	Palestine Liberation Organisation
PRD	Partido de la Revolución Democrática (Party of the Democratic Revolution)

PRI	Partido Revolucionario Institucional (Institutional Revolutionary Party)
SEDENA	Secretaría de la Defensa Nacional (Department of National Defence)
SEMAR	Secretaría de la Marina (Department of the Navy)
SHCP	Secretaría de Hacienda y Crédito Público (Department of Finance and Public Credit)
SIEDO	Subprocuraduría de Investigación Especializada en Delincuencia Organizada (Assistant Attorney General's Office for Special Investigations on Organised Crime)
SPP	Security and Prosperity Partnership
SS	Secretaría de Salud (Department of Health)
SSP	Secretaría de Seguridad Pública (Department of Public Security)
STFRM	Sindicato de Trabajadores Ferrocarrileros de la República Mexicana (Mexican Railway Workers Union)
STPS	Secretaría del Trabajo y Previsión Social (Department of Work and Social Security)
TAESA	Transportes Aéreos Ejecutivos (airline operating executive planes)
UNAM	Universidad Nacional Autónoma de México (National Autonomous University of Mexico)
UNCTAD	United Nations Conference on Trade and Development
UNDP	United Nations Development Programme
WACL	World Anti-Communist League
WTO	World Trade Organization

Acknowledgements

Peter Watt wishes to thank Richard and Julie Watt for their invaluable criticism, help and encouragement in the preparation of this manuscript. He would also like to thank Sophie, Isla, Leo and Hugo, for their infinite love and kindness. Thanks also to Professor Phil Swanson for his unfaltering encouragement and friendship. Finally, he owes immense gratitude to Brigid Frömmel and to Eileen Bradley, both of whom died too young and to whom he dedicates this book.

Roberto Zepeda would like to thank Luis Astorga for his crucial insights into the nature of narcotrafficking in Mexico. Thanks also to Steve Ludlam for his insights, comments and suggestions, all of which were indispensable. He is indebted to Pascale Baker for having taken valuable time out from writing her PhD to read and comment on parts of the manuscript and to John Smith and Amelia Moore for reading and suggesting changes to sections of this book.

Both authors wish to thank Ken Barlow, editor at Zed Books, who carefully read the manuscript and provided important feedback.

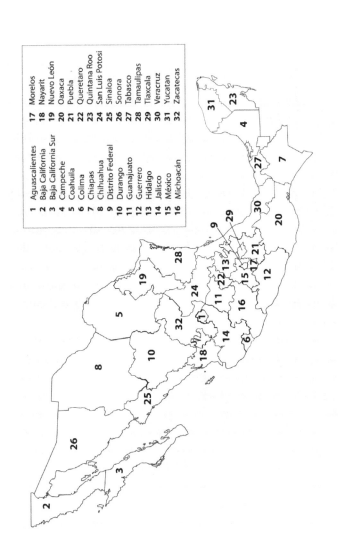

1	Aguascalientes	17	Morelos
2	Baja California	18	Nayarit
3	Baja California Sur	19	Nuevo León
4	Campeche	20	Oaxaca
5	Coahuila	21	Puebla
6	Colima	22	Queretaro
7	Chiapas	23	Quintana Roo
8	Chihuahua	24	San Luis Potosi
9	Distrito Federal	25	Sinaloa
10	Durango	26	Sonora
11	Guanajuato	27	Tabasco
12	Guerrero	28	Tamaulipas
13	Hidalgo	29	Tlaxcala
14	Jalisco	30	Veracruz
15	México	31	Yucatan
16	Michoacán	32	Zacatecas

The states of Mexico

Introduction

In May 2011 a caravan of protesters made its way north through twelve states and across 3,000 kilometres from Cuernavaca to Ciudad Juárez, now reputed to be the most violent city on the planet. The caravan, which attracted thousands of supporters everywhere it stopped, had as its principal slogans *'Estamos hasta la madre!'* (We have had it!) and *'No más sangre!'* (No more blood!). These banners voiced public despair at the horrendous escalation of violence throughout Mexico during the presidency of Felipe Calderón (2006–12) following a crackdown on organised crime directed by the Department of Public Security (SSP), led by Genaro García Luna, and the Secretary of the Interior, Francisco Blake Mora (killed in a helicopter crash in November 2011). The protesters denounced the government's counternarcotics programme, a principal factor in creating the climate of instability that has left many sectors of the population feeling helplessly vulnerable to violence perpetrated by drug cartels, the army and the police. This popular outcry defined a pivotal moment. It demonstrated the widespread belief that the government itself, and not just organised crime, was directly responsible for the carnage endured in places like Culiacán, Tamaulipas, Ciudad Juárez and Tijuana. It became a form of resistance to the intimidatory tactics of criminal gangs, while at the same time revealing the fundamental and counterproductive illegitimacy of the government's strategy.

The protest movement was led by the poet, Javier Sicilia, whose son, Juan Francisco Sicilia Ortega, had been brutally murdered along with six other young men by members of a drug cartel in Cuernavaca in March 2011. Sicilia's movement attracted enormous attention despite the climate of fear and terror which pervades those areas of Mexico where organised crime has effectively challenged the authority of the state. Sicilia declared he would stop writing poetry and instead dedicate his energies to creating a movement to oppose the apparently irrational cruelty of organised crime and of the institutions supposed to counter it. 'The world is no longer worthy of the word,' he wrote in his last poem, 'poetry no longer exists in me.'

A huge increase in violence attributable to the war on narcotrafficking and organised crime has become one of the most alarming developments in Mexico in recent years. According to statistics compiled by the national newspaper *Reforma*, 39,274 people have been killed in narcotrafficking-related incidents since Felipe Calderón assumed the presidency in 2006. Other statistics place the death toll much higher (around 60,000), taking into consideration the thousands of 'disappeared' and the sinister and numerous discoveries of *narco-fosas*, or 'mass narco-graves' (Zeta 2011). As we write, in December 2011, these figures are increasing rapidly and show no sign of a slowdown. The gruesome picture emerging from the bare statistics is at startling variance with the rhetoric that surrounded Mexico's political transition to democracy little over a decade ago.

After only ten days in office, President Calderón increased the deployment of troops and police on the streets to almost 50,000 – more, even, than the British government sent to invade and occupy Iraq. That the war became the defining feature of the Calderón presidency, and was launched immediately after he was sworn in, had the effect of drawing attention away from the highly controversial 2006 election, where it appeared there had been a fraudulent count to prevent centre-left candidate Andrés Manuel López Obrador of the Party of the Democratic Revolution (PRD) from winning. Similar dubious practices had occurred in the 1988 elections, when it appeared that the left-of-centre candidate of the National Democratic Front (Frente Democrático Nacional), Cuathémoc Cárdenas, was set to oust the Institutional

Revolutionary Party (PRI – Partido Revolucionario Institucional) from the presidency for the first time since its founding in the wake of the Mexican Revolution. In 2006, the memory of fraudulent elections was still vivid and mass protests demanding a recount were organised in Mexico City's central square, or *zócalo*. Even before Calderón assumed power in December, there had been huge displays of popular activism challenging the legitimacy of the new government and demanding greater democratic participation. The National Action Party (PAN – Partido Acción Nacional), after winning the 2000 elections, had introduced what many believed would be a democratic transition in Mexico after seventy years of PRI rule. But by 2006, it was clear that the PAN had not delivered the changes it had promised. On the contrary, it had extended the Mexican state's commitment to neoliberal economic policies, furthered the rights of foreign investors and increased Mexico's integration with and subordination to the US economy. Rather than deal with the grievances of millions of Mexicans by attempting to redress the severe economic inequalities that neoliberalism had exacerbated, the strategy of the new regime was to deflect attention from social injustices by waging a seemingly endless war within its own borders.

◆

It is not within the scope of this book to analyse trends in the scale of the export of narcotics from Mexico to the United States. Statistics on drug trafficking are by nature fickle, given the clandestine and extra-statal environment in which the industry is forced to operate, and we do not pretend to offer far-reaching insights into a topic that deserves a separate study. Instead, we focus on the development of the industry and look at the political and economic decisions of policy makers as key factors in allowing organised crime to flourish over the last hundred years. We also argue that official corruption and complicity with the drug trade has contributed significantly to the influence and power of organised crime syndicates.

In order to analyse the development of variables in the economy, labour markets, narcotrafficking, crime and public security, we accessed databases from Mexican governmental agencies, the presidential office and international bodies. When primary sources did not provide the necessary data we made use of secondary sources. The data were used to explore the patterns, fluctuations and comparisons found within such indicators to elucidate the performance of the economy, features of labour markets, and the evolution of some aspects of security and narcotrafficking.

While Mexico has advanced in recent years towards an ostensibly more democratic political system and public access to official information is guaranteed by the state, the availability of basic official data in a number of areas is still very limited. One of these areas is the security sector, specifically in relation to the number of people executed in narcotrafficking-related attacks. The official bodies of the federal government do not provide regular data, and similarly there exists no national official board which gathers and publishes information on the total number of narco-executions. Therefore, at times, we rely on reports in national newspapers, which have tallied narco-executions based on information gathered by news agencies. There is, however, some variation between newspaper databases that collect statistical information about executions.

According to the newspaper *Reforma*, for example, the number of narco-executions in Mexico reached 39,274 between 1 December 2006 and 25 November 2011. *Milenio*, on the other hand, reports 45,308 narco-related deaths for the same period. The government does not produce reports counting narco-executions, at least none for public viewing.

Furthermore, statistical data released by official institutions demonstrate little coherence and are often contradictory. Such reports are published sporadically, often making it very difficult to check data in the government publications made available to the citizenry. In some cases, the figures provided by the government on the number of people executed by narcotraffickers are slightly higher than those presented by the media. As media organisations like *Reforma* collate data in a seemingly more thorough and systematic manner than government agencies, we have for the most part opted to use their figures.

Some of the most insightful work on the current crisis in Mexico has been carried out by a number of outstanding investigative journalists, who often complete their work at great personal risk. For Mexico is at present among the most dangerous countries on Earth in which to be a reporter. In contrast, academic engagement with the topic (with some notable exceptions) has been limited. It is for this reason that we draw heavily on the work of a number of Mexican journalists and news periodicals. Those of us who wish to understand the terrible crisis currently afflicting Mexico are indebted to those courageous individuals working in the Mexican media who attempt to make sense of the current explosion of violence.

In this book we attempt to demonstrate that the current expansion of powerful drug cartels and the consequent escalation of violence in Mexico did not arrive out of the blue. In fact, as long as there have been prohibition laws, there has been smuggling of contraband across the border. Reports from media organisations like *Televisa* in Mexico, CNN in the US and the BBC in the UK tend to present the 'drug war' in Mexico as a mysterious and inexplicable conflict in which the government (with the help of its ally, the United States) and the army attempt to defeat the evil tactics and poisonous influence of organised crime. Within this narrow and misleading representation of the drug war, state actors who perpetrate violence and abuse human rights are rarely ascribed agency, and thus are afforded complete immunity by influential mainstream media organisations. Consequently, the drug war is seldom given the historico-political context and analysis it surely merits.

We argue that reality is quite different from the notion that this is a war in which good on one side tries to defeat evil on the other. Instead, we argue, the drug traffickers have often benefited from accords and agreements with political power and big business, so that the supposed division between the sides is often shifting, fluid and at times scarcely visible. In fact, drug cartels could not have grown as they did without the complicity and assistance of politicians, police chiefs, the army and the security agencies. Drug trafficking in Mexico has always been an alliance between white-collar professionals – the respectable and well-dressed politicians and business people of the Harvard- and Yale-educated Mexican elite – and the unschooled delinquents of the criminal underclass who hit the news each time there is a counternarcotics 'sting'. Somehow, Mexican political and business leaders have managed to maintain an air of respectability and decorum internationally, an image reinforced by the BBC and CNN version of history, which so champions and endorses the interests of major trading partners and political allies of the Anglo-American empire, while demonising political enemies and counter-hegemonic challenges. Countering the pervasive myth that there is a clear dividing line between the authorities and organised crime is thus one of the ambitions of this book, and is essential to understanding the history of drug trafficking in Mexico.

Major drug traffickers like Pablo Acosta, who worked out of Ojinaga in Chihuahua until the 1980s, Rafael Caro Quintero, Ernesto Fonseca Carrillo and Miguel Ángel Félix Gallardo of the Guadalajara cartel could not have expanded their businesses without police and military corruption, and assistance and protection from Mexico's then federal security agency, the Dirección Federal de Seguridad (DFS). Similarly, the activities of the individual who became possibly the richest criminal in history, Amado Carrillo Fuentes, surely benefited from official corruption and complicity when he landed his fleet of Boeing 727s packed with cocaine originating in Colombia in Mexican airports. Similarly, it stretches the realms of credulity that the man who replaced the dead Osama bin Laden as the world's most wanted fugitive, Joaquín *El Chapo* Guzmán Loera, the leader of the Sinaloa cartel – who escaped from a maximum security prison in 2001 and up to now has managed to evade the Mexican army, the federal, state and municipal police forces, and the security and intelligence agencies – continues to enjoy life and liberty without some level of official complicity. We are to believe, apparently, that *El Chapo* Guzmán is so shrewd, so clever, that, although he has become one of the world's richest men, laundering his funds through Mexican and US banks, he manages so low a profile that, even with a multi-million-dollar budget, the security forces keep losing his trail.

What are the motivations for those who become involved in the narcotics industry in Mexico? This is, after all, particularly in recent decades, an industry which chews up and spits out human lives violently and brutally. To begin with, the cultivation of opium poppies and marijuana plants has generally been far more profitable than growing food crops. If the eradication and disruption of illegal drug markets were a priority for government, one way in which to counter them might be to remove the conditions which make running the risk of growing or distributing illicit drugs the preferred option in an unregulated market. Instead of employing the army to destroy crops and arrest and violently repress growers and traffickers, one might think a more obvious and sustainable strategy would be to investigate measures that could alleviate the extreme poverty in which so many Mexicans live. Yet this latter approach has not been a priority for central government. On the contrary, the growth of trafficking and Mexican crime syndicates seems to correlate closely with the implementation of those governmental policies which, particularly in the last three decades, have led to the increased impoverishment of many Mexicans.

We view the prevalence and persistence of drug-related crime as arising from a combination of factors that have nourished its development, though we do not pretend to account for all of these. Indeed, the topic of narcotrafficking in Mexico has such multifarious aspects and is so huge, so contradictory and so astounding that we can only hope to scratch the surface of what has become a pressing and necessary area of research. Nonetheless, we offer some ideas about the past, present and future for the reader's consideration, and hope we have elucidated the history of the drugs problem and the process by which Mexico has arrived at its current precarious situation. For example, we look at the world's largest market for narcotics, located in the United States, which borders a country whose geography and climate are ideal for the cultivation of marijuana and poppies. So long as demand exists, it is likely that Mexico, where poverty is rife, will be able to satisfy US consumer demand. Traffickers have always benefited from the corruption of the political class, police, military and security agencies, whose members have often been deeply complicit in drug trafficking. None of this could have happened without the backing or tacit consent of certain bankers and business elites, who have aided traffickers in laundering monies or investing their fortunes in real estate.

In fact, during the rule of the PRI, it would appear that the government actually controlled much of the trade and entered into pacts with traffickers to ensure the state took its share of the profit. This arrangement maintained a relative stability until the last two decades, during which the monolithic PRI edifice has started to crumble and power relations have begun to shift. It was a sinister development when Mexico's political system switched to a multi-party democracy in 2000 and a number of cartels used the transition to empower themselves, moving in to capture elements of the state and to assume control over them.

Poverty and unemployment have also made a significant contribution to the success of the cartels, enticing many Mexicans to seek work in the informal economy's largest sector, the drug trade, thanks to government policies that have created a cheap and flexible labour force willing to take risks in order to make a half-decent living.

Furthermore, counternarcotics programmes have been used as a form of social control. Government spending on the militarisation of counternarcotics programmes has seen the military using resources allocated for narcotics control to suppress agrarian and peasant movements as well as left-wing guerrilla groups. We argue that all of these factors in combination have led to the catastrophic events of recent years that have seen an unprecedented escalation of violent (and other) crime.

The fact is that the narco-industry is a profit-making enterprise that shares several of the features of the model extolled by the Harvard Business School. We remind the reader that this same industry follows many of the same precepts as Microsoft, Goldman Sachs, General Motors, BP and the entire gamut of multinational corporations where profit exists for the sake of profit and human and environmental costs are merely external to the irrational and merciless laws of the market. Journalist Charles Bowden (1998) has rightly called the current mayhem and brutality of the Mexican narcotics industry, of which Ciudad Juárez is the depraved epicentre, the 'laboratory of the future'. Bowden (2010a) notes that Juárez, by the 1960s, had already become the poster child for the future global economy – an economy in which production, in order to satisfy human need, is a totally alien and subversive concept. This is the world of sweatshops and inequality, of rule by force, in which the only rights are those stolen from somebody else. The future has arrived and it looks ugly. But it would be foolish to believe it came from nowhere and that the present and the immediate future are merely the products of a series of unfortunate yet innocent historical coincidences.

This book attempts to examine why and how Mexico arrived at this critical juncture, because we believe that by understanding the past we can shape and mould a more dignified future for everyone, not just those with the biggest guns and the best political contacts. Because the future should not be a testing laboratory which devastates cultures, communities, entire nations and the natural environment for the sake of profit, but should be one that can be shared and enjoyed by all.

1 Drug Trafficking in Mexico – History and Background

Our perceptions of narcotics as a menace to social stability and a public health risk are often regarded as relatively recent, though they do in fact have precedents in the period of European colonial expansion in the Americas. One reason we think of many drugs as dangerous nowadays is that the chemical makeup of several narcotics with a long history of relatively harmless medicinal, ritual and recreational use, such as those based on the coca leaf, which became increasingly available to consumers in the nineteenth and twentieth centuries, has changed radically, usually as they were adapted and made more powerful for modern medicinal purposes. For example, the risks associated with chewing coca leaves, which are mild in comparison to those of snorting cocaine or smoking crack cocaine, should hardly be treated identically, with the same intense alarm, by public health authorities. But in different periods of the twentieth and twenty-first centuries, panic has ruled; in these times governments have devised drug policies that approach the smuggling and distribution of alcohol, coca leaf, cocaine, cannabis, opium, heroin and methamphetamine in a similar manner, as if they were all virtually interchangeable in their impact on individuals and on society as a whole. Most of these policies demonstrate a common outcome: if we assume that anti-drug policies have as their principal aim the protection of public health, an increase in public security and the suppression of criminal activity, then most have failed in all three respects. Perhaps one of the starkest and most timely examples is the anti-drug policy in Mexico.

Official and public ignorance about the effects of consuming narcotics have been a salient feature throughout the history of

Mexico's varied anti-drug policies, and may have contributed to government responses that have proved both destructive and devastating. The situation has been aggravated by corrupt politicians, who have relied on misinformation and misleading propaganda to implement policies that at times had less to do with the eradication of illegal crops and interdiction of contraband than with the empowerment of elite political and business interests. In Mexico's current 'war on drugs', the cliché that truth is the first casualty of war could hardly be more appropriate.

Misinformation about and fear of the effects of mind-altering substances is scarcely a recent phenomenon. In 1772, one of Mexico's most influential intellectuals, José Antonio Alzate y Ramírez, claimed that consuming cannabis leaves and seeds made one go mad, leading eventually to communion with the Devil. Not everyone was put off by such diabolical results: Isaac Campos (2011: 17) notes that in the eighteenth century users considered 'communion with the Devil' and the supernatural to be one of cannabis's principal attractions. Indeed, alarmist rhetoric about the plant in political discourse and popular mythology seemed only to arouse further curiosity among prospective cannabis aficionados.

In South America, sixteenth-century Spanish colonialists had been stunned by the predominance of the coca leaf and its importance to Andean cultures. Members of the clergy and the creole elites reacted as they did to so many cultural practices of the colonised: they associated coca use with the heathen customs of the savages – further evidence of their barbaric nature and of the moral duty of Spain to intensify and widen the colonial conquest of American lands and cultures. Yet the degradation associated with the plant did not prevent influential Spaniards and members of the clergy from capitalising on the sale and distribution of coca. The Spaniards recognised the potential for commercialising the plant, given its prevalence in aboriginal cultures for use in medicine, work and recreation, and made efforts to weigh the market of the leaf in their own favour. Indeed, the time came when the Catholic

Church, the leading financial and lending institution of the colonial period in Latin America, established a virtual monopoly over the coca leaf market in parts of the Andean region. In 1609 Padre Blas Valera wrote:

> The great usefulness and effect of coca for labourers is shown by the fact that the Indians who eat it are stronger and fitter for their work; they are often so satisfied by it they can work all day without eating. ... It has another great value, which is that the income of the bishops, canons and other priests of the cathedral church of Cuzco is derived from the tithe on the coca leaf, and many Spaniards have grown rich, and still do, on the traffic of this herb. (Valera, quoted in Streatfeild 2001: 35)

Though the Spaniards entrusted the cultivation of the plant to the indigenous communities, they made payments in coca and levied taxes on the trade (Buxton 2006: 7) so that it became one of the prime exchange commodities of the colonial economy. Thus, even in the early stages of the commodification of coca in the Andean region, it was the Spaniards who controlled the market but who consumed the least. Similarly, in Mexico it has been the powerful who have set the agenda on the alarmist discourse relating to narcotics, although they have been arguably the least qualified to do so, while simultaneously and unswervingly seeking to control the market and distribution to their own advantage.

In the late nineteenth century, comparable reports of marijuana smoking leading otherwise balanced individuals to both madness and acts of violence held sway in the yellow press and manipulated public opinion – leaving little room, as Campos points out, for the better-informed to counter the prevailing orthodoxy. Campos (2011: 18) argues that the lack of knowledge and heightened hysteria about marijuana, reinforced by the press and picked up by American wire services, ultimately had the effect of influencing US public and official opinion about cannabis, and acted as a contributing factor to US drug policy at the time.

Trafficking in the Early Twentieth Century

In the late nineteenth and early twentieth centuries, the health effects of narcotics were widely misunderstood. What today are considered dangerous, mind-altering substances were often prescribed by European and North American doctors for a whole variety of ailments. Many drugs – such as cocaine, coca wine or tonic, morphine, heroin and marijuana – were widely available in the late nineteenth century and were readily prescribed by practitioners ignorant of the possible dangers, who recommended them to patients by virtue of their many therapeutic benefits, particularly pain relief. Cannabis use, notes Buxton (2006: 4), spanned millennia in Indian and Chinese cultures for the relief of the symptoms of 'gout, cholera, tetanus, neuralgia, depression and for pain relief in childbirth'. Similarly, opium had been employed for a range of medicinal purposes, notably as an anaesthetic. Cocaine had become widely used in Europe and in the United States by the twentieth century, and was considered by many practitioners to be a wonder drug that could alleviate or cure a wide variety of complaints. It provided consumers with high energy levels and suppressed hunger and thirst. Drugs had also been commonly used to mitigate the exertions of demanding physical labour, as in the Andes where chewing coca leaves relieved the worst symptoms of physical work by increasing stamina and staving off hunger (*ibid.*: 4–5).

The widespread use of coca-based substances outside the Andean region did not occur until comparatively late. Because coca leaves are perishable, they were not much used elsewhere until the nineteenth century, when chemists like the Corsican Angelo Mariani discovered that the narcotic properties of coca could be distilled and taken with wine. Following this development and the creation of the drink, Coca-Cola, which contained coca (its popularity spurred on partly as a result of the prohibition of alcohol in dry zones of the United States), the use of coca extended well beyond South America.

In Europe, coca-based substances attracted the curiosity of medical scientists, some of whom were enticed by coca's seemingly endless curative properties. In Austria, ophthalmologist Karl Koller made a major breakthrough in 1864 when he discovered (with the help of Sigmund Freud, who never received credit) that cocaine could be used as an effective anaesthetic for eye surgery. Freud was among the most vocal European advocates of the consumption of cocaine and argued that it could be used for almost any complaint. For some time Freud recommended cocaine for curing a number of psychological disturbances in his patients. He also prescribed it for the common cold and, while its effects did indeed seem to dry out the nasal passages, it had the disadvantage that once the effects of the drug wore off, the patient would have to take even more cocaine to keep the symptoms at bay. It was also thought that cocaine could cure morphine addiction, although Freud's close friend Ernst von Fleischl-Marxow, and others to whom the drug was recommended, were unfortunate enough to develop an addiction to cocaine in addition to morphine dependency. Despite the increasingly common use of cocaine throughout Europe and in the United States, the health risks remained poorly understood, and it was some time before the authorities created legislation ostensibly designed to protect consumers (Streatfeild 2001).

Though the notion of drug abuse is a wholly modern one, its association with what were considered by political elites to be deviant elements in society – immigrants, criminals, the poor, racial minorities, prostitutes – has a longer history. In varying contexts and locations in the twentieth century, political agenda setters often considered the use of narcotics for medicinal purposes routine, while recreational consumption was disreputable and indicative of the kind of indolence they associated with people on the despised fringes of respectable society. Opium smoking, cocaine use and cannabis consumption did not conform to the work ethic and moral values of a modernising and industrialising society – values that the ruling elite attempted to instil in the population in the wake of the Mexican Revolution.

In the early twentieth century, the US authorities and press intensified the demonisation of cocaine use by associating it with Afro-Americans. They had noted that negro workers in the southern states were sniffing cocaine, not in order to endure barbaric work practices and to stave off hunger, but instead because they were intent on raping white women and assaulting respectable white males with firearms while under the influence of mind-altering substances (*ibid.*: 142–8). Racial prejudice and ignorance of the drug's properties, apparent in political discourse and in the media, would lead eventually to the criminalisation of recreational cocaine use. The US Harrison Narcotics Tax Act of 1914, for example, allowed narcotics to be used only for medical purposes.

In Mexico another alarming drug, opium, began to be imported in earnest from 1864, with the arrival of Chinese immigrant workers brought in to construct and improve the national rail network. In the late nineteenth and early twentieth centuries, opium would arrive in ports on Mexico's Pacific coast aboard boats originating in China, and the cross-border smuggling into the USA from the north of the country was associated with a strong Chinese immigrant presence. As moves towards prohibition intensified in the 1910s, so did anti-immigrant and anti-Chinese sentiment, stirred up by the rhetoric and discourse of politicians (Astorga 2003: 23). Plutarco Elías Calles, who, before becoming President in 1924 had been elected governor of Sonora in 1915, was as fervently anti-Chinese as he was prohibitionist. Sino-Mexican communities were consequently branded with the doubly unfortunate label of immigrant and smuggler. The stigma of opium's association with apparently threatening outsiders was made worse still as consumption among Mexicans themselves was low, being largely confined to Chinese immigrant communities, so that the latter were further demonised in political discourse and in the press. Nonetheless, their dominant role in cross-border smuggling would later be taken over by Mexicans, as political repression against Chinese immigrants marginalised them further in the 1920s and 1930s and inhibited their participation in and organisation of trafficking networks. By the late 1930s, as the supply from China was interrupted, Mexican growers and sellers could satisfy the increased demand for home-grown poppies.

Marijuana cigarettes, opium derivatives, cocaine and coca wine were widely available in the United States in the first decade of the twentieth century. As a result, US legislators had begun taking measures to criminalise the sale of opioids. Following the Spanish–American war of 1898, they became increasingly preoccupied with the government monopoly of opium cultivation and export in the newly independent Philippines. Additionally, Chinese migration into Europe and North America provoked increasingly negative reactions towards opium smoking, contributing to the decline in its acceptability and the creation of subsequent legislation banning the drug's use. At the Shanghai Conference of 1909, American diplomats pushed for the implementation of measures to halt the opium trade. Anti-drug legislation introduced in the United States, such as the Opium Exclusion Act of 1909, the Harrison Narcotic Law and the Eighteenth Amendment, pushed narcotics further towards the black market. Latin America had already become and continued to be the most critical drug-producing region during successive US administrations owing to the fact that cocaine, opium, heroin and marijuana could be grown and produced there and could cross the border from Mexico with relative ease. As María Celia Toro notes (1995: 7), the outlawing of narcotics in Mexico and the United States ensured that exports of relatively little value quickly became a very profitable line of business for those willing to take the risks.

The Impact of Economic Integration, Capitalist Expansion and Changes in Land Ownership

In the wake of the Mexican Revolution, the government re-established the *ejido* system of land sharing which had been under attack since the 1850s. *Ejidos* were communally controlled parcels of land that had provided even the poorest communities with somewhere to grow their crops and maintain a basic livelihood. Yet the unrelenting drive towards integration into the capitalist economy from the 1850s onwards – a process which Mexican sociologist Pablo González Casanova (1970) termed 'internal colonisation' – had pushed much of the communal land into private ownership. The Liberal Party in the 1850s had initiated a programme of capitalist expansion throughout Mexico in which land owned by the church and civil bodies would be acquired by the state and sold to those willing and able to purchase it. This had a direct effect on the *ejido* system, as much of this land was communally controlled. This reform under the presidency of Benito Juárez, which entailed the complete separation of church and state and the nationalisation of ecclesiastical property, sparked fierce reactions from the clergy and Conservatives. The Liberals, fighting the clergy, the Conservatives and a French invasion, were eventually victorious, and the reform paved the way for capitalist development and industrialisation in the late nineteenth century. But what appeared to favour the interests of small landholders in fact became an opportunity for larger landowners, or *latifundistas*, to buy up church and communal land, so that by the end of the nineteenth century, *latifundistas* like Luis Terraza in Chihuahua could own two million hectares (Gilly 2005: 4–6). By 1906 Mexican oligarchs had taken possession of 49 million hectares, a quarter of all arable land. By 1910, 95 per cent of *ejido* land had been expropriated and small farmers could no longer claim tracts without a legal title. At the same time foreign investors owned 130 of the largest 170 companies and controlled 60 per cent of the nation's capital (Gibler 2009a: 35–6).

Furthermore, the building of 10,000 miles of railway during the dictatorship of President Porfirio Díaz had the effect of opening up much of the land hitherto controlled by indigenous populations to capitalist exploitation and thus of dispossessing, in its wake, thousands of rural families. Capitalists were now provided with an improved infrastructure, via the railways and access to ports and harbours, which allowed for further domestic and international economic integration. At the same time, many indigenous people in previously remote rural areas, and now without a land title, were forced into wage labour.

It was clear that development and progress favoured the Mexican bourgeoisie, the political elite and foreign investors. The expansion of capitalism throughout the Mexican territories further marginalised swathes of the population, who either had to enter the wage economy or make a living on the black market. In the context of a system heavily weighted in favour of the interests of the ruling classes, and with a wealthy neighbour just over the northern border, the growth of smuggling as an attractive way for poorer people to make a living is not surprising.

Indeed, it was the incessant drive towards progress and the advance of capitalist expansion in Mexico – mainly to the detriment of the poor and the peasants – that provoked the Revolution in 1910, the largest social upheaval in twentieth-century Latin America, which continued throughout the decade that followed. Dissent and political protest had been criminalised and criticism of the regime harshly punished in order to maintain 'stability' via highly centralised *caudillo* rule. The autocratic government of Porfirio Díaz had sought to ensure, by means of science and social stability, economic development oriented to the export market. The outcome was that European and US investors controlled much of the economy, particularly the oil industry. Industrial workers' wages had been kept low in order to attract such foreign investment, further exacerbating economic inequalities.

However, the Revolution stalled the 'scientific' progress which the Díaz dictatorship had so forcefully developed. Then, as now, the government's insistence on an ideological economic model that unduly favoured capitalist interests was doomed to failure. In the 1910s, it led to widespread rebellion as socialist, liberal, anarchist, populist and agrarianist movements began to challenge the regime's authority.

During the most intense period of revolutionary conflict, the absence of political control by revolutionary forces, and by central government in the northern territories, allowed corrupt local military and political elites to run some areas as personal fiefdoms, prefiguring developments later in the century. The military general, Esteban Cantú, for example, who had been sent to Baja California to quell insurgent supporters of the anarchist Flores-Magón brothers, capitalised on the relative isolation of the state from the metropole – cut off by the Gulf of California, the desert and the region's mountainous terrain. As state governor he created his own laws, collected his own taxes and prohibited the use of Mexican currency. His personal fortune was similarly boosted by his involvement in extortion, gambling and prostitution. Furthermore, as central government was preoccupied with defeating widespread insurgency throughout the territories, its weakened state allowed for several incursions across the border by US military forces. Northern political and military leaders exploited the government's constant fear of a US invasion and were accorded increased powers by President Carranza to offset what he saw as an imminent threat (Toro 1995: 9). An environment in which leaders like Cantú could rule as they pleased, combined with new legislation in both the USA and Mexico that prohibited the sale of opium, allowed powerful actors in the political elite and the military to take advantage of the climate of lawlessness and the high prices for contraband that prohibition ensured. Furthermore, there was a constant supply of peasants and farmers dispossessed by 'scientific' economic progress and development who were willing to grow poppies and marijuana or become involved in their distribution.

By 1914 counternarcotics legislation in the United States had led to the first major organised offensives against the smuggling of contraband from Mexico. Prohibition in both countries encouraged an illegal industry to develop and become a major source of revenue for those involved in it. The more the authorities on both sides of the border attempted to control the import of narcotics, the greater the risk incurred in smuggling and consequently the higher the selling price of the final product. In northern Mexico, in regions blighted by extreme poverty, hardship and inequality, smuggling provided handsome profits. Indeed, it seems that some politicians who were involved in the incipient market in narcotics were in favour of prohibition precisely because they knew that legislation, ostensibly designed to curb the consumption of illegal substances, guaranteed greater financial return (Astorga 2003: 17). If there is one constant throughout the history of smuggling from Mexico into the United States, it is that prohibition has always led to enviable profit margins, particularly in a land marked by official corruption and a lack of legitimate employment opportunities.

Though political governors such as Cantú were smuggling significant amounts of opium by sea from the port of Ensenada to Los Angeles and San Francisco, they relied on a network of corrupt customs officials and low-level traffickers to complete these transactions. Cantú used his position of power and relative independence from central government to operate smuggling operations out of Baja California.

US consumers provided a demand and a market for contraband; Mexico offered fertile territory for the production of opium poppies and marijuana, and vast and relatively empty northern territories that facilitated the transport of illegal goods over the border. Perhaps most importantly, then as today, Mexico had no shortage of unskilled labour, which often had little choice but to accept whatever employment came its way. And so long as narcotics were illegal and successive administrations attempted to combat smuggling, the US government would play a significant role in internal Mexican political affairs. Indeed, the line between anti-narcotics operations and the shaping and manipulating of the political economy of Mexico by its powerful northern neighbour is often quite blurred.

Given the economic disparities between rich and poor, which had deepened during the Díaz dictatorship, it was no surprise that the informal black market was thriving. Chinese immigrants would smuggle opium from Ciudad Juárez across the border through tunnels. These might begin in a house in Juárez and end in another in El Paso's Chinatown. An added advantage of having a network of tunnels was the relatively easy escape this provided into another country – and therefore another jurisdiction – whenever the authorities on either side made searches of houses. But smuggling, though relatively minor by today's levels, was hardly confined to newly arrived immigrant populations. Juárez and El Paso were, and still are in many ways, one and the same city both geographically and culturally, and also because so many Americans and Mexicans worked (and work) 'next door'. The Border Patrol on the US side was not established until 1924 and, although prohibition agents had begun to appear in the early 1920s, the border was so enormous that its geography undermined any attempt to control illegal trade (Campbell 2009: 55–6).

In the United States, the prohibition legislation, which banned the sale of alcoholic beverages following the Volstead Act of 1919, which was in force for fourteen years, also played into the hands of Mexican traffickers of contraband who moved in to satisfy much of the popular appetite for illicit booze. While illegal breweries and distilleries operated within the United States, during the Prohibition era huge amounts of contraband alcohol were imported from Canada, the Caribbean and Mexico. Northern Mexico, with its porous and mostly remote border, proved ideal for the onward shipping of illegal goods. So long as there existed a steady demand, supply was likewise plentiful. When the sale of alcohol became legal again, Mexican smugglers of contraband used already existing networks to switch their focus instead to exporting marijuana and heroin to the US drug market, taking advantage of the fact that, unlike coca, marijuana plants and opium poppies could be grown and processed in Mexico (*ibid.*: 40–1).

In the first two decades of the twentieth century, Mexican smugglers sold cocaine to US buyers, but gradually this trade fell off and was overtaken by morphine, opium and heroin. This decline was probably due to anti-cocaine health campaigns and legislation within the United States, triggered by a steady flow of reports on the pernicious physical and psychological effects of consuming the drug.

Mexico prohibited the production and sale of marijuana in 1920, and of poppy in 1926. Again, fear and ignorance about the actual effects of consumption were a pervasive aspect of the official discourse about drugs on both sides of the border. In the USA, during the economic crisis of the 1920s and 1930s, the denigration of economic migrants, particularly Mexicans, constantly referred to the use of marijuana. A lack of knowledge about the drug and a suspicion of those selling and consuming it were important catalysts in transforming Mexicans in popular opinion from economic migrants – who, after all, were seeking to better their lot by crossing the border and working as ranch-hands or picking fruit – into stereotypical deceitful and indolent outsiders. In Mexico itself, although the consumption of narcotics was limited, anti-drug legislation was introduced as a result of a certain hysteria on the part of officials who were following the directives of and bilateral initiatives with the United States, where consumption and addiction rates went well beyond those in Mexico. Each drug became associated in the public mind with specific social elements. Opium smoking had become the vice of the Mexican Chinese community and the legislation reflected racist sentiment. While marijuana was associated with criminality, poverty and low-level military personnel, morphine, cocaine and heroin were linked to artists and other similar degenerates of the bourgeoisie (Astorga 1999).

By 1923, President Obregón had banned the import of all narcotics and implemented measures to limit the export of alcohol to the United States. These included the building of an airfield in Ciudad Juárez to facilitate surveillance of the frontier, and the creation of a dry zone, fifty miles wide, on the northern border. By 1925, enforcement in Mexico against dealers and smugglers of contraband items – alcohol, opium, heroin and firearms – became much more stringent, in agreement with the US government, as power was extended to the judicial authorities to prosecute smugglers. More restrictive measures still were passed into law in 1927, when President Calles banned the export of marijuana and heroin outright. These measures were extended to growers and to those processing the poppies into heroin and opium (Toro 1995: 8). By now, the consolidation of legislation prohibiting the cultivation, production, import and export of narcotics had effectively criminalised the entire industry. Throughout, however, bilateral efforts to curtail smuggling were undermined by official involvement in the drug business and the attractive and lucrative returns that prohibition guaranteed.

The Post-Revolutionary Government and Smuggling

To some extent, the growth of the market in illicit substances can be related to the structure of the state that followed the revolution. A guiding principle of the Mexican Revolution had been an anti-feudalist current, which sought to abolish land ownership for wealthy and foreign corporations and redistribute it among *campesinos*. In the post-revolutionary period, however, the bureaucratic class that took control of the political system had satisfied only some of the demands of the Revolution. The Partido Nacional Revolucionario, founded in 1929, introduced important agrarian reforms and programmes that contributed to a limited redistribution of wealth. In order to maintain a hierarchical and centralised political system and to avoid mass-based challenges to its authority, however, the ruling party sought to co-opt mass organisations. In this way, the state could influence and pressurise various sectors – *campesinos*, *obreros* (rural workers) and industrial workers alike – and exert a certain amount of control over them by keeping them within the party fold so as to minimise potential dissent. Avoiding domestic conflict had the added advantage of keeping on board international investors and corporations, which still had massive interests in Mexico, despite the Revolution's partial support for natonalisation. The regime's control thus rested on negotiation – both with its own population and with national and foreign capital.

The party had managed to compromise with various political groups by addressing some of their demands. In the 1930s, for instance, a number of significant social gains had rewarded the intense activity of peasant movements. President Lázaro Cárdenas introduced some far-reaching reforms, including the redistribution of land, expropriation of petroleum companies and advances in education. These were all important developments for rural Mexico and Cárdenas attempted to include broader sectors of the population in the ruling party. He changed the name from the Partido Nacional Revolucionario to the Partido de la Revolución Mexicana in 1937 – it was not until the administration of President Ávila Camacho that the ruling party became the paradoxically termed Partido Revolucionario Institucional (PRI – Institutional Revolutionary Party), a name which encapsulated the party's sense of permanence while presenting itself as a progressive force. One of the important props underpinning one-party rule in Mexico was Cárdenas's support base, which was strengthened by its enrolment of popular and agrarian sectors of the population. By making room for the representation of these groups within the party, political leaders hoped to offset the danger that a rural insurgency might pose a challenge to its continued dominance. This inclusive system contributed to the longevity of PRI rule and distinguished it from other one-party states (Newell and Rubio 1984: 63–4).

Nationalising the oil companies and the railroads, as well as redistributing land and giving the party a corporatist structure, meant that Cárdenas and his party had a base of tacit support among popular labour and peasant organisations. MacLachlan and Beezley (1999: 353) argue that including diverse sectors of the population in the political sphere gave the ruling party a sense of legitimacy and extensive support, although it should be noted that these groups were unable to function effectively outside the influence of the ruling party. Groups and organisations that had previously operated independently had now been drawn into a corporate structure where their influence was severely limited by a top-down organisation of power (Hamnett 2006: 255).

What later became the PRI attempted to include everyone – Marxists, Liberals and Conservatives – within its structure (Brewster 2005: 13). Intellectuals of both right and left often had close associations with the party, which minimised threats to its political monopoly since potential opposition by the intelligentsia was weakened, not by repression, but by its inclusion in the party apparatus. Critical intellectuals, with few opportunities for making themselves heard elsewhere, found themselves either attracted into the orbit of the single party or working with it by invitation.

The result was a seemingly eternal one-party political system that consolidated itself by holding a monopoly of power, addressing some demands and using repression and political violence to suppress others as it saw fit. During the seventy years of its rule, the PRI held on to power with a tentacle-like, country-wide grip. Its desire to control the drug industry was no exception. Indeed, the federal narcotics reserve, a branch of the Department of Health, attempted to impose a government monopoly on the drugs trade, an ambition the government made concerted efforts to achieve in 1938–39 – but met with fierce resistance from the US authorities, who enforced a retaliatory embargo on all medical drugs to Mexico. Mexican government moves to manage the trade were also hampered by the Marijuana Tax Act, introduced in the United States in 1937 (Musto 1991). While this did not criminalise marijuana, it took a levy from sellers and distributors and allowed the authorities to prosecute those who avoided the tax. It also contributed to the disreputable associations of marijuana consumption in the USA, aided by a campaign led by a number of politicians and the press barons – among them William Randolph Hearst, who can claim to have introduced the word 'marijuana' into the English language. As a result, the Mexicans abandoned the plan to monopolise the market, at least formally, but would eventually allow drug smuggling to flourish through a tacit understanding between traffickers, the army, the police and politicians (Toro 1995: 11).

As Luis Astorga (1999) notes, the consolidation of power in the presidency and in central government, the fragmented and disorganised nature of political opposition, and the co-option of social movements and unions by the corporatist state allowed PRI officials to exercise an unofficial *de facto* monopoly of the narcotics industry with total impunity. Politicians were drawn to the easy money that trafficking represented and used their power to create an institutionalised protection racket. Furthermore, legislative and judicial bodies were dependent on the executive, an alignment of power which, as Astorga points out, meant that, prior to the Second World War, no governor faced prosecution for illegal trafficking, despite numerous reports in newspapers and widespread suspicions indicating their involvement. Immunity from prosecution for politicians in northern states, who at times had massive stakes in the trade, meant that some appointed to enforce anti-drug legislation colluded with traffickers and dealers and took a cut of the profits.

Clearly, the contradictory nature of participation in the trafficking of drugs by the military, the police and political officials – some of whom attempted to enforce legislation while others either acquiesced or were active participants in crime – meant that the interdiction of illicit exports was frequently compromised.

When, after the Second World War, the supply to US consumers of heroin (most of which came from Europe) had been interrupted, Mexican smugglers attempted to bridge the gap in the market. During the War, the United States had encouraged Mexico to increase its production of poppies in Sinaloa, to be used for treating Allied soldiers (Dillon and Preston 2004: 327). In addition, the demand for marijuana in the United States was increasing. The Mexicans were able to take advantage of the post-war disruption of traditional overseas routes and the growing market for marijuana (Toro 1995: 11), while the poverty resulting from lack of employment opportunities in the northern states meant that many farmers could earn more by growing opium poppies rather than corn, virtually on the

USA's doorstep. Gum extracted from poppies grown in the lush Sinaloa mountains was transported to Chihuahua, where it was processed in clandestine laboratories before smugglers exported it as heroin from Juárez or Ojinaga into the United States (Poppa 1998: 6). In the United States, competition from the mafia, who imported heroin from Italy, Turkey and France, was still strong enough to keep Mexican exports of the product relatively small in global terms. In fact, it was not until the 1970s (following a reduction in the quantity of heroin exported by the Corsican mafia in Marseille, and passing through Mexico en route) that Mexico became one of the principal suppliers of heroin to the USA.

At the same time, smuggling practices from Baja California were firmly established. In the Gulf of California, for example, illegal drugs could be purchased from Japanese fishing boats. Often the products would be wrapped in waterproof packages, which could be inserted inside fish. Boxes of fish stuffed with contraband would be marked so they could be recognised by the intended recipient. Illegal substances could thus cross into the United States unbeknown to the customs authorities. There was little reason for anyone involved to inform on their fellow workers to the authorities. Each actor – the Japanese fishermen, the Mexican *atuneros*[1] who made contacts with the Japanese, the Mexican buyers, the carriers, and US buyers – enjoyed relative independence and each had an interest in ensuring maximum financial return. A characteristic of the narcotics market at the time was that each individual in the chain complemented and depended on someone else. If the illegal activities of one or a group of individuals were discovered by the authorities on either side of the border, the interests of all would suffer. This dynamic, often underpinned by official involvement and protection, allowed the traffic of contraband to operate relatively unhindered.

---

1 Tuna fishermen.

The Cold War Period

Following the Second World War and the development of Cold War policies in the West, the Miguel Alemán government created the domestic secret police service, the Dirección Federal de Seguridad (DFS), the National Security Directorate, and made Alemán's close friend and adviser, Colonel Carlos Serrano, who was also implicated in drug trafficking, director of the organisation. From the outset, the primary purpose of the DFS was to weaken labour movements and pro-left organisations. Less than a year after the founding of the organisation, for example, it played a key role in attacking the Mexican Railway Workers Union (STFRM) (Scott 2009: 178). The surveillance and repression of unionists, Marxists, Communists and other notable subversives by DFS agents allowed Mexico's democratic façade to appear stable, and limited organised working-class or left-wing challenges to centralised political power.

The DFS took as its model the US Federal Bureau of Investigation (FBI) and the Central Intelligence Agency (CIA), also founded in 1947. Indeed, the creation of the DFS had been a proposal of the US government. Both governments had a shared interest in keeping a lid on organised dissent and populist political movements in Mexico. The DFS and the CIA shared information on suspected subversives, and anti-narcotic operations were frequently used as a device for quelling social movements and justifying the repression of political adversaries. In the states of Guerrero and Oaxaca, for example, military suppression of social protest and peasant movements was, and still is, tangled up within the discourse of fighting drug production and smuggling.

Throughout the Cold War, the largest CIA operation in Latin America was in Mexico City. According to Philip Agee (1975), a whistleblowing CIA operative who had been stationed in Mexico, the collaborative nature of the relationship between the two governments was such that even the highest-ranking officials, including presidents Gustavo Díaz Ordaz and Luis Echeverría

Álvarez, supplied information to the CIA on 'subversives' in Mexico. Nonetheless, from the outset, misgivings about those in charge of the DFS had apparently been felt by officials at the US embassy in Mexico City, who raised concerns in their cables to the US State Department that senior members of the organisation were involved in the trafficking business (Astorga 1999). Similar concerns do not seem to have been shared by the CIA, which, it seems, was fully aware of the DFS involvement in illegal activities and noted its preference for this organisation over other intelligence agencies in Mexico (Scott 2009: 179). It would be naïve to pretend that the CIA merely turned a blind eye to trafficking when their top-level counterparts in the DFS were heavily embroiled in the narcotics business. CIA intelligence must have known about this defining aspect of its sister organisation in Mexico. Furthermore, it is difficult to imagine that trafficking by the DFS could have carried on for so long without the tacit consent, if not the collaboration, of the CIA. As Peter Dale Scott (*ibid.*: 174) has observed, 'the US used both the Mexican DFS and their drug traffickers as assets for violence against the Latin American left'. Howard Hunt, who was stationed at the CIA branch in Mexico City in the 1950s, worked closely with the DFS in gathering together influential right-wing and neofascist political figures to join them in defeating what they perceived to be the threat of Communism in the continent. These willing recruits would later organise into the World Anti-Communist League (WACL), which, throughout Latin America in the 1970s, came to be associated with right-wing death squads and the DFS. The WACL was also heavily involved in trafficking activities in Latin America, a practice that was overlooked so long as it assisted in targeting subversive elements. Furthermore, it appeared that anti-Communist organisations such as the WACL were funding the subversion of left-leaning governments and political coups – as in Bolivia and in Argentina – with profits from cocaine trafficking (*ibid.*: 180–1).

So long as the DFS acted as an enforcer of anti-left wing repression, minor issues like its control of the flow of narcotics into the United States were tolerated. The CIA counted on DFS spies to provide it with information on Soviet, Eastern Bloc and Cuban officials in Mexico. The PRI, with its long-established expertise in riding at least two horses at once, had refused to sever ties with Cuba, unlike other governments in the region. While the PRI and the Cuban Revolution maintained a warm relationship, Mexico was in a position to provide inside information to the CIA and the US government.

Reports of high-level involvement in and coordination of the distribution, export and sale of narcotics by DFS agents continued throughout the next forty years as they operated in a climate of total impunity. Indeed, from its beginnings, the DFS essentially coordinated and was embroiled in the largest trafficking operations in Mexico, often with CIA collaboration and direct involvement (Buendía 1988: 24–6). Small-scale and independent traffickers, who prior to the Second World War had operated with relative autonomy, increasingly found that they had to cooperate with larger crime syndicates and official organs – that is, with the police, the military, PRI officials and the DFS. Official protection allowed the stronger actors in the industry to become more powerful, shielded by the authorities so long as they made their monthly payments up the chain of command. A national organisation with lavish resources, the DFS made every effort to manage the organisation of trafficking throughout the country, making it into an industry over which the organs of the state exercised a decisive control. With state institutions – the DFS and the military and police forces – maintaining a strong measure of control over the narcotics industry, they also held a monopoly of violence. If the excesses of traffickers met with government disapproval, agencies like the DFS could intervene with force at the behest of the political class.

From the inception of the agency in 1947, the Mexican political police now had the remit to intervene in what was, in many senses and in most countries, an issue of public health. Responsibility for reducing the influence of the narcotics trade concurrently shifted, in the same year, from the Department of Health to the Procuraduría General de la República (PGR), the Attorney General's Office (Astorga 1999). Drug control strategies were thus increasingly viewed as a political rather than a health issue, and moved further and more firmly into the territory of criminality. In the post-war period, drug control could be used for a number of political purposes, many of them harshly repressive, by criminalising public protest and political activism through associating, and therefore discrediting, particular movements and individuals with the scourge of drugs. It is worth underlining here that the government's prioritisation of drug eradication policies bore little relation to the rates of consumption in Mexico itself. As a public health issue, in relative terms, drug taking in Mexico has never been an area of prime concern. Consumption of narcotics, particularly cocaine and marijuana, from the nineteenth century to the present day has been a much more significant problem in Western Europe and the United States. The most plausible explanation of the prevalence of anti-drug legislation in Mexico is the country's proximity to the United States, where the 'war on drugs' has a long history and has often been associated with political repression and institutionalised racism. In Mexico, as in the USA, anti-narcotics discourse and policy have served more often than not to create a climate of fear of the unknown which has served to justify and legitimise political violence against marginalised sectors of society.

According to researchers at the non-profit NGO, Libertad de Información México AC (LIMAC), the state spied on five million Mexicans between 1947 and 1985, when the DFS (though not its activities) was shut down.[2] The DFS's close relationship with the CIA made sense in the light of the international context of the Cold War and the various ideological crusades against Communism, which, in Mexico, became a synonym for any social movement that challenged the established order. For, in the 1970s, the PRI

---

2 Interview with Adela Cedillo, LIMAC, Mexico City, 5 August 2005.

administration was exceptionally preoccupied with what it saw as a Communist threat on its own soil. Mexican 'democracy', it believed, could function only with the aid of propaganda, the support of domestic and foreign spying agencies, and the selective use of force.

Sergio Aguayo Quegada (2001) notes that the CIA had little need to interfere directly in Mexico's oppositionary politics, because the DFS was so effective in repressing left-wing groups. The interests of the CIA and the DFS were very similar: in their view, the possibility of a Communist takeover, represented by various social movements, posed a real threat to the legitimacy of 'democratic' governments. It is in the context of the Cold War and fanatical anti-Communism that we should consider the political propaganda strategies of the Mexican regime in which anti-drug rhetoric played an important role.

After the Second World War, the Mexican army was used more and more as a tool of social control. Although the PRI power structure had attempted to co-opt and compromise divergent political interests, repression during successive PRI regimes had targeted the poor and vulnerable, and had been used to inhibit the formation of mass political movements – perhaps one of the reasons why opposition movements in Mexico had generally tended towards fragmentation.

The army often found itself in an ambivalent position, tasked with the eradication of the drug trade while at the same time defending the interests of a powerful elite which was profiting from that very trade. The *Gran Campaña*, or Great Campaign, which began in 1948, was among the first to employ military personnel to control drug production in Mexico. From the perspective of political power, with little threat of foreign invasion, an important role for the army would be as the frontline of what Pablo González Casanova termed 'internal colonisation', the march forward of industrial expansion and capitalist development to the detriment of communal life and the cultures and traditions of Mexico's indigenous peoples. From this point onwards, the army carried out tasks previously under the remit of the federal police. In 1948–49, covering 11,000 kilometres on foot, the military had stopped in over 1,000 pueblos and destroyed some 680 illegal plantations (Toro 1995: 12–13). As well as introducing more severe eradication measures, efforts like these had the effect of bringing a military presence into everyday life and helped cement the army's role as one of the essential mainstays of Mexican national identity. Moreover, the presence of the army in remote rural areas helped instil a salutary sense of fear within the population. For the PRI, keen to maintain stability, the army – used as a tool of the state and social control – would be essential in preserving its grip on power and in the suppression of dissenting voices.

Over the next decade, the army extended its eradication measures as part of a national campaign that extended into Baja California, Sonora, Jalisco, Durango, Sinaloa, Morelos, Guanajuato and the Yucatán. Ultimately, however, these measures proved to be largely ineffectual as growers bribed officials to leave their crops alone. Similarly, soldiers burning cash crops in remote isolated rural areas themselves ran the risk of violent attack from growers, something they preferred to avoid. Besides, destroying crops in one area often led to the creation of new plantations elsewhere.

The PRI elite believed that, unlike the circumstances in other Latin American republics and colonies of European empires about to achieve independence, Mexico's relative economic stability and protectionism, together with land reform policies and social programmes, could elevate its status on the world stage to parity with the industrialised economies of France and the United States. The thrust of development left little room for those whose faces did not fit into the grand plan, and even less for those who objected or refused to conform, categories that included many in a country that retained large numbers of aboriginal communities who were yet to be – and who had no interest in being – integrated into modern Mexico. Here, the military played a key role in assuring capitalist development, which was promoted by economists and politicians alike as resulting inevitably from the nature of market forces and the march of progress, but which, as things turned out, could only be achieved by force exerted by the army. In fact, Mexico's pitiful human rights record correlates closely with the advance of capitalism, the securing of investor rights and the control of natural resources by Mexican and multinational corporations.

Social control has not been the only goal of drug policies, but clearly there is an inherent difficulty in meeting their other aims if those responsible for overseeing eradication have themselves been involved in trafficking opium, heroin, cocaine and marijuana. This being the case, what are the other, publicly unacknowledged considerations that have impacted on the effective execution of anti-drug policies?

The current 'war on drugs' has its roots in the 1970s, when significant changes in policy took place in both Mexico and the United States. They occurred in response to four principal developments.

First, a government ban in Turkey, whence most opium destined for the United States originated, was introduced in the late 1960s. Eradication measures had similarly been increased, severely debilitating the 'French Connection' between New York, Marseille and Turkey (Toro 1995: 15–16). Consequently, traffickers looked elsewhere for potential suppliers to satisfy US demand. Mexico was the obvious choice, given its proximity to the United States, its pliant and corrupt political class, DFS involvement in trafficking, a geography and climate which virtually guaranteed a quality product, and an underclass of agricultural and low-level workers always in need of employment, some of whom were willing to take enormous risks.

Second, in the late 1960s, the demand for marijuana from US consumers had increased dramatically. Marijuana suddenly went from being a relatively marginal product to a mainstay of mainstream youth culture. In 1962 only around 4 per cent of American adults aged 18–25 had smoked marijuana. By 1967, partly influenced by the Beat generation of the 1950s, but mainly by the Hippie counterculture, this had increased to 13 per cent, and many among this number now smoked the drug regularly. Suddenly Mexico had become the principal supplier of two of the three globally best-selling narcotics to the world's largest drug market. Further, it could cultivate both on the very doorstep of that market, with which it shared a two-thousand-mile and largely empty and porous border. In 1972, estimates suggest that Mexico supplied between 10 and 15 per cent of the US market for heroin; by 1975, this had increased to 80 per cent. In addition, Mexico could now satisfy the ever-widening demand for marijuana and its booming market. In 1975, the country was supplying about 95 per cent of all marijuana consumed in the USA (Toro 1995: 16). For Mexican traffickers, these developments were akin to striking gold. The extension of the US market in heroin and marijuana provided growers with a stable price and constant demand – market advantages with which traditional crops like beans, corn, vanilla and almonds simply could not compete.

Third, in 1973 US President Richard Nixon founded the Drug Enforcement Administration (DEA). This can be seen in part as a response to the increasing quantity of narcotics entering the United States. But the creation of the DEA was also a highly political manoeuvre that gave the US government increased leverage over domestic dissent and international politics. The Civil Rights Movement, the anti-Vietnam war protests, and the birth of the feminist movement were leading to an increasingly open and more democratic political culture in the United States. For Nixon and for the American establishment, however, rebellious white youths and Afro-American civil rights activists represented a threat to the established socio-political order. Worse, marijuana consumption among these groups, especially among white middle-class youth, had increased to an unprecedented extent. But, for Nixon, the problem was clear. His top aide, H. R. Haldeman, wrote in his diary after a briefing with the President in 1969 that in Nixon's mind the 'whole problem is really the blacks. The key is to devise a system that recognises that, while not appearing to do so' (cited in Cockburn and St Clair 1998: 73).

Another prime concern for the Nixon administration was the growing prevalence of marijuana use among US soldiers in Vietnam. Worse still was the number of Afro-Americans, 12 per cent of the troops but as much as 25 per cent of combat units, who were becoming ever more sceptical about the war, inspired by the Civil Rights Movement and anti-war protests at home. The number of desertions increased dramatically, so that by 1971 a quarter of soldiers had gone AWOL (Geier 2000). For those who stood with Nixon, the problems were the 'blacks', in and out of the army, the working-class white soldiers who were disobeying authority, the hippies, and the anti-war activists – and all of these problems, they believed, were regularly high on marijuana.

Thus, in 1969, the Nixon government introduced Operation Intercept, a programme to interdict the traffic of marijuana over the US/Mexican border. When put into practice, Operation Intercept, in which US customs officers conducted detailed searches of all traffic crossing the US border, outraged the Mexicans, who had diplomatically agreed to the plan but had not anticipated that the Nixon administration would apply it without first consulting the then President, Díaz Ordaz. The result was quite disastrous, particularly for licit Mexican trade, which could endure an embargo much less easily than the United States. But the interruption to the flow of marijuana northwards seemed equally futile, given the economic conditions that made its cultivation so attractive. The US agency, the Bureau of the Budget, noted that marijuana 'offered individual farmers up to 40 times the income that any legitimate crop might provide' (Doyle 2003a: 47). As marijuana represented some 9 per cent of Mexico's exports, stopping the trade was going to be difficult.

Fourth, in Mexico by 1968, large-scale political activism was expressing itself in popular calls for justice and equality. This had precedents in the railroad workers' strike of 1958–59 led by Demetrio Vallejo, and in the mid-1960s in strikes by teachers and doctors. Political protest was no longer confined to rural and blue-collar workers. By the 1960s the number of students attending university in Mexico had tripled. In the latter half of the decade many campuses became hotbeds of political discussion and activism; and many of the intellectuals of the 1968 generation emerged from these institutions. The mass movement – led by students but including a large sector of workers and peasants, frustrated by what they saw as an outdated oligarchy – demanded greater popular participation in government.

It is worth recalling that the Mexican political elite has always been characterised by a paternalistic, class-conscious conservatism. The prospect of marijuana-smoking Mexican hippies, Marxists, subversives and feminists assuming a prominent role in the political sphere was quite terrifying. President Gustavo Díaz Ordaz (1964–70), who notoriously ordered the massacre of students at the Plaza de las Tres Culturas in Tlatelolco in 1968 – estimates of the death toll ranged from thirty to three hundred – was personally outraged by the behaviour of the students, whose insubordinate political activities in the street threatened to tarnish Mexico's image on the world stage just weeks before the government was to showcase the capital in hosting the 1968 'Olympics of Peace'.

Members of the PRI *núcleo duro* were increasingly troubled by the street protests and the influence of student leaders and intellectuals. However, if an urban movement was so far insufficiently threatening to warrant immediate repressive measures, in the countryside a number of peasant and armed guerrilla movements were asking for trouble by demanding changes to the socio-economic order. Perhaps the most influential of these were the Brigada de Ajusticiamiento and the Partido de los Pobres led by Genaro Vázquez and Lucio Cabañas in rural Guerrero. In the late 1960s and early 1970s, militarisation of rural areas of Guerrero reached astonishing levels. At most, Lucio Cabañas was aided by around 200 other guerrilla activists. By 1971, then President Luis Echeverría (1970–76) had dispatched 12,000 troops to the region. In 1974, the year of Cabañas's assassination by the army, it had reached 24,000, equivalent to a third of the Mexican armed forces (Watt 2010: 53). Repression was exemplary and created a climate of terror throughout rural areas occupied by the army and under the rule of martial law. During this period, in the municipality of

Atoyac de Álvarez in Guerrero alone, the military disappeared some 650 people.

Such was the Cold War hysteria about guerrillas, Marxists, Communists and subversives that the subject of repression and human rights abuses in rural areas was almost entirely absent from mainstream political debate until very recently. The notion of a *guerra sucia*, or dirty war, struggled to gain legitimacy amid government claims that the militarisation of rural areas was a response to the threat posed by ideologically motivated subversives to stability and national security. Exploiting public ignorance about the true nature of guerrilla activities and fear of narcotics, government propaganda associated all types of political activism with criminality and frequently with drug trafficking.

While the government-initiated massacre of students in 1968 had received plenty of attention from metropolitan dissidents and intellectuals, the daily terrorising of peasants and disappearances in Guerrero were met with a tremendous silence. The contrasting exposure afforded to the Tlatelolco massacre in the international press and domestic dissident publications had severely damaged the reputations of the army and government. As the hunt for Cabañas proved unfruitful, the army terrorised the most marginalised and vulnerable peasants in remote rural areas, using the justification that they were the support base for the guerrilla movement. Removed from the scrutiny and interest of the Mexico City media, the army could carry out operations in Guerrero with total impunity and, importantly, control the message that made it into print via *boletines de prensa* distributed to the major papers – namely, that it was heroically defending the country against drug traffickers and murderous political subversives. According to one internal army document published in the 2006 *Informe Histórico a la Sociedad Mexicana* (Historical Report to Mexican Society), an official report released by the government of Vicente Fox examining the government's role in systematic political repression and human rights abuses during the *guerra sucia*, 'army operations in the state of Guerrero achieved one of the most important victories with the death of Lucio Cabañas Barrientos and we think that this will have varied and significant repercussions with regard to the Armed Forces: it will increase its prestige in national public opinion and will surely influence the population to feel that [the army] is a loyal supporter of legally constituted authorities and capable of maintaining order when the circumstances demand it' (Carillo Prieto 2006: 404).

Following the assassination of Cabañas, a report of the Secretaría de la Defensa Nacional (SEDENA – Department of National Defence) justified the military occupation by 24,000 troops of swathes of rural Guerrero by associating Cabañas with the most 'negative groups in the region'. In particular, it claimed, Cabañas was 'afforded protection' by 'swindlers' and 'drug traffickers'. Notably, the context of why guerrilla fighters existed at all, and whether Cabañas and Vázquez represented legitimate grievances, was as absent in media reports as in internal military and government documents. The army's right to occupy rural areas and subject the population to terror and psychological warfare appeared to be beyond question. The official discourse, by repeating and emphasising delinquency, criminality and drug trafficking, decontextualised the emergence of guerrilla movements in Mexico for public consumption. Such justifications also paved the way for the most violent period in Mexico since the outbreak of revolution in 1910. There has since been belated recognition in some quarters that the crackdown in Guerrero was more to do with 'rural poverty and unrest' than with drug production (Toro 1995: 18). However, even at the time of repression, one high-ranking federal police agent was jubilant about the authorities' activities in rural Mexico, while tacitly admitting that narcotics production in Guerrero and Oaxaca was a minor problem, putting it thus: 'We're really attacking the poppy fields in Oaxaca, Guerrero and other states; and when we finish wiping them out we're going to launch an all-out drive against the critical triangle, because that's where it's at' (Craig 1980: 349).

Many intelligent and reputable commentators were taken in by the army's spin on events in the countryside. Even some of the most independent-minded journalists – many of whom had criticised the government for the massacre in Tlatelolco – regurgitated the triumphalist discourse of politicians and military generals in relation to the crackdown on the guerrillas. The 'army had strictly fulfilled its duty', noted President Luis Echeverría subsequently, a tone echoed by Julio Scherer, best known for his reportage of human rights abuses and official corruption, who wrote an apologetic editorial in *Excélsior*, repeating the mantra that Cabañas the guerrilla was little more than a '*delincuente*' (Rodríguez Munguía 2007: 141–2).

Playing on public ignorance about the threat of Communism and associating guerrillas and dissidents with long-held fears about the deranging effects of illicit substances were effective tools for discrediting political enemies. Nevertheless, rhetoric about drug trafficking as the country's major security problem became much more intense after the Cold War, when the ideological currency of fighting the Communist threat had lost its purchasing power. Perhaps the most pertinent aspect of repression in Guerrero is that it continues to the present day, despite the loss of political excuses, and uses the crackdown on narcotrafficking as a rationalisation of and public relations strategy for a permanent military presence in remote rural areas.

With widespread political dissatisfaction in urban areas and the countryside, the emergence of armed guerrilla insurgents, and an increase in the export of heroin and marijuana northwards, it was not long before the Nixon administration focused intensely on Mexican domestic affairs. Mexican 'stability', touted by the political elite, was contradicted by high levels of poverty and economic inequality, which increasingly led to public and organised expressions of discontent and rage (Schmidt 1991: 82).

President Luis Echeverría, who had been Secretario de Gobernación (equivalent to Interior Minister or Home Office Minister) in 1968, and who more recently was accused of and arrested for ordering the massacre in Tlatelolco that year, escalated the repression against opposition movements when he took office as President

(1970–76). Indeed, Echeverría's public rhetoric for internal and international consumption and his private opinions differed radically. In private, his conversations with President Nixon reveal an unswerving commitment to suppressing challenges from left-wing organisations. It is probably no coincidence that around the same time US drug policy began to spend massive resources on the drugs war in Mexico.

In contrast to the views he shared with Nixon, Echeverría made speeches in the early days of his presidency about Third World independence, of which he saw Mexico as a leader, and was a vocal supporter of Cuban sovereignty (Landau 2003). Similarly, he publicly supported Salvador Allende in Chile and opposed US expansionism in Latin America. Mexico boycotted the General Assembly meeting of the Organization of American States (OAS) in 1973 over human rights abuses committed by the Pinochet dictatorship. Echeverría's Mexico accepted political refugees from Chile, Spain and Guatemala, further embellishing its apparently liberal credentials.

This was important window dressing because Echeverría could be seen to support progressive movements abroad, appealing to the left he and his predecessor had previously alienated, while in reality doing something quite different at home. Underlining Mexico's change of direction under his leadership, at least at the rhetorical level, Echeverría later condemned Zionist expansion at the United Nations, criticising Israel's further incursion into Palestinian territory and its repression of the Palestinians, and allowed the Palestine Liberation Organisation (PLO) to open an office in Mexico City (Muñoz 2006). Echeverría adopted an unequivocally critical stance on the question of the Occupied Territories.

Mexican politicians regularly criticised and attacked US imperialism in Latin America, yet there was a clear understanding between the two governments that Mexican 'stability' was a top priority and that discreet support (or failing that, neutrality) for US foreign policy and wars was one of pragmatism which suited both sides. US administrations were willing to allow Mexican politicians to sound off in public so long as the relationship of cooperation in areas vital to both governments remained intact in reality.

Between 1971 and 1974, a series of bombings and kidnappings of politicians and business leaders took place throughout Mexico. The US consul was taken hostage by the Fuerzas Armadas Revolucionarias (Revolutionary Armed Forces – FAR), while President Echeverría's father-in-law, José Guadalupe Zuno, was the victim of a kidnapping. When Eugenio Garza Sada of the Monterrey Group was kidnapped by the Liga Comunista 23 de Septiembre and killed in an ensuing gunfight initiated by his bodyguard, and Lucio Cabañas and the Partido de los Pobres (Party of the Poor – PDLP) kidnapped the PRI candidate for the state governorship, Rubén Figueroa, and held him for one hundred days, mounting pressure came from the business community to crack down on insurgents (Doyle 2003a: 27–8). Such developments also caused concern to the Nixon administration.

In 1972, Echeverría met with Nixon to discuss his preoccupations with the influence of Communism in the hemisphere and the repercussions of domestic dissent. Both presidents were obsessed with the Communist 'threat' as well as with controlling organised dissent domestically. Recordings of their conversation demonstrate that Echeverría's stance in private was diametrically opposed to his public statements. According to this conversation, he clearly saw Allende's victory in Chile, as well as the continuing influence of the Cuban Revolution, as a threat to stability throughout the region. Referring to leadership of the Third World, he told Nixon, 'If I don't take this flag in Latin America, Castro will,' adding that, 'I sensed this also when I was in Chile and it can be felt in Central America, and among young people, among intellectuals – that Cuba is a Soviet base in every sense of the word, both militarily and ideologically, and that this is going on right under our noses.' In a reversal of his public comments, Echeverría told the US President that he saw Cuba as an instrument of Soviet penetration into the United States and Mexico.

This ideological ground was fertile for a significant US involvement, and the commencement of a permanent drug war (supported by the establishment of the DEA) provided a suitable pretext. Similarly, a new role for the Mexican military, clamping down on both insurgents and drug traffickers, was intended to win back the legitimacy the army had lost in Tlatelolco in 1968.

As declassified internal CIA documents obtained by the National Security Archive at George Washington University demonstrate, both presidents Díaz Ordaz and Echeverría as well as Fernando Gutiérrez Barrios, head of the DFS, had worked as informants for the CIA under the LITEMPO programme. They provided information on alleged subversives and Communists in Mexico to the agency, information that the DFS also held (Morley 2006). This provided the CIA with direct and practically unrestricted access to Mexican intelligence on opposition movements. Likewise, it is hard to imagine that intelligence on Mexican drug traffickers, apparently a matter of pressing concern to the US government, was not shared between the two agencies. This then raises the question of why the CIA, with such an interest in liquidating rebel, Marxist and guerrilla groups to ensure Mexican stability, seemed quite happy to tolerate the potentially destabilising effects on US and Mexican society of high-level involvement in the drug trade by officials in the DFS and federal police (we discuss this further in Chapter 3). Indeed, as Anabel Hernández has pointed out, 'in those years to belong to a guerrilla or dissident group was much more dangerous than becoming a narcotrafficker' (2010a: 119).

One politician with a keen interest in regaining the legitimacy the army had lost at Tlatelolco was Javier García Paniagua. He had been Defence Secretary at the time of the massacre and was keen to re-establish a role for the military which would win back public confidence. When he later became chief of the DFS in 1976, President López Portillo entrusted him with oversight of the *guerra sucia* against dissident and opposition groups, a responsibility which was sure to gain the army some respect. Yet García Paniagua also envisioned an improved DFS: while cracking down on insurgents and subversives, a parallel role for the secret police would be to control the narcotrafficking business throughout the Mexican territories, not in order to clamp down on criminals, but to profit from their enterprise. In addition, DFS influence over the drugs trade meant that some of the profits could be siphoned off and destined for the fight against subversives (*ibid.*: 121–2). Luckily, Fortune smiled on his project in that, during raids against rebels, the DFS's paramilitary wing, the *Brigada Blanca*, repeatedly came across remote rural warehouses used to store narcotics. Seizing on the opportunities provided by such discoveries, which were made under the pretext of searching for insurgents, the DFS could run its own protection racket and take a substantial cut of the drug-trafficking profits (Dillon and Preston 2004: 328). Thus, during the 1970s and early 1980s (during the administrations of Luis Echeverría and José López Portillo), when more than 1,200 people deemed to be subversives were disappeared, while others were murdered, tortured or incarcerated (Castellanos 2007), the secret police opportunistically increased their own involvement in the narcotics trade, under cover of eliminating dissidents whom they regarded as the real criminals.

Government policy in using the DFS and army to combat opposition groups was successful in so far as it could simply liquidate those involved and intimidate potential adversaries. In the corridors of political power, there was little disagreement on how subversives and guerrillas should be treated. But efforts to reduce the cultivation, production and export of drugs were undermined both by official participation and complicity in the trade, and by the absence of sustainable economic alternatives for the poor.

The Other Operation Condor

The economic crisis which beset the Luis Echeverría *sexenio* had been developing in the preceding years and became more pronounced in the 1970s. Disillusionment with the PRI had increased, particularly since 1968, and Echeverría attempted to elicit renewed support through populist economic measures.

Harsh inequalities remained persistent in Mexico and poverty was rife, despite the lauded 'economic miracle' which had taken place between the 1940s and 1960s. Growth had averaged around 6 per cent for a number of consecutive years, but wealth distribution continued overwhelmingly to favour the rich. Growth was limited to 2 per cent in the rural areas, which were home to 58 per cent of the population – a figure that declined dramatically as the decade continued (Craig 1980: 354), in part explaining why so many farmers turned to illegal crops which they could sell at a profit, and which were less subject to price fluctuations.

For the poorest 50 per cent, economic conditions had actually worsened during the economic miracle: in 1950 they had owned 19 per cent of the country's wealth, but between 1963 and 1969 this fell to 15.7 per cent. The top 20 per cent of the population increased their share of the nation's income during the same period, while the top 5 per cent benefited even more. People in rural areas saw their incomes decline, as did industrial workers in the urban areas. Poverty in the countryside obliged huge numbers to migrate to the cities, which posed a new set of urban problems: overcrowding, housing shortages and lack of adequate infrastructure and services. In response to the growing demand for drugs in the United States, difficult economic conditions and inflation, other rural workers moved from growing traditional crops to poppies and marijuana, particularly in the northern states. Besides, between 1960 and 1970 unemployment had risen by 487 per cent and spiralled higher still under Echeverría (Schmidt 1991: 20–1).

Government spending increased in an attempt to restore control over the economy and neutralise the discontent that had characterised the latter half of the 1960s. Programmes were introduced to bolster ailing businesses and reduce unemployment through state intervention and subsidies. Yet at the same time, most people in the cities had little purchasing power, while many of those in rural areas operated outside the cash economy.

Higher business taxes were to pay for government solutions to these problems as it was spending more than the revenues it received. As a result, domestic and foreign companies were reluctant to invest, which in turn negatively affected growth levels (Cothran 1991: xiv–xv).

These remedies were far from revolutionary, though they did provoke opposition from big business (Lustig 1998: 17). Mexico's position in the world economy – one of dependency on foreign markets and capital – meant that even relatively small measures of wealth redistribution would lead to capital flight. While Echeverría's programmes may have had positive results for a great number of people, these were undermined by Mexico's position of relative weakness in the world system.

Equally, Echeverría's relatively superficial solutions to quelling popular dissatisfaction with social and economic conditions were unsuccessful. One manifestation of this was in the comparatively low number of people turning out to vote. In the election that had brought Echeverría to power, for example, 34 per cent of those registered to vote abstained, 25 per cent of the votes cast were annulled, and a further 20 per cent went to other political parties (Shapira 1977: 567). The demonstration culture that had peaked in the 1960s had by no means disappeared, despite the massacre of students in the Plaza de las Tres Culturas. Some of these students had become radicalised and joined the armed insurgent movements that emerged in the late 1960s and early 1970s, which were another symptom of a profound social malaise; not since the 1930s had there been so many violent attacks on the state and the rich.

One business was booming, however. By the mid-1970s in the *triángulo crítico* or *dorado* (the 'critical' or 'golden' triangle in the northern states of Sinaloa, Durango and Chihuahua), according to the government's own figures, 600,000 square kilometres were being used to grow marijuana and poppies, and there were some 30,000 opium plots. Many of these exceeded forty acres (Craig 1980: 347–52). Any eradication programme which would seriously tackle the widespread cultivation of illegal crops would have to take place on a massive scale. In recognition of this, the Echeverría government drew up plans for Operación CANADOR (Combate Contra el Narcotráfico) – later to become Operation Condor – to destroy illegal crops in the *triángulo dorado*.

Appropriately, José Hernández Toledo, who had commanded military operations at the Tlatelolco massacre, the occupation of the National Autonomous University of Mexico (UNAM) and the repression of student protests in Morelia and Sonora in the late 1960s under Díaz Ordaz and Echeverría, was entrusted with the military side of the operation. An expert in repressive measures, he noted that there were enough armaments in the mountains to create a 'small revolution', but assured the politicians that within months the campaign would achieve the eradication of illegal crops in the region (Astorga 2005: 115).

The operation pooled a variety of resources, doubling the number of federal police and sending thousands more troops to the *triángulo* (5,000 soldiers and 350 members of the Federal Judicial Police – PJF). The United States supplied 76 aircraft and invested $150 million, with Mexico initially investing $35 million in what was intended to become a campaign that would end only when poppy and marijuana crops were completely eradicated (Streatfeild 2001: 375; Craig 1980: 347). Condor also gave the green light to the formalised and permanent presence of US agents in Mexico. Some thirty US agents were dispatched to Mexico to oversee the plan and assist with identifying illicit crops (Toro 1995: 18).

One of the most significant new developments was the aerial spraying of crops with herbicides. The government had denied publicly that it was intending to use Paraquat, also known as Agent Orange, in northern Mexico. But this was not what had been decided in private, following meetings between Pedro Ojeda Paullada, Mexico's Attorney General, and Sheldon Vance, director of the Cabinet Committee on International Narcotics Control and adviser to Henry Kissinger (Astorga 2005: 114). This was an unprecedented technique in Mexico, and, while promising to eradicate thousands of illegal plantations, it also threatened to destroy legal crops, and therefore the livelihoods of farmers; pollute the groundwater and the soil; and put at risk the health of those who came into contact with the chemicals. It emerged that the government had been conducting its own 'experiments' in the aerial spraying of herbicides in rural Sinaloa and Guerrero in preparation for the launch of Operation Condor (Craig 1980: 347). The chemical in question, Paraquat, has been linked to Parkinson's disease; lymphoma; cancer; liver, eye and kidney damage; and asphyxiation if ingested. While the US government was supplying Mexico with the chemical, American drug users were consuming small quantities of Paraquat whenever they smoked marijuana originating from fumigated areas. According to the US government's National Institute on Drug Abuse (NIDA) about a fifth of all marijuana (around five hundred tons) smoked in the USA was contaminated with the chemical and some tests sampled contained 44,000 times what was considered to be safe for humans, something which caused irreparable lung damage. But, as Dan Baum comments, 'because there existed no addict lobby for pot smokers, nobody in the US made a fuss about that' (1996: 107). The risks to US marijuana smokers, to the public health of Mexicans living in areas near fields targeted for fumigation, and to the ecology, did not prevent politicians from pronouncing with confidence on the indisputable benefits of aerial spraying. Attorney General Pedro Ojeda Paullada claimed that 'the Government of Mexico will under no circumstances conduct or condone operations that could have an adverse effect on the country's ecology'. 'But,' he went on rather crucially, that 'does not mean that we should not use herbicides' (Craig 1980: 346).

In a sense, Operation Condor, which began as Echeverría was about to leave office and was continued under his successor, José López Portillo, was a success, at least if measured by the number of plantations eradicated. Prior operations had seen groups of soldiers (sometimes as few as six) patrolling remote areas on foot and destroying crops by beating the plants with sticks. They were often attacked by armed peasants who opted to guard their livelihoods by force rather than escape into the forest. On other occasions, heavily armed employees of trafficking organisations would attack soldiers in order to defend their crops. Aerial spraying, on the other hand, could destroy vast plantations quickly and effectively, and in the first year of the operation over 21,000 opium fields were eradicated.

In 1976, one of the leaders of the operation claimed that 'before mid-year we are going to end completely cultivation in this country' (Toro 1995: 17). Such optimism was somewhat misguided. Certainly, Operation Condor had destroyed most of the opium and marijuana crops in the critical triangle on an unprecedented scale in its first three years. But unless the reasons why people became involved in trafficking narcotics in the first place – and why so many high-level players could operate with impunity – were addressed, the campaign was unlikely to achieve its stated goals in the long run.

Aerial spraying also encouraged the 'cartelisation' of the drug market. Those with the resources and capacity to do so planted new, smaller plots in remote areas, which were more difficult to detect, as far as away as Chiapas and Veracruz. Certainly, the use of defoliants had had a huge and devastating effect on poppy and marijuana cultivation and severely restricted the amount of both crossing the US border. By 1979, three years after the inception of Operation Condor, the amount of heroin entering the United States had almost halved. But this apparent success was countered by the fact that demand for the product was constant. Scarcity of heroin on the market meant that suppliers could get away with selling a poorer quality and more impure product, and also pushed the price up so that a milligram's street value rose from $1.26 in 1976 to $2.25 in 1979. For the producers and traffickers with the best political contacts, the largest networks, and sufficient resources, and for those who had adapted to survive the initial years of this new phase of anti-drug policy, this sharp and sudden rise in the price of their exports was both rewarding and tantalising. Similarly the reduction of Mexico's marijuana-producing capacity by around 70 per cent merely meant that Colombian growers and traffickers capitalised on the endless demand from the US market (Craig 1980: 358–9).

Better-resourced traffickers could defend plantations by attacking crop-spraying planes with gunfire. Operation Condor put their small-time competitors out of business and thus rewarded the most daring risk-taking producers and allowed the most dangerous elements of the smuggling industry to become more powerful. Similarly, these groups had the greatest bargaining power with the police, military, the DFS and politicians, and could thus buy protection.

Alberto Sicilia Falcón, for example, had paid bribes to the authorities to divert government eradication programmes away from his own plantations and towards the elimination of his competitors in Sinaloa so that he could establish a monopoly over the marijuana trade. When Sicilia Falcón was arrested his Sinaloense competitors moved in to Guadalajara and paid for their competitors in turn to be put out of business by eradication campaigns. 'The DFS did much more than protect the most notorious traffickers', write Peter Dale Scott and Jonathan Marshall (1991: 40); 'It brought them together as a cartel, centralised and rationalised their operation, snuffed out competitors, and through its connections with the CIA, provided the international protection to ensure their success.'

Concurrent with the DFS's persecution of dissidents, activists and guerrillas were major and regular trafficking hauls by police vehicles on behalf of the Guadalajara cartel. In the late 1970s, a fleet of six hundred DFS tankers was used to cross the US border (around twelve would cross every day) stuffed with marijuana. Mexican and US border officials were bribed to allow the trucks to arrive in Phoenix and Los Angeles unhindered. The DFS, often under the usual rubric of going after political subversives, would help by cracking down on smaller competitors, thus allowing the Guadalajara cartel to monopolise the market. In return for protection, the cartel had to provide the DFS with 25 per cent of its profits (*ibid*.: 40).

What initially seemed to weaken the base of high-level crime in Mexico in fact encouraged emerging crime syndicates to become better organised and to rely more heavily on official cooperation. These factors, combined with the onset of neoliberal economic policies, which escalated the levels of inequality and poverty, with a concomitant reduction in social services and a weakened infrastructure, bringing ever larger numbers of the rural poor into the urban areas, would contribute to an increase in the export of marijuana, heroin and cocaine and the empowerment of drug cartels over the following decade.

Furthermore, in a twist worthy of a Hollywood fiction, it later transpired that some of the planes ostensibly sent out to spray crops with herbicides were instead spraying water and fertilisers on illicit plantations. And some officials were apparently using some of the $150 million supplied by the US government and intended for the operation, to line their own pockets (Streatfeild 2001: 375). According to Peter Dale Scott and Jonathan Marshall (1991: 38), in *Cocaine Politics*:

> Informants reported that some Mexican officials used the planes for joy rides and pleasure trips, while other officials shook down drug cultivators in exchange for protection from spraying. Reports of this fraud made it into occasional press reports, but these were buried under the State Department's press releases about the Mexican miracle.

The principal victims of anti-drug policy were not the high-level growers and traffickers, but the rural poor. While the government was exalting the achievements of the campaign by adding up the total number of fields destroyed, nobody was counting the social costs of eradication. In the municipality of Badiraguato (the birthplace of the world's most wanted trafficker, Joaquín *El Chapo* Guzmán Loera), for example, around 30 per cent of the population's livelihood depended on the production of illicit crops. Growing legal crops scarcely provided a living, and so many former growers migrated to urban areas in search of work. Then there was the largely unrecorded damage to health of spraying defoliants. And the quasi-permanent presence of the army: Amnesty International denounced the investigative methods of the Federal Judicial Police used in anti-narcotic operations, which included beatings, the application of electric shocks, burns to the skin, rape and the forced inhalation of carbonated liquids via the nasal passages (Astorga 2005: 118).

The agrarian sector was already in crisis, with the average farmer's income falling, and areas under cultivation reduced by around 20 per cent. Mexico's economy had shifted from a net exporter to an importer of food. Richard Craig summarised the problem succinctly:

> Unable to survive off the land, desperate campesinos are flooding the cities, abandoning *ejido* and private plots, seizing haciendas, executing local *caciques*, streaming across the border as illegal immigrants, and becoming drug entrepreneurs. All these activities are disconcerting to Mexico City. But only one of them to date, involvement with narcotics, has caused deep official concern *and* determined action. This has led some writers to conclude that Mexico's war against the poppy may be more accurately termed a war against the peasant and the real or imagined guerrillas of the sierras. (1980: 355)

For Craig, the problems which arose from drug eradication – intended as a campaign to reduce the number of illegal crops – were essentially concerned with restraining and limiting the activities of the poor and disenfranchised, and offsetting the possibility of social revolt. The campaign allowed the army to establish itself as a quasi-permanent force in areas which had witnessed important social movements and guerrilla mobilisations – Guerrero and Oaxaca – and in states where economic desperation was contributing to a generalised climate in which 'people had lost all respect for authority' (Schmidt 1991: 82). If, as was indeed the case, the government was unprepared radically to restructure an economy that reinforced a massive inequality benefiting only those at the top, it would have to be maintained by the use of coercion and violence. Whether intended or not, a consequence of the militarisation of these zones was that it became much more difficult for independent growers and smugglers to operate without cooperation and even oversight from the state. As a result, the government's monopoly on violence and the drug trade would be assured in the years that followed.

Three contributory factors undermined bilateral drug eradication and interdiction programmes in the 1970s. There was the grinding poverty and unemployment in the northern states, which led so many people to seek alternatives to the legitimate economy in the black market. Second, the world's largest market for narcotics was on the doorstep of these regions. Demand was unlikely to go away, particularly because US anti-drug policies overwhelmingly favoured prohibition, incarceration, eradication and interdiction over rehabilitation and addressing the social and economic root causes of trafficking and addiction. Anti-drug legislation in both countries had failed to stop the cross-border flow of drugs. A third factor was official corruption and a political monopoly of drug smuggling. While Mexican/US counternarcotics operations were presumably designed to reduce the supply of drugs, official protection of the major players in the market was a principal reason for the increasing power of crime syndicates.

A perfect example of the authorities' cooperation with major traffickers is provided by Alberto Sicilia Falcón, one of Mexico's major criminals and a Cuban exile who had quit the island for Miami in 1959. Here he was trained by the CIA to participate in raids on Cuba and deliver weapons to anti-Castro forces there. Following his move to Mexico in the 1960s, he was responsible for establishing the largest cocaine shipments ever to leave Mexico. Enjoying CIA and DFS protection, Sicilia Falcón developed an operation based in Tijuana that is estimated to have generated $3.6 million every week. In addition, Sicilia Falcón was connected politically to the family of President Echeverría's wife, María Esther

Zuno de Echeverría – who had ties to the European heroin trade. By the early 1970s Sicilia Falcón was regarded as one of the continent's most important and influential traffickers (Cockburn and St Clair 1998: 355). But at the same time that presidents Echeverría and Nixon were ratcheting up counternarcotics discourse and policies, a major exporter of illegal drugs and importer of illegal arms such as Sicilia Falcón could have a coterie of DFS agents armed with AK-47s protecting his Roundhouse in Tijuana; his five-billion-dollar-a-year enterprise (laundered via Mexican and US banks) could thus, with bilateral security agency backing, continue unhindered.

One has to wonder why the government allowed such high-level protection of criminals when it was, with the other hand, attempting to undermine the drugs business. This is what is often referred to as the 'schizophrenic' nature of the Mexican political system – appearing to do one thing, but doing the opposite. Or rather, in an even more astonishing act of prestidigitation, doing one thing and its contrary simultaneously.

But there were good, if not valid, reasons for such seemingly contradictory political moves. While the DFS ran the paramilitary death squad, the *Brigada Blanca* or White Brigade, which President López Portillo was forced to disband in 1980 following increased exposure of the group's activities against leftists, criminals like Sicilia Falcón appeared to enjoy protection from senior officials within the organisation (Shannon 1988: 180–1; Weinberg 2000: 351; Grayson 2010: 137). DFS protection was granted as a result of Sicilia Falcón's anti-Castro and anti-Communist activities on behalf of the CIA. One of Sicilia Falcón's closest partners and friends, dating back to their participation at the Bay of Pigs, was José Egozi Bejar, who had worked for the CIA and the DFS. According to Cockburn and St Clair (1998: 355–6),

> During the [later] investigation of Sicilia Falcón, DEA agents inter-viewed Egozi. He admitted that he had introduced Sicilia Falcón to political contacts in the Mexican elite, helped him set up a network of bank accounts to launder his drug proceeds and had once given the drug lord a CIA catalogue of weapons. They also worked together

in an attempt to finance the Morgan super-rifle, a high-powered gun made by a Los Angeles-based firm that the CIA wanted put in the hands of its covert armies in Latin America.

Sicilia Falcón's role in repressing progressive political movements was not limited to the Americas, however. Following the *Revolução dos Cravos* in Portugal, which represented both a victory against fascism and European colonialism in Africa, Egozi employed Sicilia Falcón's power and connections to supply an arms shipment worth a quarter of a billion dollars for a CIA campaign to overthrow the newly formed democratic government (Scott and Marshall 1991: 34).

Miguel Nazar Haro, then chief of the DFS and infamous for his role in the 1968 Tlatelolco massacre of protesters in Mexico City, intervened. Sicilia Falcón knew a great deal about government and DFS involvement in the drug trade and Nazar Haro's intervention prevented this from coming to light. Nazar Haro himself, an FBI investigation alleged, was profiting from a car-stealing ring in Los Angeles and San Diego, which they estimated was worth some US$30 million (Shannon 1988: 183). Once the cars were stolen, they were taken across the border and dropped off at the DFS office in Tijuana. When Nazar Haro was arrested in San Diego in 1981 following an FBI investigation into his activities, it was the CIA who secured his release, stressing that he was an 'essential, repeat, essential contact for the CIA station in Mexico City', particularly important for the 'security of the United States' in providing 'counterintelligence' and in fighting 'terrorism' (Aguayo Quezada 2001: 236). Nazar Haro's lawyer secured the US$250,000 bail and authorisation to travel; he crossed the border back into Mexico and never returned to the United States. Twelve years later, in 1994, he was arrested and imprisoned in Mexico for his involvement in the activities of the *Brigada Blanca*, and in particular for his role in the disappearance of Jesús Piedra Ibarra, the political activist son of human rights campaigner, Rosario Ibarra de Piedra (Grayson 2010: 137).

The tolerance afforded high-level traffickers demonstrates that subverting challenges to Western hegemony was a higher priority for the CIA, the DFS, and the Echeverría and López Portillo administrations than eradicating illegal crops. The Echeverría government's progressive mask – its rhetorical support for the overthrow of fascism in Europe, the anti-colonial movements in Africa, and the Cuban Revolution, its rejection of US imperialism in the region and self-promotion as an advocate and leader of Third World nationalism – concealed a *realpolitik* that backed exactly the opposite. In the following years, as discussed in Chapter 3, the subversion of leftist politics by drug traffickers backed by the CIA and DFS reached unprecedented proportions.

While Mexico's 'schizophrenic' politics in relation to narco-trafficking was, on the one hand, grounded in ideologically deter-mined considerations during the Cold War, on the other, the sheer scale of the business and the profits it generated for government bodies and corrupt officials meant that its illegal activities would be tolerated.

The PRI exercised a monopoly over the trade, often called *la plaza*. *La plaza*, literally referring to the central square of a village or town, took on a broader meaning concurrently with the expansion of the drug market. Whoever controlled *la plaza* enjoyed the protection of the police and army, so that incursions from competing traffickers were met with fierce resistance from the authorities. Those who held definitive control were the politicians, who would offer protection to traffickers in return for regular payments. For police chiefs, being appointed to a particular area could prove extremely lucrative. Some would bribe their bosses in order to secure a placement in Tijuana or Guadalajara, for example, where the profits for corrupt police willing to provide protection for the cartels were considerable. As Terrence Poppa remarks, 'Cops were poorly paid and were expected to supplement their income by fair means or foul. Politics and government service had become roads to riches, terrific rackets if you were on the inside. That system could be bent to work to the advantage of the trafficker if he knew how to cultivate the right authorities and become a member of the club' (1998: 64). One police chief reportedly paid the Mexican Attorney General more than a million dollars in order to be stationed in Guadalajara so that he could control the *plaza* there. This was after he had apparently paid six million dollars to be posted to a job in Tijuana (Streatfeild 2001: 376).

In *Drug Lord*, the life story of Ojinaga's most renowned trafficker, Pablo Acosta, Poppa demonstrates that typically the traffickers who were arrested were the independents who refused or failed to pay tribute to the relevant authorities (1998: 44). Each time this happened, it appeared as if the police were seriously going after criminals and also provided captivating statistics for the press. 'That most of the seized narcotics were then recycled', notes Poppa, 'sold to favoured trafficking groups or outrightly smuggled by police groups was irrelevant. The seizures were in fact made and there were headlines to prove it' (1998: 45). Those shrewd enough to understand who really held power dutifully paid off the police, army and PRI every month. In return for protection, they would supply information on independent smuggling operations.

The army would protect plantations, while the PJF looked after shipment, and the DFS dealt with the traffickers and kept them under control. For every kilo of contraband produced, traffickers could pay a tax of sixty dollars; twenty dollars to the military leaders of the given area, or *plaza*, twenty to the federal police chiefs and a further twenty to the DFS (Hernández 2010a: 121). Those who refused to pay such taxes often found themselves out of favour with the authorities and would end up murdered or in prison. Often, such rogue traffickers would be reported by or dealt with by fellow traffickers, who did not see why they should pay taxes to the authorities while others could flout the rules.

High-profile arrests or assassinations of major traffickers tended to occur if the individual charged with running a particular *plaza* ceased making regular payments or had created enough of a public profile to attract unwanted interest from the press, the DEA and the US government. For Pablo Acosta, for example, it was when reports of his exploits were published in the US media that he was considered a liability by the Mexican administration and became expendable. He was eventually shot dead by a joint squad of federal police and FBI agents led by Comandante Guillermo González Calderoni, who, ironically, sold *plazas* to high-level traffickers.

Until then, Acosta had been given privileged access to the political elite and the DFS. He and other major traffickers in Mexico carried *La Charola*, the badge of DFS agents which exempted them from unwelcome legal scrutiny. Poppa notes that the badge 'carried by Acosta and other protected drug traffickers throughout Mexico, allow[ed] them to operate with impunity. [It] allowed them to carry weapons and instructed civil and military authorities, as well as private citizens, to cooperate "so that the bearer may carry out his legitimate duties"' (1998: 74). This made criminals like Acosta untouchable and 'American agents . . . also learned that the commissioned officers working under the new federal police *comandante* were in fact thugs selected by Pablo from the ranks of his own gunmen and bodyguards. These men were also given police credentials' (*ibid.*: 75).

Manuel Salcido, a larger-than-life character known as *El Cochiloco*, or 'Crazy Pig', boss of the Guadalajara cartel, who held the *plaza* in southern Sinaloa and who by the early 1970s was one of the chief traffickers in Mexico, employed the services of the federal police in order to send a clear message to rivals. In 1973 he paid them a quarter of a million pesos to eliminate six young traffickers belonging to the rival Braulio Aguirre gang, who were competing for control of southern Sinaloa. The six men were kidnapped, killed with machetes and burned. When Salcido was subsequently arrested and incarcerated, one editorial lamented that 'there is an undue marriage between narcotrafficking and those responsible for combating it'. Such were the links that in 1975 Salcido paid off the Culiacán prison guards so that he and his associates were allowed to leave the prison, prompting state governor Calderón's lukewarm assertion that, 'this makes us think that there is something murky going on' (Astorga 2005: 113–14).

Only months later, when *El Cochiloco* attended his father's funeral in Mazatlán, surrounded by around a dozen heavily armed men, no members of the authorities were on hand to arrest the escaped convict. Salcido's presence at the funeral was public and took place in broad daylight (*ibid.*: 114). Such blatant disregard for the rule of law cleared up any 'murkiness' about the leniency afforded to *plaza* holders and sent a clear message to residents of the area about police and government enthusiasm for cracking down on narcotraffickers.

According to one former military general interviewed by Anabel Hernández, in the 1970s no large-scale plantation of poppies or marijuana was possible without the unequivocal permission of government. No consignment of narcotics could be exported without the explicit approval of the army, the DFS and the federal police. During Operation Condor owners of plantations which had received official approval flew flags on their fields to signal to pilots not to fumigate but to spray water instead. Hernández's informant also claims that in order to avoid their being robbed by rivals, loads of contraband would be accompanied and protected by the Policía Federal Judicial (PJF) (2010a: 118–19). Interestingly, such was the profit to be made by selling contraband on the US market that the sale of drugs for domestic consumption was strictly forbidden and harshly punished, something which perhaps explains why Mexican rates of consumption have always been relatively low. The same informant reveals that, every month, traffickers sent cases full of cash to the Attorney General's Office, the final destination being the presidential residence of Los Pinos in Chapultepec in Mexico City, a practice that appears to have spanned a series of administrations (*ibid.*: 124–5).

One of the most significant innovations in trafficking into the United States involved the use of aircraft – developed initially as part of major smuggling operations by the trafficker Pedro Avilés Pérez, the first Mexican to transport large quantities of cocaine from Colombia to Mexico en route to the United States. When he was assassinated in 1978, the method was adopted by Miguel

Ángel Félix Gallardo, Ernesto Fonseca Carrillo and Rafael Caro Quintero, who later formed the Guadalajara and Sinaloa cartels. They established major links with Colombian crime syndicates, shipping cocaine by air to Mexico before taking it across the US border. Sinaloa, in addition to being a major producer of opium and marijuana, was the corridor from South America for cocaine landed en route to the USA. Again, without official protection, the growth of the Guadalajara cartel would have been stunted.

In spite of the apparent initial effectiveness of the eradication campaigns of the 1970s, all of the problems associated with official complicity in – and, in some cases, oversight of – organised crime remained; and so did the poverty which persuaded people to work in the drugs industry. As stronger trade links evolved with Colombian cartels supplying cocaine, these underlying conditions, far from being addressed, were further exacerbated by the economic crises and neoliberal policies of the 1980s – as we discuss in the next chapter.

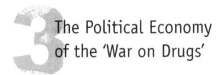

The Political Economy of the 'War on Drugs'

The notion that the narcotrafficking industry existed in parallel to and entirely separately from the state, as Mexican politicians always claimed, has little credibility. As we showed in chapters 1 and 2, since the beginning of the twentieth century the smuggling of contraband into the United States has benefited from official backing, complicity and collusion, despite legislation and campaigns to eradicate production and interdict shipments.

Even politicians who purported to be in favour of cleaning up public life in Mexico either found the task too daunting or ended up with the taint of corruption about them. Such a fate befell Miguel de la Madrid, who entered the presidency in 1982 with an extensive media and public relations campaign ambitiously titled *La Renovación Moral*. The new government would crack down on corruption, abuse of power and those in government who were using their posts to enhance their business investments. The *Renovación* was very much a public relations campaign designed to present the new government as morally sound and different in outlook and practice from its predecessors, and to distract public attention and scrutiny away from the severe Mexican economic crisis. 'Either we govern or we do business', de la Madrid asserted in his inauguration speech. To do both was 'immoral' and the position of public servant did not give anyone justification to 'loot' (Delgado de Cantú 2003: 444). One of de la Madrid's first moves was to remove and prosecute a number of corrupt public officials. Among the first was Jorge Díaz Serrano, accused of abusing his post in the national petroleum company, PEMEX, for the purposes of financial fraud during his time as director. Arturo Durazo Moreno, who had been chief of police for the Federal District (Mexico City) under López Portillo, was accused and found guilty of stockpiling illegal arms, tax evasion and extortion. Both later served custodial sentences. By 1985, sanctions had been applied to 163 public officials who had been judged to have abused their positions (*ibid.*: 445). Whether the *Renovación Moral* was a genuine attempt to address the corruption of public officials or merely a public relations stunt is a matter of conjecture, but the record clearly shows that both domestic and international pressures were such that anti-corruption measures like those introduced by de la Madrid could only scratch the surface of a huge problem. Furthermore, the benefits of institutionalised corruption to those involved were so substantial, the profits so huge, that serious attempts to deal with the problem would require radical structural and economic changes in order to make corruption seem an unattractive, unacceptable and unpalatable option. Yet in the economic crisis which consumed the economy in 1982, the de la Madrid government opted for a programme of economic restructuring that made corruption easier, more attractive, more acceptable and more palatable.

In this chapter we examine the extent to which narcotics were an integral component of PRI hegemony and the economic restructuring and implementation of neoliberal policies which began in 1982, following the debt crisis. We look at how the Colombian cocaine traffickers over the same period strengthened their links with Mexican crime organisations as they sought new shipment routes to the United States. Finally, we discuss the internal political contradictions in both countries underlying the tangled relationship between the US and Mexican administrations as they conducted what was meant to be a joint war against Communism and drugs. It was the mixing of all these elements into a socially toxic brew that enabled crime syndicates to increase their power in Mexico.

Traffickers and the PRI

By the early 1980s the number of cultivated plots eradicated by the army had shrunk, partly because growers had dispersed their operations, often to smaller fields, which were more difficult to detect. The army's earlier successes in destroying crops had not been sustained: for example, when DEA agent Enrique Camarena was captured, tortured and killed by members of the Guadalajara cartel, evidence led straight back to the ranch of Rafael Caro Quintero in Chihuahua where a storehouse of thousands of tons of marijuana – a massive and unsuspected cache – was discovered.

If it were true, as has been suggested, that the narcotics trade flourished in a parallel and autonomous existence divorced from the state, traffickers would not have needed constantly to seek, and very often obtain, official backing and protection from the authorities. The notion that the involvement of high-ranking DFS officials in overseeing and coordinating much of the drug trade was kept secret from politicians is just not plausible. A more likely explanation is that those whom Echeverría had entrusted with the crackdown on urban guerrillas and subversives were acting within the parameters of what was acceptable to the political elite. Again, it seems highly improbable that presidents Echeverría and López Portillo, and the inner circle of the presidential elite, were unaware that major drug traffickers were being protected by the country's chief intelligence agency, and that the activities of criminals like Alberto Sicilia Falcón – who himself had links to the Echeverría family – were unknown to the political hierarchy.

Then there was the issue of impunity, which was virtually guaranteed to traffickers who paid tribute in order to control a given *plaza*. So long as the DEA did not overly pressurise the Mexicans, and traffickers were shrewd enough to stay out of the public eye, impunity for murder and smuggling was frequently assured.

It could be that these were blindspots of the judicial system. But again, this seems unlikely. No impunity was afforded to the illegal activities of urban dissenters and rural guerrilla movements. In fact, the security agency's repressive measures also extended to crackdowns on activists involved in peaceful protest and activism (Aguayo Quezada 2001). This discrepancy between judicial measures, legal and extra-legal, applied to guerrillas on the one hand and major traffickers on the other, again indicates that state involvement in narcotrafficking, a constant dating back to the early twentieth century, had continued and become stronger in the 1970s and 1980s.

Terrence Poppa recounts how events on the ground could be played out in establishing mutually convenient relationships between criminals and law enforcers. When a vacancy for the Ojinaga *plaza* arose, local traffickers voted on who should run it. They voted for Victor Sierra. Sierra then required permission from the *comandante* in Chihuahua to run the *plaza*. After arriving for his business appointment in Chihuahua, Sierra spent three days being tortured by the *comandante*'s subordinates, during which time they asked him for all manner of information about his past and his entourage. Poppa writes:

> Then on the third day, a miracle happened, the *comandante* offered him the *plaza*! Sure, Victor had talked, but he had put up resistance, and it took more than usual to break him down. The *comandante* informed him he was satisfied that Victor had *huevos*, and it was apparent from the interrogation that he had contacts and a solid organisation.
>
> 'You go ahead and work the Ojinaga area, but have ten thousand dollars right here on this desk every month. And I want the first payment the day after tomorrow.' (Poppa 1998: 68)

Soon, the *comandante* was demanding higher monthly payments as, he explained, he himself was being pressured from above. Before long, Victor Sierra was paying thirty-five thousand dollars per month in return for political and legal protection. This one example indicates that traffickers during the 1980s were far from independent agents: they were, on the contrary, paying tribute to their protectors and taking orders which came down the chain of command from high-level officials.

As Poppa tells us, such arrangements, depending upon tacit agreements between officialdom, the police and *plaza* holders, could provide vital services for a price. Pablo Acosta, among the most important Mexican traffickers in the early 1980s, relied on the army to protect his plantations and shipments. Poppa (*ibid.*: 85) notes that, without the army, Acosta would have been unable to conduct his business, which, by the mid-1980s, was responsible for exporting sixty tons of Colombian cocaine annually to the United States. In one sting, which was reported widely by the media as a 'blow' to *narcotraficantes*, the military were filmed burning a field of Acosta's marijuana. Poppa claims that Acosta had actually been granted permission to harvest the potent tips of the plants (a variety called *sinsemilla*, grown only for the tips) before soldiers arrived (*ibid.*: 76). Acosta had received military credentials from General Luis de la Soto García Rivas, passed on as a gift from the commanding general of the Fifth Military Zone in Chihuahua, Juan Arévalo Gardoqui, who later became Minister of Defence during the supposedly cleaned-up administration of President Miguel de la Madrid. Both Gardoqui and José Guadalupe Zuno Arce (whom the DEA knew was involved in smuggling narcotics and who was the brother-in-law of Luis Echeverría) had been complicit, as it subsequently transpired, in the 1985 murder of Enrique Camarena, a DEA agent who had been investigating the involvement of the political class in narcotrafficking.

Stanley Pimentel (2007: 181) has termed the problem of narco-trafficking in Mexico an 'elite-exploitative' model, in which the traffickers were under pressure from, indeed forced by, the legitimate authorities to accept and sell loads of seized drugs, were constantly threatened and taxed, and compelled to pay a percentage of profits to officials. According to Pimentel,

> criminals are rarely permitted to retire; they are either killed or imprisoned while other family members are allowed to take over. In this model, the organized criminal system is called upon to support the oligarchy. Control and initiation comes from the top, from the

so-called legitimate power holders and their social control agents, and the drug lords, like good 'cash cows', are protected, milked (taxed), and when no longer useful, are imprisoned or sent to the slaughter. (*Ibid.*)

The PRI era was permeated by this kind of clientelism, in which the *patrones* (those of elevated political status) provided benefits to their 'clients' (individuals or groups with a lower political status) (Cornelius 2003: 492). These benefits could include protection, support in political struggles against rivals, and opportunities for political ascendancy or economic prosperity. In exchange, clients provided loyalty and useful services such as voter mobilisation, political control and solutions to the problems of their patrons within the official party or governmental bureaucracy (*ibid.*).

In this way corporatist arrangements were not only negotiated between the state and organised groups like unions and employer associations, but also embraced criminal organisations. As we saw in the previous chapter, the relationship between drug traffickers and the ruling party had strengthened following the Second World War. Their connection was coordinated by the Mexican Ministry of the Interior and the Federal Judicial Police, and reinforced existing, government-established, patron–client relationships with drug traffickers (O'Neil 2009). As Shannon O'Neil points out, 'this arrangement limited violence against public officials, top traffickers, and civilians; made sure that court investigations never reached the upper ranks of cartels; and defined the rules of the game for traffickers'.

O'Neil's picture of this consensual backscratching between the authorities and criminal organisations was confirmed more recently when Socrates Rizzo Garcia, the former PRI governor of Nuevo León, claimed that the wave of violence which has engulfed the country in the first decade of the twenty-first century resulted from the breakdown of agreements between the PRI federal government and the narcotraffickers. Equally, he acknowledged that, during the PRI era, agreements between the federal government and drug cartels had determined the narco-routes of every cartel in the country and claimed that the control of narcotrafficking organisations was overseen by the presidential office (Coronado 2011).

As we demonstrated in Chapter 2, the security services had long been deeply involved in narcotrafficking. A reasonable observer of events might not therefore find it remarkable that in Mexico the state backed and encouraged the repressive measures of the police and security services against political dissenters and the rural poor, while dodging the question of the law enforcers' failure to deal effectively with the cartels. Clearly, the climate of impunity for human rights abuses, for which the alleged perpetrators were almost never prosecuted, let alone investigated, was not accidental. It is worth considering which individuals or sectors most benefited from intimidating and coercing civilians. In a society that now has among the highest levels of economic disparity in the world, the political class and economic elites oversee a system that privileges the few while excluding the majority. As Mexico has become ever more unequal, the pressures on government to perpetuate these arrangements have become greater, as growing dissent and social movements have challenged the authority of the state. While, on the one hand, there has been, since the late 1970s, a kind of democratic opening at the societal level, on the other, successive regimes have had recourse to increasing levels of violence as a form of social control.

It was not as though, in the 1980s, the state had suddenly become corrupted by the increased power and presence of narco-trafficking organisations. In fact, the state and traffickers had a long history of collaboration and it was generally state actors who supervised the entire business. In the 1980s this mutually convenient relationship intensified as conditions became even more favourable for accumulating greater profits and power with the onset of neoliberal reforms. The three main sectors to make massive gains from free market economic reform were the domestic political and business elites, international investors and organised crime.

Consumption in Mexico

According to the Secretary of National Defence in the de la Madrid administration, Juan Arévalo Gardoqui (later indicted for drug trafficking and the murder of DEA agent Enrique Camarena), 'In Mexico, unfortunately, between 18 and 20 per cent of the population are drug addicts, especially young people' (Astorga 2005: 129). Such a bold assertion was not corroborated by the government survey begun soon afterwards, in 1988, the Encuesta Nacional de Adicciones (ENA) of the Secretaría de Salud (SS – Department of Health). The study found that only 2.1 per cent of Mexicans had taken one or more illegal drugs in the preceding twelve months. Measured by those who had consumed drugs more recently, in the previous month, the figure dropped dramatically to 0.9 per cent. In a comparative study of Latin American countries, Mexico's consumption of marijuana and cocaine was the lowest. In terms of actual addiction rates Mexico could count, per head of population, fewer than a tenth of those defined as drug addicts in the United States (Astorga 2005: 130). Clearly, the government's own statistics contradicted politicians' public pronouncements. One might wonder why the Secretary of National Defence would want to give such wildly exaggerated figures for drug dependency in Mexico. It is tempting to suggest that it was part of the propaganda campaign to tarnish the image of youthful political dissidents by associating them with a drugs culture that had to be eradicated.

The fact was that the vast majority of the addicts who consumed narcotics originating in Mexico lived abroad. If the consumption rates among Mexicans had been high, traffickers would simply have catered to the domestic market and avoided the risk and organisational costs of maintaining cross-border distribution networks. This was not the case, because Mexico's addiction rate was relatively insignificant in comparison to that of the United States, where consumption was high and where there were wealthy customers willing to pay a high price for narcotics. If the extraordinarily expensive and generally ineffective war on illegal drugs in Mexico was not being waged against domestic addiction, which was comparatively unimportant in terms of both numbers and overall social impact, then we must look to the country's neighbours to the north and the south, and Mexico's relationship with them, for an explanation.

The Economy, Free Trade, the Washington Consensus and the Cartels

Miguel de la Madrid and the technocratic elite
The presidency of Miguel de la Madrid (1982–88) marked a watershed in Mexican politics as the economic model advanced by the state resulted in a transformation of the PRI power structure (La Botz 1995: 101). The PRI abandoned its national revolutionary project and ideology, dismantled the state corporatist structure, and discarded economic protectionism in favour of what became known as free trade, neoliberalism or the Washington Consensus. As David Harvey (2005: 99) has commented, 'De la Madrid was reform-minded, less embedded in the traditional politics of the PRI and had close relations with the capitalist class and foreign interests.'

Mexico had had one of the most protectionist economies in the region, which, since the Cárdenas administration in the 1930s, had been based on an import substitution industrialisation (ISI) model. This meant that certain protections were afforded to domestic industrial development. Nonetheless, in Mexico, as elsewhere, ISI policies failed to advance a model of economic development which would pull Mexico up from its status as a developing economy, owing to the fact that it remained highly dependent on imports of goods which could not be produced domestically. Although the country was still largely reliant on international trade, tariffs on imports and exports, limits on foreign ownership, a relatively high investment in social programmes and subsidies to farmers and on foodstuffs added up to at least a modicum of protectionism.

The economic crisis which was crippling the economy by 1982

was largely caused by the sharp rise in interest rates on loans that Mexico was repaying to New York banks, which had profited massively from the oil boom of the 1970s. This burden, combined with a decline in oil prices, meant that Mexico was unable to repay its debts. This position of vulnerability provided an opportunity for the US Treasury to step in and offer to rescue the Mexican economy by bailing out the lending banks. The conditions laid down in return for the bailout required a massive restructuring of the Mexican economy. The International Monetary Fund (IMF) imposed a structural adjustment programme that demanded the privatisation of public services, cuts in government social programmes, the further opening of Mexico to foreign direct investment (FDI) and increasing the quantity of exports in order to generate enough dollar currency to pay back loans and interest to US banks (DuRand 2010: 235–6).

During the 1970s, for the first time in the post-war period, the Mexican economy had been faced with an adverse international context.[3] Furthermore, the ISI model was showing signs of exhaustion as its core policies were not able to generate economic growth. As with other Latin American countries, Mexico's economic growth during the 1970s often relied on external borrowing (Skidmore and Smith 2005: 58). Attempting to overcome structural weaknesses in the economy generated by the ISI model within the context of an international economic crisis, the Mexican government decided to expand its activities, including an increase in the number of parastatals, or government enterprises run on commercial lines. The administrations of Echeverría (1970–76) and López Portillo (1976–82) had enlarged the role of the state in the economy with relatively high public spending. As a result, the public sector deficit increased steadily, rising from around 2 per cent of GDP in 1971 to 10.9 per cent in 1982. The current

---

3   US policies under President Richard Nixon drastically affected Mexico; they included a 10 per cent surcharge on all imports and the replacement of the gold standard by the dollar. Because the peso had always been pegged to the dollar, the peso became unstable. Inflation did more damage. By 1973 the economy was in severe distress (Foster 2007: 208).

account deficit rose from $928.9 million in 1971 to $6,220 million in 1982, which represented 3.2 per cent and 3.5 per cent of the GDP respectively (Chávez and Huerta 2003: 64).

Although the economy spun out of control in 1982 with the debt crisis, there had been signals of weakening since the early 1970s (Aspe 1993: 13). Additionally, in 1976 the national currency had undergone a devaluation, in contrast to stability in the rate of exchange in the three previous decades. Since 1954 the rate of exchange between the US dollar and the Mexican peso had been 12.5 pesos to 1 dollar, but this rate collapsed to 20: 1 in 1976 and to 70: 1 in 1982.

Previously, in the 1970s, the government had faced a choice of whether to open up the economy and prioritise exports, or to reinforce the nationalist model which had held sway since the 1940s. The government chose the second option and economic policy included the expansion of parastatal enterprises while relying on oil exports as a major source of income. Unfortunately, the governments of Echeverría and López Portillo failed to achieve a balance between public revenues and expenditure. What by the early 1980s was viewed by technocrats as an obese state apparatus had long since become a burden upon Mexican businesses, inhibiting their ability to adapt to the international crisis of the early 1970s, characterised by high inflation rates and economic stagnation (stagflation).

In the late 1970s, under the government of López Portillo, oil wells had been discovered and the economy had found new momentum. The exports of oil were greater than before, climbing from $500 million in 1976 to $13 billion in 1981, and the Mexican economy had grown 8 per cent annually in this period. When oil prices were high, oil exports were the main source of government revenues; for instance, in 1982 Mexico depended on oil for 75 per cent of total export income (Edmonds-Poli and Shirk 2009: 251). However, this was not enough to support government programmes and the state suddenly became dependent on financial loans from international institutions to sustain the economy. These loans were covered by the income generated from high oil prices, helped to some extent by the relatively low interest rates paid to foreign banks and international financial institutions (Aspe 1993). Thus, the sound operation of the economy depended on external factors over which the government had no control: high oil prices and low interest rates. As a result, Mexico's foreign debt increased from $4.2 billion in 1970 to nearly $20 billion by 1976 and to almost $59 billion by the end of 1982. Unfortunately, a large percentage of this debt had been contracted on a short-term basis, at high interest rates (Levy and Bruhn 2006: 161–2). Mexico's external debt, which accounted for 31 per cent of GDP in 1980, increased to 39 per cent of GDP in 1981 (Schlefer 2008: 169).

Some domestic problems were alleviated in the short term, even as the public finances became weaker as external debt increased and the economy became more vulnerable to international conditions. It was not a surprise that a debt crisis emerged in Mexico, in the light of the fragile foundations on which its economy was built. 'In the early 1980s,' comments Ruth Collier, 'sharply rising interest rates combined with falling oil prices [made] Mexico the first among the debtor nations to enter financial crisis' (Collier 1992: 80). The debt crisis of 1982, initiated in Mexico and expanded through all Latin America, was so severe that Mexico had to modify the main parameters of the economy. In a perhaps understandable knee-jerk reaction, the government suddenly changed direction: opening its economy to international markets became its main strategy for economic recovery. As Gavin O'Toole (2007: 442) suggests, 'The debt crisis was a turning point because it called into question the viability of ISI in Latin America, which had become dependent on a continuous infusion of capital, and so strengthened the hand of neoliberals.'

While the year 2000, when the PRI was defeated in a general election, is generally regarded as the most important political transition in contemporary Mexican politics, the adoption of the neoliberal economic model by de la Madrid in 1982 seems more significant in retrospect.

Although Mexico's political system was dominated by a hegemonic party during most of the twentieth century, there were diverse political currents within the party. Presidents often adopted different kinds of policies, depending on the political orientations of those in federal government (Skidmore and Smith 2005: 252). The solid political structure that had enabled the PRI to remain in power for seven decades dated back to the presidency of Cárdenas (1934–40), which had acted as a moderating force between diverse social and political groupings. Through it the bourgeois elite that took power following the Mexican Revolution had been able to curb challenges to its dominance from outsiders by co-opting them into the corporatist party structure.

The corporatist state had enjoyed an all-pervasive grip on political power, acting as arbiter and manager of divergent interests from unions, to peasant organisations, to the business elite. This was equally true for the drugs trade, over which the party exercised a similar hold via arrangements between local politicians, the army, police and the DFS over who controlled *plazas*. Narcotrafficking had been absorbed into this corporatist framework, an aspect of its relationship with the state of mutual benefit to the political class and those working in the industry. It is striking that the state's abandonment of this form of organisation appears to have contributed to the independent growth and power of organised crime syndicates as the neoliberal project progressed and developed, and as the role of the state in economic activities declined, a subject to which we return in Chapter 5.

In 1982, with the election of de la Madrid and in response to the economic crisis, the political orientation of the PRI – which until then had attempted to cater, at least on some levels, to differing political beliefs and interests – changed direction in favour of a fiercely right-wing free-market ideology. The policies resulting from this *volte-face* were intensified and reinforced during the subsequent administrations of presidents Salinas (1988–94) and Zedillo (1994–2000).

The rise of the technocrats among the political elite (Demmers 2001: 163) was linked to the growing power of the Presidential Office, the SPP (Ministry of Planning and Budget), and the PRI's institute, IEPES (Institute of Political, Economic and Social Studies). In the late 1970s and the early 1980s, an institutional change took place in favour of these agencies and at the expense of the Ministry of the Interior (Secretaría de Gobernación) and the PRI.

By the mid-1980s, as Miguel Ángel Centeno (1994: 40) has shown, the technocrats had achieved not just a behind-the-scenes influence, 'or control within limited policy areas, but commanded the helm of the state as a whole'. This was a massive shift in Mexican politics away from corporatism and government intervention and control; it established a new relationship between the state and capital that endures today. The rise of the technocratic elite would have been impossible without the maintenance of networks of patron–client relationships, known as *camarillas*. These networks cemented the new political system, assured the integration of the newly emergent elite, facilitated its rise to power, provided the channels through which its members centralised control of resources, and contributed to the development of a new political mentality later known as *salinastroika*.

Unlike previous PRI leaders, the technocrats did not emerge from mass political organisations, such as unions or other structures within the party, but rather came into the party at the top, working in the IEPES think-tank or in the shadow cabinet of the elected President (La Botz 1995: 103). As La Botz points out, this was a political vanguard which aimed to take control of the party and the state in order to transform Mexican politics and society in line with the increasing dominance of international free-market politics. Most importantly, the 'technocrats believed in neoliberal capitalist economic values, such as privatisation of the economy and integration into the world market', and 'were committed, above all, to bureaucratic and economic efficiency as the highest goals' (*ibid.*).

However, the impacts of this process and the subsequent restructuring of the economic model during the 1980s mainly affected the working class and the poor, and were manifested in a decrease in real wages, a reduction in social benefits, the reorganisation of collective labour agreements in large-scale businesses, repression of labour unrest, official policies from the local boards of conciliation and arbitration clearly favourable to employers, and the flexibilisation and weakening of labour unions (Zapata 1995: 45).

Neoliberalism and the drugs trade

Neoliberalism in Mexico, as elsewhere, was characterised by the supposed retreat of the state. The technocrats who rose within the party under de la Madrid argued that economic failures, such as chronic inflation and slow economic growth, were caused by the state's overly dominant role in the economy. Their rhetoric asserted that new economic measures would halt and then reverse the trends towards 'big' government and state intervention that had typified much of the twentieth century (Heywood 2003: 54–5). These policy prescriptions also came to be known as the Washington Consensus. Among them were the harmonisation of macroeconomic indicators, especially inflation and the reduction of public deficit, but also fiscal discipline, tax reform, liberalisation of trade and foreign investment, privatisation and deregulation.

Neoliberalism pushed the Mexican economy further towards integration with that of the United States and reoriented the ISI model towards one based upon exports. Mexico thus became more dependent on the USA, closer economic ties entailing closer political links and cooperation, which allowed the US government to become increasingly involved in Mexico's drug policy.

While the implementation of neoliberal reform represented a set of economic policies and practices, it was just as much a political and hegemonic project. According to Duménil and Levy (2004), neoliberalism was the expression of the desire of capitalists and the institutions in which their power was concentrated to restore economic and political dominance, which they viewed as having been in decline since the Great Depression and the Second World War, following the establishment of the welfare state and Keynesian protectionism. Far from being inevitable, the Washington Consensus, or neoliberal project, was a highly political act (*ibid.*: 1–2) prompted by actors who would benefit massively from such a shift. For David Harvey (2005: 19), more than anything else neoliberalism was a 'political project to re-establish the conditions for capital accumulation and to restore the power of economic elites'. Indeed, neoliberalism was effective in revitalising global capital accumulation, and it succeeded remarkably well in restoring the power of economic elites. Similarly, Saad Filho and Yalman (2009: 1) noted that neoliberalism was 'the contemporary form of capitalism', which was 'based on the systematic use of state power to impose, under the veil of "non-intervention", a hegemonic project of recomposition of the rule of capital in most areas of social life'.

Such was the 'recomposition' that during the period 1982–94, about eighty state enterprises were privatised in Mexico (MacLeod 2005: 42–5). As discussed above, neoliberal policies require the stabilisation of macroeconomic indicators, particularly the control and reduction of inflation rates and public deficit. Control of inflation therefore was one of the priorities of the Mexican government, while other aspects, such as the stimulation of employment, were sidelined, thus impacting on the creation of formal jobs, most notably in the public sector. In Mexico, though inflation was reduced, the reforms also resulted in the erosion of workers' real wages. Meanwhile, cutbacks in social spending, including cutting subsidies on foodstuffs and in other areas, in the first stage of neoliberal reforms, were especially harmful to the living standards of the working class.

Deregulation of the economy also led to the flexibilisation of the labour market, meaning that many of the protections afforded to workers by unionisation and legislation were abruptly removed. Increased unemployment and poor union representation weakened the average Mexican's bargaining power. The technocrats of the new elite portrayed flexibilisation as a way to deregulate labour and, supposedly, increase productivity, but in reality it was used as a tool to remove the benefits workers had gained through the Keynesian policies of the previous forty years (1930s–1970s). Neoliberalism contributed to the restructuring of capitalism, providing the essential means by which capital started to remove many of the compromises that had been made during the Keynesian era: for instance, the government's commitment to a full employment policy, which had increased the power of trade unions (Gamble 2001: 131).

As a result of the economic collapse generated by the debt crisis of 1982, Latin American countries (including Mexico) required external assistance to overcome domestic problems, mainly the payment of foreign debt. International financial institutions, particularly the World Bank and the International Monetary Fund, set conditions in return for loans whose main thrust was the implementation of neoliberal policies, creating pressure to open up economies to foreign investment (Stiglitz 2002: 37–8), which generated a major economic transformation.

To what extent was neoliberalism relevant to the increasing influence of organised crime in Mexico? One of the principal effects of reorienting the economy towards the export market was on food production. In 1960, Mexico had been almost self-sufficient in food, but one effect of switching to the production of cheap food for export was that small-time farmers no longer had a domestic market. Mexico accepted more and more imported foodstuffs from the United States. There, the US government subsidised large-scale agribusiness and sold its surplus to poor countries. Ironically, it was reluctant to impose the same economic measures at home as it demanded abroad. Cheap, US government-subsidised imports, which undercut local producers, had the effect of devastating small farmers, who no longer had a stable market for their crops. Luis Astorga (2005: 132) recounts how by the mid-1980s in the areas around Culiacán, traffickers would recruit day labourers by driving around in trucks and announcing to potential workers via megaphone that they could earn anywhere between four and five thousand pesos per day by going, as it was called, 'apple picking'. Such was the appeal in many of the *colonias* of the city and the surrounding villages that all the unemployed men disappeared during the day, leaving only the women and children. Clearly, this had a deleterious effect on farmers producing legal crops, who paid labourers only 660 pesos per day. Consequently they resorted to employing labour from outside the state as the bargaining power of those locals working for the illegal trade had increased thanks to the high prices fetched by marijuana and heroin compared to foodstuffs. A corollary of these trends was that traditional farmers saw that breaking the law could provide a far better livelihood than growing crops such as beans, tomatoes or corn.

Another striking aspect of the neoliberal economy since 1982 has been the unprecedented transfer of wealth to the rich. In the case of Mexico, which shares a border with the country whose consumer market for narcotics is the largest in the world, poverty exacerbated and perpetuated both drug production and export. Neoliberalism had the effect of putting ever more small agriculturalists out of business while the burgeoning market for marijuana and poppies provided practically their only viable alternative to bankruptcy and flight from the land. The prevalence of drug production, combined with economic reforms that essentially excluded much of the rural workforce from legitimate commercial activity, meant that it was very difficult to create sustainable alternatives within the formal economy (Scott 2009: 185). As the poverty aggravated by neoliberal structural adjustment programmes pushed people into the informal black market, conflicts, grievances and disagreements were increasingly resolved without legal representation and without recourse to the law. Furthermore, competition between rival trafficking organisations was by nature exercised in an extra-legal environment in which those best able to resort to force and violence and willing to employ them with the utmost brutality, and those with the largest stocks of armaments, would dominate a market unregulated by the rule of law. Narcotraffickers capitalised on the opportunities provided by the 'free market', the flexibilisation of the labour force and the loss of union and legal representation which the Washington Consensus so eagerly encouraged. The guiding principles of the 1980s free market, as introduced by Reagan and Thatcher, prioritised accumulation of profit over social welfare, ruthless competition over cooperation, the orienting of domestic production towards export, the sanctification of private property and wealth over community and civic responsibility, the extension of investor rights over worker representation, and the entitlement of the wealthy and powerful to exploit cheap labour and the natural environment to the detriment of the human rights of marginal, disenfranchised and aboriginal peoples. All of these propositions – the cornerstones and guiding principles of free-market ideology – also formed the dominant ideology of crime syndicates operating within the same socio-economic context. Just as powerful states intervene by force in the Third World, using violence to guard and maintain their economic advantage, so the narcotraffickers acted in Mexico to protect their assets.

In the free market, writes Cliff DuRand (2010: 235–6), 'The only actors allowed are individuals who are guided not by altruism, conscience or compassion, or even enlightened self-interest, but only by their own self-seeking benefit-maximising proclivities.' According to this perspective, distinctions between the actions of legal and illegal capitalists become quite blurred. In the ideology of the free market, 'The only legitimate role for the state is to maintain or establish the conditions for a market to operate.' With the introduction of neoliberal reform in 1982, the state had indeed created the necessary conditions for the 'free' market in narcotics to operate by allowing transnational corporations to dominate the market while removing protections and subsidies for the poor.

In *The Corporation* (2004), Joel Bakan discusses the destructive consequences inherent in the workings of corporate capitalism. What economists call 'externalities' can refer to the social or environmental consequences of transactions between corporations and/or individuals. Thus when tobacco corporations sell cigarettes to consumers, the damage to the health of smokers is an externality and is irrelevant to the transaction. That the smoker is likely to pay for the externalities with his or her health does not affect the integrity of the original transaction. That the real costs are social – public health and taxpayers must foot the bill – is not the concern of the corporation. Bakan concludes that if the corporate institution were a real human being, it would share the profile of the psychopath. Subordination of compassion and empathy for the sake of profit turns societal breakdown and human suffering into a mere 'externality' to the workings of the market. This certainly sounds like the profile of many a modern corporation, and exactly describes drug cartels.

The Colombian connection

The 'war on drugs' became a defining characteristic of US domestic and foreign policy, which, between 1981 and 1989 under the Reagan and Bush 1 administrations, was reflected in federal expenditures. In the first half of the decade the South Florida Task Force attempted to limit Colombian cocaine and marijuana shipments being landed on the coast for distribution in Miami. In the latter half of the decade the US focus shifted to their Mexican border as trade routes switched from the Caribbean basin to Mexico in consequence of the pressure exerted on traffickers in Florida. Seizures of cocaine in the United States rose from 2 tons in 1981 to 100 tons by 1989 (Toro 1995: 31), encouraging Colombian traffickers to make the move into Mexico where they had existing criminal contacts. Mexico proved fertile ground for the expansion of the narcotics industry, being a country where the police, DFS and political class were corrupt enough to take a cut, where the Mexican cartels took all the risks by transporting the goods across the border themselves, and where there was a cheap and flexible labour force. In addition, seizures of cocaine in the USA, while a setback, had the effect of hiking up the price, thereby guaranteeing increased rewards to sellers and their official contacts.

Colombian cartels had, in the main, imported coca and cocaine from Bolivia and Peru, but by the late 1970s and 1980s they began to circumvent this trade by increasing their own domestic production of cocaine. In addition, the quality of Colombian marijuana was considered superior to its Mexican counterpart, for which reason it had been in constant demand in the US since the 1960s. By now, Colombia could grow the three crops necessary to produce the world's major illegal narcotics: poppies, marijuana and coca. As well as being a nation that enjoys an ideal climate and terrain for growing all three crops, Colombia's Caribbean coastline allows relatively easy export northwards.

At the same time in Mexico even more workers faced extreme poverty and unemployment. Already scarce, ever fewer opportunities were now available for unemployed young people looking to better their lot. This allowed the relatively small Mexican cartels to take advantage of an endless pool of cheap labour. As the Mexican cartels grew and became better organised – with networks and distribution lists throughout Mexico, the Americas and now Africa and Europe – they became less dependent on their Colombian counterparts. The Colombians were happy to let the Mexicans run the riskiest element of the operation. Transporting the goods to the US, where the sentences, if caught, were severe, and where it was more difficult to bribe officials, would almost always be the job of relatively junior Mexican cartel workers.

New business relationships were established between Colombian organisations looking for alternative routes to the US and Mexican organisations hoping to capitalise on the opportunity for profitable collaboration that Reagan's drug war had provided. As we have seen, interdiction by the US authorities in the Caribbean meant that the price of cocaine had increased thanks to its relative scarcity on the market. As they found Caribbean operations becoming more risky and expensive, it made sense for the Colombian and Mexican cartels to compensate by shipping larger consignments overland. Thus, by the middle of the decade, some 30 per cent of all cocaine consumed in the US passed through Mexico (Toro 1995: 31).

By the early 1980s, the Guadalajara cartel was charging the Colombians as much as 50 per cent of the profits for exporting cocaine into the United States. With official protection, the organisation was able to expand its influence and resources rapidly. It was the Guadalajara cartel that nurtured the millionaires and billionaires who became the most powerful traffickers on the continent: Manuel Salcido Uzueta (*El Cochiloco*), Hector *Él Güero* Palma, the Arrellano Félix brothers, Amado Carrillo Fuentes (*El Señor de los Cielos*), who became the most powerful trafficker in Mexico in the 1980s and early 1990s, and Joaquín *El Chapo* Guzmán, since the late 1990s Latin America's most powerful mafia boss, all originally operated out of Guadalajara.

During the 1980s Félix Gallardo, Caro Quintero and Ernesto Fonseca were bringing in $5 billion every year (Cockburn and St Clair 1998: 349). The crackdown on trafficking from Colombia to Florida had not stopped the flow of drugs moving north. Put simply, the huge profits – the result of high prices for drugs caused by prohibition – made trafficking an attractive option in a context within which the neoliberal programme was making it ever more difficult for small-time food producers to grow and sell, while unemployment soared and the inequality gap widened. Within this context, narcotrafficking was unlikely to go away, and the chief effect of the crackdown in the Caribbean had only been to push the major smuggling routes westward to Mexico. Félix Gallardo, who was working for the Medellín cartel in Colombia headed by Pablo Escobar Gaviria, Gonzalo Rodríguez Gacha and Jorge Luis Ochoa, used his position to increase the flow of narcotics – particularly cocaine – passing through Mexico, a move that benefited the Colombians, the Guadalajara cartel, high-ranking members of the DFS, the Federal Police, and the Mexican and US banks responsible for laundering the proceeds. All had a shared interest in the trade's success and were profiting handsomely from such easy earnings.

US Involvement in Mexico

Manuel Buendía and Enrique Camarena

Mexican politics in the 1980s were dominated not only by a severe economic crisis but also by the rise of narcotrafficking as a major problem for Mexico in its relationship with the United States. When US DEA agent Enrique 'Kiki' Camarena Salazar was kidnapped and killed by Mexican narcos Rafael Caro Quintero, Miguel Ángel Félix Gallardo and Ernesto Fonseca Carrillo (*Don Neto*), the event triggered a crisis in US–Mexican relations regarding the drug war. Tensions were deepened when the DEA launched Operation Intercept II and Operation Leyenda (to investigate the murder of Camarena), and intensified its operations and surveillance in Mexico. Narcotrafficking became the prime government concern at the negotiating table with the US, even in the midst of the Mexican economic crisis and while salaries and incomes were being pulverised. Most significantly, the Camarena murder highlighted the importance of narcotrafficking to the underground economy and the power of drug traffickers *vis-à-vis* state institutions. In response to calls both from the US government and within Mexico, Miguel de la Madrid would later announce that narcotrafficking had become a problem of national security.

In 1984 (the year preceding the execution of Camarena), investigative journalist Manuel Buendía had been researching the ties between the DFS and high-level traffickers. Buendía was interested in the workings of the intelligence agencies and had cultivated warm and extensive relations within the DFS. The DFS had even provided him with a permit to carry a gun. Buendía began publishing the kind of article few journalists dared touch. He had written about the CIA in Mexico and its relationship with the DFS but, in May 1984, he published his first story on a subject that had hitherto been strictly off-limits – the DFS and its political involvement in the drug trade – in which he suggested that the influence of the narcos had infiltrated the police and reached the upper echelons of the Secretaría de Gobernación. According to a DEA report, Buendía's investigations led him to suspect that Manuel Bartlett, then Secretario de Gobernación (Secretary of the Interior) Miguel Aldana Ibarra, the director of the anti-drug enforcement programme of the Federal Police (PJF), and Manuel Ibarra Herrera, former head of the PJF, worked closely with drug traffickers (although they were never prosecuted). Buendía had also received information detailing the use of Rafael Caro Quintero's ranch in Veracruz as a CIA/DFS training camp for guerrilla fighters involved in overthrowing the Sandinista government in Nicaragua (Hernández 2010a: 94–5). In his column *Red Privada*, which he published in the daily newspaper, *Excélsior*, Buendía had also uncovered information on a German arms dealer and ex-SS officer, Gerhard Mertins, whom the CIA was apparently using to send armaments to the Nicaraguan Contras (*ibid.* 2010a: 98–9). Furthermore, Buendía had received a dossier detailing the ties of the DFS chief, José Antonio Zorrilla Pérez, to the Guadalajara cartel (Aguayo Quezada 2001: 239). Later it emerged that Zorrilla Pérez and the bosses of the cartel had collaborated in the subsequent murder of Buendía, for which Zorrilla was eventually prosecuted and incarcerated. Two police commanders who both reported directly to Manuel Bartlett, Secretario de Gobernación, turned out to be associates of the leaders of the Guadalajara cartel, Ernesto Fonseca, Félix Gallardo and Rafael Caro Quintero. Later evidence revealed that leaders of the cartel had been given DFS badges by means of which they could fob off unwelcome judicial and police investigations.

The murder of one of Mexico's most celebrated columnists in broad daylight in Mexico City provoked shock and outrage and contributed to the closing of the DFS the following year. Leaving his office on 30 May 1984, Buendía was shot five times in the back at point blank range. Manuel Bartlett, one of the protagonists of Buendía's investigations into alleged official collusion with the drug trade, ordered the DFS itself to investigate the crime. DFS agent

Rafael Moro Ávila Camacho, a relative of ex-President Manuel Ávila Camacho, was eventually prosecuted and incarcerated for the murder of Buendía, along with Zorrilla Pérez.

Buendía had not been allowed to finish his research. In the following year, the DEA agent, Enrique 'Kiki' Camarena, who had been pursuing a similar line of inquiry to that of Buendía, was also murdered. Camarena had been investigating the Guadalajara cartel bosses and their protection by the Mexican police. This had led to the discovery of ten thousand tons of marijuana (the largest such seizure until then) at Caro Quintero's El Búfalo ranch in Chihuahua. This was equivalent to eight times the amount of marijuana that US government studies had estimated Mexico produced annually, found on only one day and at one ranch. It was also estimated to be roughly the equivalent of what the US marijuana market consumed in one year (Scott and Marshall 1991: 37). The cartel's bosses had become increasingly concerned by Camarena's investigations, as had a number of politicians and members of the DFS whom the DEA agent had linked to the cartel. Perhaps Camarena underestimated the dangers of prying into the affairs of corrupt PRI officials with interests in narcotrafficking. In any case, his investigation was cut short in 1985 when, according to eyewitnesses, he was kidnapped by armed DFS agents (Cockburn and St Clair 1998: 349). His tortured and mutilated body (he had apparently been killed when a screwdriver was rammed through his skull) would later appear in the grounds of a ranch in Michoacán one month after his capture.

Camarena and his pilot, Alfredo Zavala Avelares, had been taken to the ranch of Félix Gallardo and subjected to a torture session that lasted some thirty hours while interrogators attempted to extract as much information as possible about DEA operations before eventually killing them both. Throughout, Camarena had been injected with doses of amphetamines lest the continual beatings should make him lose consciousness.

Two days after Camarena's kidnapping, DEA agents in Mexico discovered that Rafael Caro Quintero was headed for the airport in

Guadalajara and contacted Mexican federal agents to arrange his arrest in order to question him. DEA agents were stunned when the Federal Judicial Police allowed Rafael Caro Quintero's private jet to take off from Guadalajara for Mexico City. The DEA agents had contacted the *Federales* after a tip-off and had expected that this would be the ideal opportunity for a high-profile sting against one of Mexico's most powerful kingpins in the drugs business and a massive blow to the cartel. As Comandante Armando Pavón approached Caro Quintero's aircraft, which was protected by armed guards, the two men shook hands and talked for a few moments before the plane prepared for departure. In exchange for $300,000, Caro Quintero's plane had been given the green light to take off, which it did moments later, with the wanted man on board (*ibid*.: 349).

The Guadalajara cartel in the 1980s controlled shipments of cocaine into the United States of truly stunning proportions. The bosses – Caro Quintero, Gallardo and Fonseca – were apparently earning five billion dollars a year. According to information gathered by the DEA, Félix Gallardo was laundering 20 million dollars every month through the Bank of America in San Diego (*ibid*.: 349).

As a result of growing doubts about their ally's commitment to the 'war on drugs', politicians in Washington and the US ambassador to Mexico, John Gavin, began to release the names of officials they believed to be connected to the narcotrafficking business. Meanwhile DEA agents were becoming increasingly frustrated by and concerned about both DFS's closeness to and the CIA's laxity towards major drug traffickers (Aguayo Quezada 2001: 241).

Even following his later arrest, Rafael Caro Quintero was allowed to run the Guadalajara cartel from prison – using, appropriately enough, a cell phone. Nevertheless, US pressure for a thorough investigation of the murder of Camarena eventually led to his interrogation, ironically, by Sergio Saavedra Flores, an ex-DFS officer and member of the federal police. After Caro Quintero had been treated to the *tehuacanazo*, a favoured DFS technique in cross-examinations which entailed forcing carbonated water laced with jalapeños into the suspect's nasal passages, he revealed that the DFS director Zorrilla Pérez – himself protected by the CIA – was the intellectual author of the assassination. Caro Quintero's interrogation revealed things that were potentially embarrassing to the DFS, the federal police, Minister Manuel Bartlett and the entire political establishment. The interrogator's methods had been overly efficient and Saavedra soon realised that a more cautious approach would be needed to aid the cover-up which followed. Eventually, Saavedra himself disappeared. Some thirteen people connected to the Camarena case were murdered in the months that followed, three of them defendants (Cockburn and St Clair 1998: 352). As a result of the ensuing cover-up led by agents within the DFS, the exact details of Camarena's detention and murder never emerged, though Rubén Zuno Arce (brother-in-law of Luis Echeverría), Honduran trafficker Juan Matta Ballesteros, who had worked for both the Colombian Medellín cartel and the CIA (by running arms and money to Contra training camps in return for being allowed to deliver shipments of drugs to the United States), Miguel Ángel Félix Gallardo and Ernesto Fonseca were all implicated and sentenced for their involvement following pressure and investigations by the DEA. Zuno Arce, it was revealed, had sold Rafael Caro Quintero the house in which Camarena was murdered and he appears to have ordered Camarena's kidnapping in order to protect Juan Arévalo Gardoqui, then Minister of Defence (Camarena's investigations had led directly to Gardoqui). Camarena's interrogation at the hands of the Guadalajara cartel had been recorded and parts of this were played at the court hearings in Los Angeles into the murder. The interrogators had pressed him on what information he possessed on Defence Minister Gardoqui, his ties to the Guadalajara cartel and to what extent he knew of the role of the CIA in drug trafficking (Hernández 2010a: 109).

The murder of Camarena exposed both the Mexican government and the DFS to the sort of embarrassing scrutiny they much preferred to avoid. So, in 1985, the de la Madrid government ceased DFS operations and closed the agency down. It was replaced in 1989 by the Centro de Investigación y Seguridad Nacional (CISEN – National Security and Investigation Centre). The name change and reorganisation meant little: political repression of opposition groups, spying and corruption continued unabated, only under a different banner.

Given the events described above and the security organisation's closeness to the most prominent drug barons, it is hard to believe that senior commanders of the DFS were unaware of political complicity and involvement in the illegal narcotics trade. The DFS included elite presidential Military Staff Guards (EMP) and paramilitary groups. Besides, the President and the PRI leadership enjoyed near absolute power over the organisation as Stanley Pimentel (2007: 179) observed:

> Everyone from the lowly police officer on the street, to the mayor of the city, the governor of the state, to the Minister of Finance, or the Attorney General himself, are all indebted to the party bosses, and ultimately, to the President. No controversial action was taken by one patron, without checking with his/her patron, and on up the line. Many decisions that normally would be made by a deputy secretary would be referred to the President, who appointed that individual, for the final say . . .

The 1985 closure of the DFS would eventually contribute, however, to a weakening of the state's control of the drugs trade, something which, in the 1990s and 2000s, allowed the consolidation of even more powerful criminal organisations, which we discuss later, in Chapter 5.

The road to victory goes through Mexico

Although neoliberalism entailed increasing control of the politics and markets in the Global South by powerful Northern economies, articulate and organised challenges to US economic imperialism in Central America found expression in the late 1970s and 1980s. The revolution, led by the Frente Sandinista de Liberación Nacional

(FSLN), which had come to power in Nicaragua in 1979, not only overthrew the US-backed puppet dictator, Anastasio Somoza, but rejected the existing economic and political model in favour of greater investment in social programmes and education, and a redistribution of wealth. These moves threatened to destabilise US hegemony and economic dominance in the region. In addition, US planners were apprehensive that the revolution would spread to El Salvador, Honduras and Guatemala, where the peasants were becoming progressively more radicalised, and imprudent Catholic priests were preaching Liberation Theology. In order to halt the independent course being taken by the Sandinista government and to head off the possibility of economic and political self-determination throughout the region, Washington invested in groups of Nicaraguan exiles and ex-members of Somoza's National Guard, essentially a proxy army of US power, which became known as the Contras.

Jeane Kirkpatrick, US ambassador to the UN, declared that 'Central America is the most important place in the world for the United States today' (LaFeber 1993: 5). President Ronald Reagan's speeches demonised the Sandinista regime, associating it with all manner of brutalities, torture, rape and anti-Semitism (Kenworthy 1995). Equating the 'free market' of neoliberalism with freedom and democracy (a mantra which has become a permanent fixture of political discourse in the West, despite its questionable basis), Reagan further argued that the Sandinistas were preparing a 600,000-strong army and were intent on invading the United States. They could reach the Mexico/Texas border in three days, had weapons of mass destruction, and were bent on using them against the free world, he claimed. That Nicaragua had neither the wherewithal – as a country of three million mostly impoverished peasants and only insignificant military resources – nor the volition to launch an invasion of the country with the most powerful military force in world history, was irrelevant. As Reagan claimed, not only did the Sandinistas 'sponsor terror in El Salvador, Costa Rica, Guatemala, and Honduras', they had 'become involved themselves in the international drug trade. I know every American parent concerned about the drug problem', he maintained, 'will be outraged to learn that top Nicaraguan Government officials are deeply involved in drug trafficking' (cited in Appendix, *ibid.*: 170). Lest the American public be in any doubt about the threat posed by the Nicaraguan regime, Reagan claimed there was an 'old Communist slogan that the Sandinistas have made clear they honour: "The road to victory goes through Mexico"' (*ibid.*: 124).

However, as Eldon Kenworthy points out, 'Whatever cocaine flowed through Nicaragua to the United States was minuscule compared to that smuggled into the United States by Contra suppliers, a connection Oliver North is thought to have prevented the DEA from investigating' (*ibid.*: 125). In contrast to the stated reasons for intervention and support for the proxy Contra army, Reagan did hint at more plausible motivations for intervention, which were 'our vital security interests', stating, correctly, that, 'through this crucial part of the Western Hemisphere passes almost half our foreign trade, more than half our imports of crude oil'.

Just as institutions like the IMF, World Bank, the Inter-American Development Bank (IDB) and the European Common Market could be used to impose economic neoliberal reform in the Third World, so equally they were used as political tools against countries whose governments resisted such pressures. The US government ordered the same institutions to withhold loans to the Sandinista government and cut off trade, American investment, and trade programmes to the country (Blum 2003: 291).

US refusal to allow an independent course for Central America and its fear of losing political and economic control of the region was at the heart of its foreign policy. If economic integration of the Global South could not be achieved by consent, the 'free market' would be applied by force. Furthermore, should the proxy army of Nicaraguan exiles prove insufficient for terrorising Nicaraguan civilians, an alliance of Mexican traffickers, politicians, DFS agents and CIA operatives could be enlisted to provide assistance.

As reports of the Contra army's shocking human rights abuses began to surface in the United States in 1982, and when Congress passed an amendment by Democrat legislator Edward Boland, the US government was forced to reduce the funds available for bringing down the Sandinistas. To replace the shortfall, Lieutenant Colonel Oliver North hatched a plan to supply arms to Iran in exchange for money which would be sent to Central America to rid the region of the Communist 'cancer'. North's justification was that if the war on Communism had to be funded by illegal arms sales to Iran and by cocaine money, it was because the threat posed by the Sandinistas was so extreme that other strategic, moral and political considerations paled by comparison.

When Oliver North was summoned to appear before the Irangate hearings in 1987, some protesters held up a banner upon which was written, 'Ask about the cocaine smuggling' (Streatfeild 2001: 338). As Gary Webb, investigative reporter for the *San José Mercury News*, revealed in 1996, in a series of articles entitled 'Dark Alliance', the Reagan administration and the CIA – via covert funding of the Contra army in Nicaragua derived from illegal arms dealing and drug smuggling – had been, to a great extent, directly responsible for the enormous amounts of crack cocaine which had materialised on the streets of Los Angeles and other US cities (Webb 1998).

In exchange for transferring funds and arms to the Contras, Mexican crime syndicates, in particular the Guadalajara cartel, were essentially allowed a free pass into US cities. The highly addictive crack cocaine, a relative newcomer to the market in illegal narcotics, was appearing in abundance in disadvantaged areas of US cities, allowing Los Angeles, for example, to become the 'crack capital of the world'. US dealers were buying Colombian cocaine from Mexican traffickers and processing it into crack (Streatfeild 2001: 346–53).

The underhand operation devised by North perhaps explains CIA and DFS leniency towards the bosses of the Guadalajara cartel. Some DEA agents noted that every time they arrested a high-level trafficker he was carrying DFS badges. These credentials allowed the criminals to carry machine guns, instal wiretapping devices and interrogate detainees. Often, truckloads of drugs would be protected by DFS agents, who would use the Mexican police radio system to intercept US police surveillance to ensure safe passage over the border (Scott and Marshall 1991: 39).

As part of the Iran-Contra investigations, the Tower Commission, the Walsh Commission and the Kerry Commission were formed in the United States to investigate covert arms sales to Iran and governmental support for the Contras. They found that high-ranking members of the Guadalajara cartel, who had also been involved in the capture and murder of Enrique Camarena – Ernesto Fonseca Carrillo, Rafael Caro Quintero, Miguel Ángel Félix Gallardo – alongside members of the Colombian Medellín cartel, were providing the Contras with 'humanitarian aid' in the form of high-powered weaponry, hard cash, planes and pilots. In return, many of those who themselves had been sentenced, who were under investigation or were suspected of smuggling-related offences by the US authorities, were permitted to continue to fly planeloads full of Colombian narcotics into Mexico for onward transmission to the United States (Hernández 2010a: 92–3). It was not that the founders of the Medellín cartel, like Pablo Escobar and Carlos Lehder Rivas, had any particular interest in supporting the Contras by sending millions of dollars. Rather, circumstances created by the US and Mexican governments, the CIA, and Mexican organised crime had provided them with a remarkably attractive business opportunity. For the Medellín cartel, the instability and violence created by the US proxy army, the Contras, represented a favourable commercial climate in which to operate. The suffering of ordinary Nicaraguans at the mercy of Contra death squads was thus a mere externality to a lucrative investment.

Lawrence Harrison, an American who had worked for the DFS and the Dirección de Investigaciones Políticas y Sociales (DIPS – Office of Political and Social Investigations), later testified that the DFS acted as a private army for the Guadalajara cartel. On one occasion the DFS and DIPS had tasked him with installing a wiretapping system in the home of Ernesto Fonseca in order to spy on rivals and to hack into Enrique Camarena's DEA office. In his testimony, Harrison recalled that Félix Gallardo had told him that the DFS were working with the Guadalajara cartel to run drugs to the Contras and in return would be guaranteed protection and given free rein by the CIA to import cocaine, crack, heroin and marijuana into the United States (Cockburn and St Clair 1998: 353–4). Apparently, US planes loaded with armaments would land in Mexico, where they would refuel and then would be sent to Honduras and Nicaragua for delivery. Before their return, testified Harrison, they would load the planes with drugs originating in Baranquilla, Colombia, refuel in Mexico and then land in Florida (Hernández 2010a: 99).

Despite the Reagan administration's 'war on drugs' being a defining feature of domestic and foreign policy, it was the CIA who were using the cartels' monopoly of violence and their readiness to break the law to defeat the revolutionary Nicaraguan government. Félix Gallardo, despite running four tons of cocaine into the United States every month, was entrusted with supplying arms to the Contras. Caro Quintero's ranch in Veracruz became a training facility for the Contras run by the DFS, presumably to divert attention from the CIA should unsavoury publicity surface (Scott and Marshall 1991: 41–2). When PJF agents arrived at the ranch as a result of an investigation into activities there, nineteen of them were killed by the Guatemalan and Nicaraguan Contra trainees; many of the bodies showed signs of torture.

While both the US and Mexico were spending millions of dollars on ineffectual campaigns of prohibition, interdiction and eradication, the intelligence-gathering and security agencies in each country were actually contributing to the growth of cartels in Mexico and Colombia and facilitating the export of narcotics into the United States. The increased availability of narcotics and the explosion of crack cocaine on the streets of US cities were made possible by agencies of the same governments that had promised they were eradicating them in the interests of public health. Ultimately, the interests of profit and power, combined with Cold War hysteria, trumped the security and health of citizens on both sides of the border.

The war on Communism, which had helped create a climate of fear in the United States and which provided a superficial justification for the funding of death squads and proxy armies in Central America, also acted as an ideological distraction from the social damage done by the imposition of neoliberal reform and structural adjustment programmes. What defined both US and Mexican government programmes in the 1980s was a free-market fundamentalism, the effect of which was to transfer more wealth from the poor to the rich and to create wider inequalities and economic disparities. If the majority of the poor suffered as a result, lost jobs and saw their incomes drop, then this was regarded as merely an outcome of the 'natural' laws and workings of the free market, a mere externality rather than a government responsibility.

Yet, far from being aspects of a natural process, the workings of the free market, the Washington Consensus and neoliberal reform in Mexico relied on force and violence, government corruption and the cooperation of powerful drug cartels to reinforce political and economic influence over the US's 'backyard'. As the decade closed at least thirty thousand people had been killed in Nicaragua, the infrastructure destroyed and the Sandinista government defeated. Throughout the region about 200,000 people had been killed in civil wars in which the US government had backed paramilitary death squads to overpower the increasing influence of Liberation Theology and socialism. Mexican traffickers, who had supported US policy by supplying arms and funds to the death squads, were thus not only complicit in creating misery and suffering in Mexico, but also in Central America, for the sake of profit. No politician would ever admit it, but the 'war on drugs' had transmuted into an exercise in social, political and economic control, maintaining an unequal and hierarchical domestic and international order by force, which benefited political and economic elites. Neoliberal capitalism was backed up by violence and the repression of opposition groups, and had become dependent on the assistance of high-powered criminal organisations. This new market was anything but 'free', except insofar as it removed restraints from the accumulation of capital by the few and gave a free hand to criminals and security agencies who were able to help the process along.

We open this chapter by examining more closely how the Colombian connection functioned inside Mexico to bring unprecedented power and wealth to the illegal narcotics industry. As we saw in Chapter 3, Colombian cartels had attempted at first to work independently of Mexican criminal organisations, but with little success. In order to operate inside Mexico they would have had to create their own contacts within the established hierarchy of control, and Colombian organisations did not have the access to the police, army and politicians that their counterparts in Mexico already had. As the crackdown by the South Florida Task Force had made smuggling narcotics via the 7,000 islands in the Caribbean more risky, Colombian traffickers increasingly looked to Mexico and its well-established overland smuggling operation as the corridor for their products to enter the United States.

Colombian cartels thus entered into a business partnership with Mexican traffickers. While initially the Mexicans had often been, in essence, employees of the Colombians, by the mid-1980s they increasingly dictated their own terms, being in a commercially advantageous position to do so. Because the Mexicans had been for some time taking great risks by smuggling contraband across the border and thus facing the possibility of arrest by the US authorities, they had already developed the most secure contacts and distribution lists there (Poppa 1998: 185–7). The practice of running the *plaza* as a way of controlling the drugs trade throughout the country also meant that Mexican traffickers had the best connections at home within the political system.

The Colombians began by approaching Pablo Acosta, who controlled the Ojinaga *plaza* in Chihuahua, for assistance in receiving and exporting planeloads of cocaine destined for the US market. Acosta would receive loads at the airport in Ojinaga or on private remote runways before taking them across the Río Bravo. But he also used his control of the *plaza* simply to store merchandise for other important traffickers. Acosta exploited his protection by the military to warehouse massive loads of cocaine within his jurisdiction and earned between 1,000 and 1,500 dollars per kilo for this service (*ibid.*: 187). The Colombian connection expanded Acosta's operations massively and made him one of the most powerful traffickers in Latin America.

Amado Carrillo Fuentes, who was to become Mexico's most feared and successful drug lord, had been sent by his uncle, Ernesto Fonseca Carrillo, to enter into partnership with Acosta in Ojinaga. Carrillo Fuentes, according to the DEA, had worked for the federal government in Guadalajara, though in what capacity was unknown (*ibid.*: 241). Carrillo Fuentes's task was to organise and manage cocaine shipments passing through the Ojinaga *plaza* for Fonseca on behalf of the Guadalajara cartel. He was to turn his experiences in this role to highly profitable use.

When Acosta was killed in 1987, the *plaza* was taken over by Rafael Aguilar Guajardo, who was federal police commander for the National Security and Investigation Centre (CISEN), the organisation which had replaced the DFS in 1989. Under Aguilar Guajardo, CISEN effectively became the Juárez cartel. He used his position and resources within the organisation to gather intelligence on opponents and competitors and to avoid prosecution. In 1993 Aguilar Guajardo was assassinated in Cancún by Carrillo Fuentes, who subsequently took control of the cartel. As a result of his innovative trafficking modus operandi and ruthless treatment of competitors and opponents, Carrillo Fuentes would become the continent's richest and most powerful cartel boss (Cockburn and

St Clair 1998: 361). Carrillo Fuentes came to be known as *El Señor de los Cielos*, or Lord of the Skies, because of his fleet of 27 Boeing 727 jets that flew, loaded with cocaine, between Cali and Medellín and Mexico every week. Trafficking cocaine into the United States had by now taken on unprecedented and awesome proportions. As a result, in the early 1990s Mexico had taken over half of the Colombian market in illegal narcotics, which accounted for anything between three to eight billion dollars every year (Fabre 2009). Of course, such operations as those of the Juárez cartel had to rely on a wide and complex network of employees and bribed public servants. For example, landing 27 Boeing 727s laden with narcotics every week could hardly be kept secret for long.

Carrillo Fuentes became the world's richest trafficker in 1993: the timing was significant. In December 1992 President Carlos Salinas de Gortari (1988–94) signed the North American Free Trade Agreement (NAFTA) with the governments of the United States and Canada. The Agreement came into force in January 1994. Thus, at the same time as cartel bosses were using illegal methods to increase their influence and reap staggering profits, the NAFTA agreement was reinforcing the economic restructuring set in motion by Miguel de la Madrid in 1982, using legitimate institutions to channel wealth and power to economic elites. Of Carillo Fuentes, more later; first we will consider some of the factors that contributed to the unholy alliance between state power, big business and the cartels.

'Un Político Pobre es un Pobre Político' (A Politician Who is Poor is a Poor Politician)

'NAFTA', Harvard economist Jeffrey Sachs (2001) noted once, 'really is a beautiful thing.' Indeed, from the perspective of multi-national capital, if not of Mexico's poor, deregulation, corporate-friendly tax and low wages were very attractive. But the freedoms awarded to those making the highest profits could hardly be said to have been achieved thanks to their aptitude and enterprise.

Neoliberalism had in fact tilted the playing field in their favour. Again, the free market was not the result of a law of nature that, when allowed to function unhindered, coincidentally tended to benefit the rich. One only has to look at how the architect of Mexico's new economy, the man who negotiated and signed NAFTA, himself came to power.

Cuauhtémoc Cárdenas, the son of President Lázaro Cárdenas, had been nominated by a centre-left coalition faction within the PRI to lead the *Corriente Democrática* (Democratic Current). As discussed in Chapter 3, the PRI leadership had undergone a shift during the de la Madrid presidency and was more and more dominated by Harvard-educated technocrats whose vision of instituting further neoliberal reform and consolidating the Washington Consensus did not fit with Cárdenas's left-leaning politics. Cárdenas was subsequently expelled from the party of which his father had been a co-founder and whose leadership had led to the creation of the corporatist state in Mexico. This was a clear signal that a massive shift was occurring in Mexico's political and economic life.

In the wake of his expulsion, a leftist coalition, the Frente Democrático Nacional (National Democratic Front) was formed and Cárdenas was chosen as presidential candidate for the 1988 election. For the first time since 1929, the possibility arose that an organised opposition might depose the PRI in an election. Furthermore, Cárdenas counted on widespread political support as the outcome of his opposition to the policies of the technocrats, which were presented as being somehow the inevitable course of history, and because of the prestige and the reputation of his father. On the day of the election, 6 July, Miguel de la Madrid ordered Secretario de Gobernación Manuel Bartlett to withhold a public announcement of the election results and terminate the count (Dillon and Preston 2004: 149). It appeared that Cárdenas was winning. Suddenly, the recently installed computerised ballot counting machines mysteriously shut down. 'Se cayó el sistema' ('There has been a system breakdown') was the only official explanation. When the computers began functioning again, the Comisión Federal Electoral (Federal Election Commission) proclaimed Carlos Salinas de Gortari the official winner. This raised a number of suspicions, not least because, in the face of accusations of electoral fraud, PRI politicians in the Congress voted to keep secret and get rid of documents that, if revealed, might show Cárdenas as the winner. In any case, the PRI ruled out a recount and, as the ruling party effectively controlled the electoral commission and the army, after a period of intense political conflict, which saw the largest public demonstrations in Mexico until then, Salinas was inaugurated. 'Se cayó el sistema' began to take on a secondary meaning.

In the weeks that followed, although all ballot papers were supposed to have been burned, numerous reports emerged of ballot sheets with an extra zero added, and of 20,000 ballots favouring Cárdenas found in waste sites and riverbeds. One independent study concluded that Cárdenas had won with 42 per cent over Salinas's 36 per cent (Cockburn and St Clair 1998: 358).

Such manipulation and lack of openness in the refusal to grant a recount were reflected in Salinas's dealings with the media. A report by the NGO, CENCOS, noted that during the Salinas administration there were 645 government-instigated attacks reported against the press. In fact, as Tanius Karam (2000) points out, Salinas won the 'medalla de oro' (gold medal) for the greatest number of journalists assassinated (more than fifty) during his presidency.

To claim that Salinas's takeover of power represented the inevitable triumph of the free market and the Washington Consensus, and that the new world order enjoyed a popular mandate and widespread support, was clearly misleading. Francis Fukuyama's (1998) claim that the fall of the Berlin Wall and the supposed triumph of globalised capitalism over any alternative forms of social organisation represented the 'end of history' ignored the fact that many neoliberal governments like that of Mexico did not have popular endorsement.

Soon after Salinas took power, he ordered a series of attacks on labour unions. Labour leaders were also targeted and often subjected to false but very public accusations. For instance, Joaquín Hernández Galicia, head of the Oil Workers Union, was charged with stockpiling weapons, while Agapito Gonzáles of the Day Labourers and Industrial Workers Union was arrested on charges of tax evasion. Though the charges were dropped, the frequent attacks on strikers and syndicalists, such as Salinas's deployment of 5,000 paratroopers to attack the walk-out at the Cananea copper mine in Sonora, made it clear that the technocratic elite were fanatical about keeping wages down. Low wages and the removal of worker protections were exactly what prospective investors hoped for in the new export-oriented Mexican economy (Cockburn and St Clair 1998: 358–9).

The government of de la Madrid had implemented a relatively gradual privatisation programme (compared to that of Salinas) in order to overcome, among other things, the negative effects of the debt crisis. Privatisation in Mexico, as presented publicly by the Salinas administration, had at least three key objectives (Weiss 1996: 67). (1) It sought to improve the operating efficiency of enterprises by transferring them to the private sector. (2) It was expected to contribute to a reduction in the government budget deficit either from the sale proceeds, or from the disposal of loss-making enterprises whose losses no longer had to be covered by government. (3) The administration and its supporters hoped to foster confidence in the private sector and thus encourage new investment. Privatisation proceeded in three phases. In the first (1983–85), non-viable and non-priority state enterprises, mostly small, were either liquidated or merged within the public sector. In the second phase (1986–88), experience was built up through the sale of medium and small companies, generally in non-sensitive areas. In the third phase (1988–94), during the Salinas administration, the larger, more strategic, public enterprises were sold, such as the telecommunications company (Telmex), the two airlines, the national steel company, fertiliser and sugar companies, and the commercial banks, which had been nationalised in 1982 in the wake of the crisis (*ibid.*).

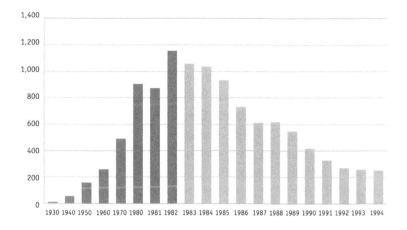

Figure 4.1. Number of parastatal enterprises in Mexico, 1930–1994
Source: MacLeod (2005).

During the ISI period, the number of parastatal corporations had increased in Mexico, but in the neoliberal era these decreased significantly. As a result of the privatisation process, the number of parastatal enterprises was reduced from 1,156 in 1982 to only 252 in 1994. Previously, the figures had increased from 259 in 1960 to 905 parastatal firms in 1980 (see Figure 4.1).

When public enterprises were privatised, collective agreements underwent modifications, removing labour benefits for workers and creating more flexible work rules at the workplaces. Furthermore, the privatisation of public enterprises, fostered by neoliberal governments, benefited a small group who became some of the world's richest people.

Thus, state assets disposed of by Salinas included the eighteen most important national banks as well as the national telephone company, Telmex. As a result of the privatisation process, 'Mexico's stock of billionaires rose from 2 to 24 during the presidency of Carlos Salinas (1988–94)' (O'Toole 2007: 448). Carlos Slim, for example, who bought Telmex, has since become the world's richest man. Those who had seen their assets grow considerably were keen to offer their support to Salinas and the PRI, and offered to help fund the PRI's next election campaign in 1993. A gathering of the wealthiest business people in the country managed to donate some $750 million in one evening; Emilio Azcárraga, owner of the network Televisa, alone pledged $50 million (*ibid.*).

Moving large shares of public assets into private hands meant that there was less and less accountability within these institutions. Now private concerns, these companies were free from the parameters and limitations of state-imposed regulation. But again, this was hardly the free market in operation. After Carlos Slim purchased Telmex, the payments for it were made with revenues generated while it was still a state-run company. Allowing companies such as Telmex, whose infrastructure and service had been paid for by the taxpayer, suddenly to go private could hardly be presented as proof of the miraculous effects of market forces. It was the taxpayer who had over the years contributed to the maintenance and functioning of these same companies. Salinas and the Washington Consensus simply passed them over to private hands. The notion that, as the rich further accrue assets and profits, the process will benefit the majority of the population, as capital 'trickles down' to the poor, is misleading. Instead, those with the largest assets tend to be the same ones who invest least in Mexico, preferring instead to entrust their dollars to the US economy where returns are far healthier. In addition, many of these funds – like those of Raúl Salinas, the President's brother – were held in offshore bank accounts where their earnings were unlikely to 'trickle down' to anyone but their owner.

In essence, under neoliberalism, the costs were social, the profits private. In the case of the sale of Telmex, it allowed Slim to create a massive telecommunications monopoly, scarcely proof that the competition of the free market means that the shrewdest and most competitive companies naturally rise to the top. Instead, it was those who had been given most by the state who were most successful. Privatisation also meant that, because the principle of publicly owned companies had been abandoned, it was much less the public's business how these companies operated, something which gave greater confidence to those involved in corrupt practices. For the banks, for example, less accountability and less control over the movement of capital made it much easier to launder billions of dollars for the cartels.

Seizing on this opportunity provided by Salinas's programme of privatisation, narcotraffickers bought up some previously state-owned companies as channels through which to launder their profits and invest (Scott 2009: 186). In Mexico, notes Guilhem Fabre (2009), corruption and organised crime thus 'played a major part in creating public debt and diverting funds to speculative overseas financial markets'. After the peso crisis of 1994–95, also dubbed the *efecto tequila* or 'tequila effect', for example, the Mexican banks had debts of over $60 billion – but these were paid by the state, not the bankers. Again, if this were the self-regulating 'free market' in action, the state and the taxpayer appeared to have a much more important role than NAFTA's proponents had promised.

As a result of the growing share of the international market in drugs shifting to Mexico, and the ease with which money could be laundered by Mexican and US banks, drug trafficking increased massively under Salinas. By the early 1990s, 75 per cent of all cocaine entering the United States passed through Mexico, while the latter could produce and supply its own marijuana, heroin and methamphetamines. Clearly there was a correlation between deregulation, privatisation and narcotrafficking. Bill Clinton evidently understood that a consequence of the NAFTA treaty would be an increase in the number of migrants crossing into the United States, and that poverty in Mexico was likely to push a greater number of people into the illegal narcotics industry. The launching of Operation Gatekeeper in 1994 and its criminalisation of migrants point to this. Furthermore, during the NAFTA negotiations, Bush 1 and Clinton had expressly prohibited members of the DEA and the US Customs Service from raising the subject of drug trafficking as a likely outcome of NAFTA (Cockburn and St Clair 1998: 359–61).

The idea that the market would regulate itself, if left to its own devices, meant that banks could launder money on behalf of criminal organisations and make massive profits doing so. Thus by the 1990s US banks were laundering around $250 billion of criminal earnings every year, funds that again were leaving the Mexican economy and being safeguarded across the border by the US banking system.

As in previous administrations, it appeared that some of the highest officials had more than questionable links to drug trafficking. One of the most notorious examples of laundering drug money was President Salinas's brother Raúl. It is estimated that Raúl Salinas had assets in offshore bank accounts of over $300 million. When he was investigated for his links to the cartels, he claimed in his defence, with astonishing insouciance, that the benefits of political and financial nepotism were such that he hardly needed to become involved in the drug-trafficking business.

In two managerial posts in government food-distribution agencies, the President's brother had been making lucrative deals. While in charge of the CONASUPO distribution network, he had bought powdered milk contaminated in the Chernobyl disaster for distribution among Mexican school children, and profited from replacing US-imported cornmeal with animal feed for sale to the poor (*ibid.*: 367–8). *El Señor Diez Por Ciento*, 'Mister Ten Percent', as Raúl Salinas was known for his commissions on government contracts and for selling access to his brother, had an important role in the democratic transition in Mexico in 2000. As Sam Dillon and Julia Preston (2004: 304) point out, however, 'His . . . was not a hero's role.' A contributing factor to the PRI debacle had been Mexicans' disgust with the level of corruption within the presidential family.

The extraordinary scale of their venality had been exposed by a year of political and drug-related assassinations and cover-ups, the most notorious being the killings of PRI presidential candidate Luis Donaldo Colosio on 23 March 1994, and of José Francisco

Ruiz Massieu, former brother-in-law of President Salinas and General-Secretary of the PRI, on 28 September 1994. Raúl Salinas was implicated in, and was convicted as the mastermind of, the latter's murder during Zedillo's presidency.

The scandals surrounding Raúl Salinas appeared to be endless. In 1995 Swiss investigators arrested Salinas's wife, Paula Castañón and her brother Antonio Castañón, as they attempted to withdraw US$84 million from accounts belonging to Raúl. The Swiss authorities began an investigation into what they suspected to be a complex money laundering operation between banks in Mexico, the United States, Switzerland and the United Kingdom. Swiss officials concluded that many of the millions he had deposited in numerous accounts in that country were profits from narcotrafficking – they froze $110 million, of which $74 million were returned to the Mexican government. Another federal investigation in Mexico claimed that, while President, Carlos Salinas had transferred $38 million into accounts owned by Raúl Salinas (under aliases) (*ibid.*: 305). Similarly, the United States General Accounting Office conducted an investigation into his financial activities in 1998 and how Salinas 'was able to transfer between $90 million and $100 million from Mexico into foreign accounts through Citibank and its affiliates' (GAO 1998: 1). Though the numerous investigations into Raúl Salinas's alleged financial activities never led to prosecution, he was subsequently sentenced to fifty years in prison following his arrest in Mexico in 1995 due to his involvement in Ruiz Massieu's murder. He was, however, later acquitted on appeal in 2005.

One company which had been privatised under Carlos Salinas was the network, TV Azteca. Subsequent investigations into Raúl Salinas's activities revealed that he had helped pay for the station via an entrepreneur, Ricardo Salinas Pliego. Raúl Salinas began paying money to Salinas Pliego via accounts in the Cayman Islands and Switzerland to make a concealed bid for control of the station. Salinas Pliego eventually won the bid for TV Azteca, privatised by his associate's brother (who also happened to be President), much to the surprise of many in the business world. After all, Salinas

Pliego had little experience of the telecommunications industry, having made his original fortune by selling stoves.

When in 1995 Raúl Salinas's Swiss bank accounts were frozen as a result of narcotics violations, Carlos Peralta Quintero stepped forward to claim that $50 million of the funds were his. The Salinas government had awarded Peralta Quintero a licence to run the cell-phone competitor to Telmex. Seemingly, Peralta Quintero had paid Raúl Salinas for securing his licence to operate – and now he wanted his money back. In the end, the funds remained frozen (Dillon and Preston 2004: 306–9).

Following testimonies of DEA informants and investigations by Swiss police, it was claimed that Raúl Salinas had met with Amado Carrillo Fuentes, *El Señor de los Cielos*, at least once in 1990 and that they had struck a business deal. One witness claimed to have given Raúl Salinas $28.7 million on behalf of the Medellín cartel to retrieve a Colombian shipment of cocaine that had been forced to land in northern Mexico. Additionally, according to the Swiss investigators, Rául Salinas controlled most of the drug shipments moving through and out of Mexico during his brother's term as President. Nonetheless, it was not the numerous accusations of money laundering that led to the conviction and incarceration of Salinas in 1999.

Many suspected that the assassination of the politician and presidential candidate, Luis Donaldo Colosio, was related to the country's growing drug trade. Colosio was shot in Tijuana while on the campaign trail for the the presidency of Mexico. He had promised to clean up corruption in government and was killed just days before he was to meet with investigators who were exploring the Salinas administration's involvement with the Gulf cartel. He had also demanded that Humberto García Abrego – brother of Juan García Abrego, one of the leaders of the cartel – be removed from a list of guests for a PRI fundraising event. Certainly, there was no doubt that Colosio's stance *vis-à-vis* corruption and political involvement with the cartels had angered the Salinas administration, which lent substance to suspicions of its complicity in his killing (Cockburn and St Clair 1998: 363). 'I have no doubt that Colosio was killed by narco-politicians or poli-narcos,' claimed Eduardo Valle, a top adviser to the Attorney General who was also responsible for investigating drug trafficking in Mexico. Valle subsequently resigned after it became clear to him that the Attorney General had no interest in investigating the case. Fearing an assassination attempt against him, he fled to the United States (Paternostro 1995). According to Porfirio Muñoz Ledo, the assassination of Colosio was perpetrated by narcotraffickers: 'this was an execution of the narcos with the support of irregular forces', and, 'it was not Colosio's speech that made him die but his refusal to negotiate with the narcos' (Albarran de Alba 2010: 11).

Following the assassination of Colosio, Salinas chose Ernesto Zedillo to succeed him as presidential candidate for the PRI. Perhaps unwisely in the circumstances, José Ruiz Massieu, secretary general of the PRI, and brother-in-law of Carlos Salinas, began pushing for further investigations into the death of Colosio, to whom he had been a close friend. In September 1994 he too was murdered. President Salinas then appointed Ruiz Massieu's brother, Mario, who was the Deputy Attorney General, to lead the investigation into Colosio's assassination. Manuel Muñoz Rocha, Deputy of the PRI, it emerged, had been involved in instigating the murder. Yet it also turned out that Mario Ruiz Massieu had had ties to the Gulf cartel, particularly to its boss, Juan García Abrego. Instead of investigating his brother's murder, Mexican federal officials maintained, he had in fact attempted to cover up the assassination in order to protect Raúl Salinas, later jailed as the intellectual author of the murder (Paternostro 1995). In 1997, in a civil money-laundering suit, US authorities seized $9 million of the $17 million he had housed in US bank accounts. Mario Ruiz Massieu was later arrested in Newark boarding a plane while carrying a case stuffed with undeclared cash. Faced with the prospect of a lengthy custodial sentence in a Texas jail, in September 1999 he took his own life (Golden 1999).

According to the 1998 report by the United States General

Accounting Office, Raúl Salinas had been laundering millions of dollars through Citibank New York, Citibank Mexico, and the bank's branches in London and Switzerland, as well as accounts in the Cayman Islands. In order to disguise the paper trail to a stash of $90–100 million, Salinas used several aliases with the agreement of the banks. Clearly, Citibank's 'know your customer' policy did not apply. In fact, without the cooperation of Mexican, US, UK and Swiss banks, Raúl Salinas would have been unable to safeguard his funds. One of Salinas's principal contacts in Citibank was Amy Elliott, who facilitated the deposits of millions of dollars under the alias Juan Guillermo Gómez Gutiérrez on his behalf. Elliott also helped Amado Carrillo Fuentes, 'Lord of the Skies', as well as the billionaire businessman and politician, Carlos Hank González and his two sons, all of whom had been accused of having links to the Tijuana cartel led by the Arellano-Félix brothers (the nephews of Félix Gallardo), to launder millions through Citibank. Another of the respectable faces of Mexican narcotrafficking, Elliott testified before the US Congress, claiming that, 'I didn't have motives to suspect that the money would be dirty' (Giordano 2000).

Bank privacy regulations meant that investigators were often unable to obtain crucial information on the laundering activities of drug traffickers. For the banks, it was too easy and, more importantly, too profitable, to avoid asking difficult questions about the provenance of the millions of dollars belonging to people like Raúl Salinas, who, after all, was supposed to be a public servant. The private banks, it seemed, were answerable to no one but their account holders. If combating the flow of narcotics from Mexico to the United States had been a priority for both governments, introducing stiffer regulation of the private banking system would have been one way of hindering illegal transactions. As a matter of fact, Carlos Salinas's privatisation of the banks, telecommunications and broadcasting had made an elite circle of supporters extremely wealthy. It simply was not in their interests to create tougher regulations on transfers of capital. The system, which was expanded by Salinas's administration, was not inclined to self-regulation or external regulation. Indeed, owing to the massive sums involved in the laundering of illegally acquired funds, among the greatest beneficiaries of the drug industry were and are the bankers themselves. And it was the Salinas administration that helped make the system work in their interests.

Roberto Ramírez Hernández, for example, who became a board chairman and then CEO of Banamex, the national bank of Mexico, which had been privatised in 1991, became one of the world's richest men.[4] Indeed, the bank privatisation sold the institutions to men who were not professional bankers (like Adrián Sada, Roberto González and Alfredo Harp Helú) but technocrats who had close links to the Salinas administration and were a key constituent support base for an ailing PRI. Banamex was by 1998 the target of an investigation by the US State Department, Operation Casablanca, which concluded that Banamex, Bancomer and Banco Confía were laundering money for the Cali cartel of Colombia and for Amado Carrillo Fuentes. Arcadio Valenzuela, the ex-head of the Asociación de Banqueros de México, had been, the DEA discovered, the boss of white-collar crime in Mexico and had facilitated the laundering of funds for Miguel Ángel Félix Gallardo and Rafael Caro Quintero. Juan García Abrego, meanwhile, had been one of Banamex's best clients. Banamex's ties to Amado Carrillo Fuentes later became the target of DEA investigations when the agency discovered in 1999 and 2001 that the ex-governor of the state of Quintana Roo, Mario Villanueva Madrid (1993–99), had been taking monies from *El Señor de los Cielos* and depositing them in a Banamex bank account, in return offering state and federal protection to the trafficker's operations (Hernández 2010a: 222–4).

According to journalist Al Giordano of *The Narco News Bulletin* (2000), Roberto Ramírez Hernández was the financial engineer for the Gulf cartel. Raúl Salinas, meanwhile, was responsible for maintaining political relations for the organisation, for obvious

---

4 Banamex was acquired by Citigroup, the same group to which Citibank belongs, in 2001.

reasons. Carlos Cabal Peniche was allegedly the financial brain of the cartel. Before Cabal Peniche was arrested in Australia, he had been granted two privatised banks (Banco Unión and Banca Cremi) by the Salinas government. Raúl Salinas owned 52 per cent of Banca Cremi. In 1990, one year before the privatisation of the banks, Carlos Salinas had created the FOBAPROA fund, ostensibly to safeguard the banking sector from insolvency during major economic crises. As Giordano notes (*ibid.*), Cabal Peniche gained massively from the FOBAPROA loans, which were never paid back, adding to the $80 billion debt with which the Mexican taxpayer was saddled. As the Swiss investigations into Raúl Salinas's financial activities revealed, at least $67 million of drug money had been laundered through the Banca Cremi. And the FOBAPROA fund, as Giordano indicates, made such operations all the easier:

> The neo-bankers . . . took full advantage of its loopholes to make loans to phony corporations – owned by themselves and their friends, often to launder drug money – that did not have the capital or business activity to pay back the loans. They took the money and ran. That the FOBAPROA fund would pay the banks for their uncollected bad loans was a money-launderer's dream; a means by which they could form paper corporations and make self-loans, never to be paid, and collect the money a second time from the government. The paper corporations were also ideal for hiding and moving drug money around. (*Ibid.*)

President Salinas's 'model businessman' had also purchased Del Monte in Mexico and was apparently using the company's infrastructure (the Salinas government had used taxpayer money to restore the Dos Bocas port in Tabasco on behalf of Del Monte) to export cocaine to the United States.

Again, not only was the public paying to enable major national companies to operate privately, but public funds were also being plundered to fund the infrastructure that made laundering – and in some cases the export of narcotics – possible. During a period in which the poverty level and the number of unemployed people had risen dramatically, the looting of public funds to assist illegal trafficking and money laundering was unlikely to impress an already disadvantaged and dissatisfied public. For the NAFTA beneficiaries, information of this kind needed to be kept safe from public scrutiny. Little wonder then, that the Salinas administration interfered so often in the working of the press, and aimed so many attacks at journalists.

Faced with mounting popular discontent and political opposition, Salinas turned to his elite support base to ensure a PRI victory at the polls in 1994. His supporters included the thirty richest men in Mexico, those who had benefited directly from Salinas's campaign of privatisation. They were invited to a fundraiser dinner in 1993 by the President, who urged the billionaires to make an investment in the PRI. Guests included Carlos Slim, now the world's richest individual. Also present were Carlos Hank Rhon, the son of the businessman Carlos Hank González, whom Eduardo Valle, an assistant to the Attorney General, Jorge Carpizo, described as '*il capo di tutti capi*', the 'primary intermediary between the multinational drug trafficking enterprises and the Mexican political system' (Reding 1995). It was Carlos Hank González who once famously said that, '*Un político pobre es un pobre político*' (A politician who is poor is a poor politician).

Hank González had also been secretary of tourism and then secretary of agriculture during the Salinas presidency. According to Valle, Hank González acted as protector of the Arellano-Félix brothers who ran the Tijuana cartel and were responsible for shipping Colombian cocaine and heroin from Asia and Pakistan into the United States. In Tijuana, the Arellano-Félix brothers could count on their operations being protected by police, the army and politicians, and were provided with police credentials in order to carry out their work without interference.

Hank González's sons, Jorge Hank Rhon and Carlos Hank Rhon, were two of Mexico's wealthiest businessmen, and both had privileged access to the political elite. Carlos Hank Rhon, for example, had been a close friend of Raúl Salinas since they studied together at university. Jorge Hank had been indirectly linked to the murder of an editor of the magazine *Zeta*, who had been investigating the family's ties to Colombian cocaine, when two guards from Jorge Hank's Tijuana racetrack ambushed and shot him, a crime for which they were subsequently convicted. In addition, the *New York Times* reported that TAESA, the company founded by the Hanks and later sold to the family's own pilots, was flying Boeing 727s into Mexico loaded with Colombian cocaine.

During President Miguel de la Madrid's *Renovación Moral*, Hank was one of several former officials considered for indictment. But de la Madrid ruled out any action, according to the former president of the PRI, Porfirio Muñoz Ledo, because he feared *un magnicidio* – a presidential assassination. Reding notes that 'Carlos Hank was merely banished from government service for the duration of the de la Madrid presidency. It was Salinas, lionised by Washington and Wall Street as a reformer, who rehabilitated Hank by naming him to the Cabinet' (*ibid.*).

As Giordano (2000) writes,

Likewise, the Hank family stands accused before the US Federal Reserve Bank of forming two banks in Texas with laundered monies. In 1993, while Carlos Hank González was Salinas's secretary of agriculture – a position that has obvious advantages in the drug trade – he met with a Citibank executive in Mexico City and said that he wanted to buy a controlling interest in the Laredo National Bank of Texas. And could Citibank arrange for the purchase – in the name of his son Carlos Hank Rhon – using $20 million dollars from 'offshore' accounts in the Virgin Islands? Citibank obliged him.

In June 2011, Jorge Hank Rhon, the flamboyant ex-mayor of Tijuana, was arrested after the military raided his home and discovered unlicensed firearms. Forty of the 88 weapons seized were high-calibre rifles. Also in the stash were 9,000 rounds of ammunition and a gas grenade (Morales and Otero 2011). If convicted, Jorge Hank could have faced a jail sentence of up to fifteen years. Forensics officials claimed that their tests 'indicated that one of the guns had been used to kill a security guard in

December 2009 and the other to kill a car salesman in June 2010'
(Tuckman 2011). Ten days later, however, a judge ordered the
release of Jorge Hank and ten of his employees.

It was the Hanks and a handful of Salinas's friends who had
become billionaires as a result of deregulation and privatisation
and of corruption tolerated or protected by the authorities. These
men were in fact the political and economic support base for the
PRI. For instance, prior to the 1994 presidential elections, each
of the thirty billionaires at the Salinas fundraiser pledged to back
the PRI presidential campaign with an average of $25 million,
a total of three quarters of a billion dollars. Banamex's Roberto
Hernández was the first to pledge $25 million. But he was outdone
by Emilio Azcárraga, the media magnate owner of Televisa, one of
the richest men in Latin America, according to journalist Andrés
Oppenheimer's (1996) account, who reportedly said, 'I, and all of
you, have earned so much money over the past six years that I
think we have a big debt of gratitude to this government. I'm ready
to more than double what has been pledged so far, and I hope that
most in this room will join me. We owe it to the President, and to
the country.'

This was politics run by and for a tiny and very rich elite.
Salinas's portrayal in the US and European media as a democratic
reformer committed to the free market clearly did not account for
how that market was fixed. Had Mexico been an official enemy of
the United States and its allies, such levels of political corruption
would have been the cause of much hysteria. But Salinas was
touted as a suitable candidate for the head of the World Trade
Organization and as the moderniser of Mexico's ailing financial
system. What this accolade failed to acknowledge was that
the growth of narcotrafficking and the extension of money
laundering were not merely consequences or 'externalities' of the
modernised system, but an integral part of its workings. And it
was the politicians and business elites, the vanguard of the new
Washington Consensus, who, rather than being the solution,
were a big part of the problem.

NAFTA

From the 1980s onwards neoliberal reforms were implemented in such a way that Mexico became the developing country where conversion into an economy oriented to the 'free market' was achieved most rapidly.

The administration of Carlos Salinas built upon neoliberal policies introduced by de la Madrid, bringing about significant political and economic changes that had further impacts on the corporatist political and economic structure. As Dan La Botz has remarked, 'The rise to power of Carlos Salinas represented a kind of counter-revolution within the Mexican government and the Institutional Revolutionary Party' (1995: 101). NAFTA represented the peak of the counter-revolution and the absolute restoration of power to private interests.

The United States government had backed military dictatorships throughout the region in the 1960s and 1970s. In Chile, for example, where the neoliberal model took hold prior to its rise in Mexico, economic restructuring and 'free'-market reform were introduced via a centralised authoritarian state that brutally punished, killed and disappeared unionists, political opposition and dissenters. Mexico differed in the sense that the introduction of similar reforms correlated with a restructuring of the traditional leadership of the authoritarian PRI, which was replaced by an elite of technocrats. Major moves towards the neoliberal integration and a system of democratic accountability – however limited – occurred after the fall of the Berlin Wall and once the potency of Cold War polarities between Communism and Western capitalist democracy had abated. Furthermore, US backing of death squads in Central America, which accounted for one of the bloodiest episodes of the late twentieth century, had proved an unsustainable feature of US 'democracy promotion' abroad thanks to exposure by human rights organisations and a modicum of coverage in the international media.

It would not take long, however, for US leaders to substitute new ideological threats as replacements for the now defunct

Communist menace. Almost immediately, any challenges to the sanctity of the Washington Consensus came to act as political and moral surrogates for the evils of socialism. Following the decline of the bipolar world system, argues John Saxe-Fernández (2004: 57), in the West the Communist nemesis was replaced by the 'enemies of the liberal market democracies'. These included international terrorists, narcotraffickers, and Third World nationalists. The new threats permitted and justified military spending and the preservation and expansion of the US military-industrial complex. Since the 1990s the fight against narcotrafficking by the United States in Latin America has been incorporated into an international agenda to protect the market and safeguard the guise of democracy (*ibid.*).

In Mexico this involved loosening the state's control of key sectors of the economy by reshuffling the political leadership to enact the priorities of the Washington Consensus. The state had been reluctant to relinquish control of the economy, recognising the possibility of an emboldened political opposition which might arise from a more fragmented political and economic system. But, by the 1990s, state actors unwilling to concede economic control to the private sector had largely been replaced by the technocrats who now occupied the PRI leadership. With key sectors of the economy firmly destined for private ownership, democratic reforms unlikely to upset the structures of economic power in any meaningful sense allowed Mexico to 'modernise', with free elections in 2000.

The NAFTA region is one of the largest free trade areas in the world. In 2006, it was home to a total population of more than 440 million, with a GDP of $US14.5 trillion. It is the second largest free trade zone, after the European Union (EU), in terms of population. However, in terms of GDP, the NAFTA region is the biggest worldwide (see Table 4.1). The NAFTA accord covers only issues of trade and its institutions are not supranational as in the European Union. For example, each NAFTA signatory decides on its own labour and trade policies. The common frontiers among the three members, rather than allowing free transit, have become increasingly closed to workers, particularly between Mexico and the United States, and the idea of a common currency appears distant.

In contrast to the EU, NAFTA represents a less ambitious effort to establish a common market for the trade of goods and services, with little interest in the development of a continental policy with an institutional framework (Stanford 2003). Integration processes in Europe and North America have been very different and spurred on by diverse interests, with contrasting social supports and different institutional levels (Curzio 2004). Yet, under NAFTA, in areas of 'security', such as combating drug trafficking and the threat of terrorism, cross-border institutional cooperation has been much more extensive.

The NAFTA region is dominated both economically and politically by the United States, which accounts for almost 70 per cent of the signatories' total population and around 85 per cent of their economic production. Furthermore, the negotiation and implementation of NAFTA was arguably less beneficial to Canada and Mexico than to the USA. For the USA, the creation of a free trade zone was a significant event, but did not necessarily herald the beginning of a new era. Far from giving the other countries greater freedom of action, NAFTA reinforced US strategic and economic dominance in the continent (Stanford 2003).

In spite of increasing economic links, major political and economic differences still prevail among NAFTA members (see Table 4.2). In terms of per capita income, the US economy is the richest in the region and economic policy is characterised by high levels of deregulation unique to the industrialised world. Meanwhile, Mexico's per capita income is about one quarter that of the United States.

Income inequality is significantly more severe in Mexico than in the USA. Both Mexico and Canada depend on the production and export of primary resources to the United States (specifically, energy) as an important economic activity; moreover, both have encouraged manufacturing industry. Mexico relies on low labour costs, whereas Canada depends upon innovative activities based on advanced technology.

Table 4.1 NAFTA, European Union and China, 2006

	European Union	NAFTA	China
Countries	25	3	1
Population (million)	456	440	1,313
GDP (US$ trillion)	12.1	14.5	8.8
Labour force (million)	218.5	209	

Source: CIA World Factbook, www.cia.gov (consulted 15 July 2009).

Table 4.2 Main features of NAFTA members, 2006

	Canada	Mexico	United States	US as % NAFTA
Population (thousand)	32,270	107,525	300,110	68.1
GDP (US$ billion)	1,114	1,067	12,360	84.8
GDP per capita (US$)	30,738	9,382	39,653	
Labour force (thousand)	16,300	43,400	149,300	71.4

Sources: Statistics Canada, www.statcan.gc.ca (consulted August 2007); US Department of Labor, www.dol.gov (consulted January 2008).

Mexico became a member of the General Agreement on Tariffs and Trade (GATT) in 1986, of NAFTA and the Organisation for Economic Co-operation and Development (OECD) in 1994, and of the World Trade Organization (WTO) in 1995. By 2007 it had signed twelve free trade agreements that involved more than forty countries (the European Union in 1999, Japan in 2004).

A major consequence was that Mexico became more dependent on and more inextricably linked to the economy of the United States. By 2006, around 85 per cent of Mexico's exports, which accounted for US$212 billion, were destined for the United States (US Embassy in Mexico 2008). A simultaneous development, for reasons which we consider below, was an increase in the export of illegal narcotics, so that it is estimated that currently around 90 per cent of the cocaine entering the United States crosses the US/Mexico land border (UNODC 2010: 74).

In spite of its economic transformation, during which it had moved from an ISI model focused on internal markets to the prioritisation of exports, Mexico's economic performance was mediocre and the labour market became even more precarious. Unemployment, according to official statistics, remained relatively low – by 2007 it was 3.4 per cent; however, the recorded rate is not a good indicator of labour market conditions in Mexico, as the large proportion of the total workforce located within the informal sector is not considered as unemployed. It is estimated that by the mid-2000s, around 50 per cent of the economically active population was employed in the informal sector.

Clearly, the problems of the country, including the exacerbation of crime and violence related to drug trafficking, have to be understood in this wider economic environment. In other words, neoliberal policies constitute part of an economic model that does not generate employment; rather, it has generated poor economic performance and has lowered the living standards of the working class. Neoliberalism in Mexico has had an exclusionary effect on the poor and economically disadvantaged. With government subsidies to small farmers and businesses curtailed, and the continuing transfer of wealth to the rich, it has become ever more difficult for the poor to participate in the formal economy. In this way, related problems like criminality, corruption and narcotrafficking have expanded since the 1980s. Police bodies are easily corrupted by criminals and drug gangs, thanks to their low salaries, while the poor, young and unemployed workforce has been readily absorbed by drug-trafficking organisations.

Neoliberal policies were not alone in contributing to economic crisis, high unemployment and low wages. For example, the government of Carlos Salinas de Gortari had maintained an exchange rate policy in which the peso was pegged to the US dollar, which had the short-term effect of reducing inflation. Usually, the exchange rate fluctuates according to certain conditions in the economy and financial markets. However, a policy of a fixed or pegged exchange rate (for instance, peso–dollar) enables the government to prevent devaluations in the national currency through intervention by the national central bank. This was how the Mexican peso became overvalued during the Salinas administration. The expected devaluation between 1989 and 1994 would have occurred had Salinas not prevented it in order to display a healthy economic profile to international financial markets, something which facilitated the negotiation of NAFTA. This meant that Mexican exports were sold at an artificially low price. Salinas continued to delay deflation even after NAFTA was signed, which further exacerbated the problem. As J. Lawrence Broz and Jeffrey Frieden (2006: 595) explain, 'given the political unpopularity of a devaluation-induced reduction in national purchasing power, governments may face strong incentives to avoid devaluing even when the result is a more severe crisis than would otherwise be expected'. For instance, 'in Mexico in 1993–4 and Argentina in 1999–2001, electorally motivated delays almost certainly led to far more drastic currency collapses than would have otherwise been the case'. Mexico thus maintained a pegged exchange rate between 1987 and 1991 as part of a programme that included a substantial reduction in government expenditure. As a result, inflation fell from 160 per cent in 1987 to less than 20 per cent in 1991, although in 1994 a speculative attack on the peso led to a sharp currency devaluation and another financial crisis (Gil-Alana and Pestana 2009).

Thus when Ernesto Zedillo (1994–2000) assumed the presidency, a major economic debacle emerged. One of his first decisions in office was to cut out the peso–dollar peg, causing the currency's value to drop by more than 50 per cent in only a few days (Steger and Roy 2010). The peso subsequently devalued in relation to the dollar between 1994 and 1995, from 5.3:1 to 7.6:1 (Banco de México 2009). This was mainly as a result of an overvalued peso, particularly in the last year of the Salinas *sexenio* (1993 to 1994), when a gradual devaluation might have been less damaging. Moreover, the adjustment of the exchange rate and the subsequent devaluation were mishandled by the Department of Finance and Public Credit (Secretaría de Hacienda y Crédito Público, SHCP), creating a climate of tension and uncertainty among international investors who decided to withdraw their money from the country.

In response to the sudden devaluation of the peso, the IMF and the United States contributed to the rescue of the Mexican economy, liberating credit for US$50 billion (Cameron and Aggarwal 1996). This financial lifeline stopped the peso from collapsing, prevented the crisis from spreading to other countries, and contributed to some economic recovery (Lustig 2001: 92). But this further demonstrated that the Mexican economy was at the mercy of the international financial institutions and subordinate to the United States, a relationship that intensified during the neoliberal project, particularly after the signing of the NAFTA treaty.

During the period of economic globalisation, finance capital became highly mobile between nations, often to the detriment of national economies. The relative ease with which financial movements are performed allows capital mobility; in some developing countries this can lead to bankruptcy. For example, in Mexico this situation is considered to be the main factor behind the economic crisis of 1994–95, which triggered the international financial crisis, or 'tequila effect'. This had repercussions throughout the world and illustrated some of the shortcomings and dangers of economic globalisation, especially when financial markets are not regulated. For instance, the peso crisis produced aftershocks in the main economies of Latin America, such as Brazil and Argentina, which also experienced severe economic difficulties.

While the Salinas administration had relied heavily on foreign investment as a strategy to foster economic development, it was short-term and unregulated. With an additional flight of financial capital in 1994 and a $70 billion loss on the Mexican stock market, the economy now faced huge problems. In the first year of NAFTA there had been a million lay-offs and a flood of bankruptcies (Scott 2009: 186).

Within a decade of neoliberal reform, Mexico had integrated into international trade and financial markets. The economy came to rely on exports mainly destined for the United States, and on attracting foreign investment. This environment, characterised by low salaries and poor living conditions, an increase in criminal violence and the recourse to drug trafficking as an alternative source of employment for unemployed and young people, became the norm.

The economic collapse of the mid-1990s had deleterious outcomes for diverse social sectors. Informal employment rose rapidly as a result of the scarcity of jobs. In 1995 alone, one million jobs were lost which could not be recovered in the formal economy. By the end of 1996, there were 8 million unemployed and 5 million working within the informal economy, out of a total labour force of 35.7 million (Fox 2006; Becerril 1996). Furthermore, after the crisis of 1994–95, workers' wages deteriorated even more than in previous years. In the decade 1987 to 1997, real wages halved (González Amador 1998). Mexican manufacturing wages fell over 20 per cent in real terms from 1994 to 1997 and by 2003 average real wages in the manufacturing sector were still 5 per cent below 1994 levels (Hufbauer and Schott 2005: 99). Indeed, despite rising productivity levels throughout the 1990s, worker remuneration stagnated in this sector of the economy (Polaski 2004).

A key aspect of NAFTA was the amendment of Article 27 of the Constitution, previously understood as one of the principal achievements of the Mexican Revolution. A condition for entering the agreement was that Mexico must undo the agrarian reform and *ejido* land sharing which had been a plank of post-revolutionary government policy. Communal *ejido* land was consequently divided up and converted into private property. To make sure the land would be sold, protections and subsidies that had provided support to small-scale farmers were removed and government price regulation of staple crops was scrapped. Similarly, under NAFTA, tariffs and quotas on agricultural imports, which to an extent had protected farmers from foreign competition, were removed (DuRand 2010: 238). At the same time, while subsidies were being removed from Mexican farmers, US agriculture continued to receive federal support, equivalent to 40 per cent of net farm income (*ibid.*). This meant that US agricultural products, like corn and beans, which had been subsidised by the US taxpayer, could now be 'dumped' in Mexico and sold at a price that at times was lower than the cost of production. Now that tariffs and quotas on foreign imported agricultural products had been removed, it became much more difficult for small-scale farmers to survive by making a living off the land. The two companies that shared control of 97 per cent of the market in corn flour for tortillas, GIMSA and MINISA, benefited massively from these new measures. The cuts made to CONASUPO meant that they could now buy cheaper US subsidised corn instead of its Mexican counterpart. These companies had close links to the government and directors were members of the Consejo Mexicano de Hombres de Negocios (Mexican Council of Businessmen). As Sergio Broholm points out, many of the individuals who directly benefited from NAFTA were in the negotiating team that made the treaty possible. Again, this illustrates the artificial character of the free market, which in the case of NAFTA was conceived by and for elite business interests.

Noting the evident tangling of interests, Broholm continues, 'the "king of the tortilla" and long-time owner of the world's largest corn tortilla manufacturer, Roberto González Barrera, has been a long-time friend of President Salinas de Gortari. With the dissolution of CONASUPO, he received all of the subsidised corn sales of the government and even furnished the ex-President with a private jet' (2010: 12).

Meanwhile, the cost of basic foodstuffs and necessities, which had been subsidised by the state as a means of price control, rose suddenly. The price of milk, tortillas, petrol, electricity and public transport shot up at the same time that wages were being slashed. The government-subsidised CONASUPO stores, which had made daily necessities available to poor communities, were simultaneously closed down (Bacon 2006). Producers were thus dealt a double blow. On the one hand they had to compete with cheap imports (many of which *were* subsidised) and on the other they lost the guaranteed outlet that the CONASUPO stores had provided.

The perverse irony of the logic of the 'free market', which resulted in Mexicans buying from abroad the agricultural foodstuffs they had produced for centuries in their own backyard, was lost on the Zedillo and Salinas administrations, but not on those farmers most affected by such policies. The price of corn dropped by around 50 per cent following the NAFTA agreement, and the number of people living in poverty rose by a third. Likewise about half the population had almost no access to basic necessities and services (Chomsky 1999: 122). Mexico had gone from being almost food self-sufficient in 1960 to a situation in which it imported 40 per cent of its food (DuRand 2010: 238). Also noteworthy is the extent to which Mexican workers under neoliberalism were increasingly alienated from the goods they were producing for the export market. The products of the apparel factories in *maquiladora* sweatshops were destined for the foreign market and not for domestic consumption, just like the narcotics that were produced to satisfy demand abroad.

Thus, in the six years following the introduction of NAFTA, two million farmers abandoned their land, migrating to urban areas, the *maquiladora* belt on the border, and the United States (Gibler 2009a: 95–6). In the same year that NAFTA came into force, US President Bill Clinton enacted Operation Gatekeeper, a programme of immigration control to be enforced by the Immigration and Naturalisation Service (INS). To support the new legislation Clinton tripled the INS's annual budget to $4.6 billion in 1994, a measure that subsequently made the border more militarised and increasingly dangerous for economic migrants at a time when the transfer of goods was being made ever easier. As migrants, desperate to find work in the United States because of the impact on their lives of free trade policies, were forced to cross the remoter and less guarded areas of the border territory, more of them died as a result of the extreme heat and cold of the desert. In the first few years of the operation, migrant deaths increased by 500 hundred per cent (Akers 2001).

Investment in improved highways and rail services from Mexico to the US border was also intended to facilitate cross-border trade – but played into the hands of drug traffickers, too. 'The North American Free Trade Agreement', notes Victoria Malkin (2001: 120), 'has played a major role in the rise of narcotrafficking cartels in Mexico, as trade routes could now be used to smuggle narcotics across the border with much more ease.' In this way, 'narcotraffickers follow an economic logic that has flourished in the region and is reinforced by the current neoliberal policies, which reward entrepreneurial solutions'.

Just over a decade after the NAFTA agreement was implemented, some 50 per cent of the Mexican population had fallen below the poverty line (Gibler 2009a: 95–6). A corollary was that a further 3.3 million children under the age of 14 were forced into work. Provision of basic social services, a pledge of post-revolutionary governments, was similarly cut, so that fewer people now have access to free health care and education than prior to 1980 (*ibid.*).

Of course, much of the political rhetoric that touted the

benefits of the NAFTA treaty was highly misleading. For example, in the first six years of NAFTA, two thirds of exports were in fact intra-firm trade (Kose, Meredith and Towe 2004: 16). This meant that companies could part-assemble goods in China and then move them to Mexico, where *maquiladora* workers would complete the assembly process, before the final product, always under the ownership of the same corporation, was exported to the United States to be sold. This was hardly trade, as, although it constituted moving goods from one factory to another one located in a different country, the profits accruing from the operation benefited only the economy of the country in which the owners of both factories were based.

Mexican workers, who had suffered tremendous setbacks as a result of neoliberal reforms and restructuring, were attractive to foreign investors precisely because they were cheaper to exploit than their US and Canadian equivalents. With manufacturing focused on the export market, there was little benefit to Mexican society. Raúl Delgado-Wise (2004: 593) has highlighted the inherent inequalities that the globalised economy intensified for Mexican workers, noting that 'The concept of shared production inherent in intra-firm trade does not, of course, mean shared profits.'

Harmonisation of the Mexican with the US economy involved creating the conditions by which the workforce was forced to be 'flexible', a euphemism for having no choice but to accept poor working conditions and remuneration. For Delgado-Wise, the *maquiladora* belt is little more than an economic colony, with the Mexican police, courtesy of the Mexican taxpayer, providing the 'security' necessary to make investment in Mexico seem attractive to foreign speculators. Under neoliberalism, among Mexico's principal exports was its cheap labour. As agricultural goods, manufacturing and profits were exported abroad, so their labour became virtually the only resource Mexican workers possessed. And just as products destined for export contributed little to the Mexican economy, the same could also be said for significant amounts of labour time in the *maquiladoras*, a situation which

Delgado-Wise describes as 'manpower for foreign capital' (*ibid.*: 593).

Furthermore, the influx of a cheap and flexible labour force to areas located on major trafficking routes in northern Mexico proved particularly advantageous to expanding drug cartels.

'A Guy of Absolute Unquestioned Integrity'

Support for Ernesto Zedillo's candidacy against the Partido de la Revolución Democrática (PRD – Party of the Democratic Revolution) candidate, Cuauhtémoc Cárdenas, was not limited to Carlos Salinas's fundraising dinner. A number of reports claimed that the Colombian Cali cartel had such an interest in maintaining PRI rule in Mexico that they had contributed $70 million to the campaign, while Raúl Salinas's business associate, Carlos Cabal Peniche of Banco Unión and Banca Cremi, reportedly found $40 million to donate to the cause (Cockburn and St Clair 1998: 371–2).

Zedillo's contribution to the 'war on drugs' was to grant the military an increased role in policing matters, a trend which continues into the present. The military would take on the fight against the cartels, but also, crucially, a greater role in the repression of popular opposition and grassroots political movements. Just as in the 1970s, when the war against rural guerrilla movements had defined policies of internal repression, so the army would be used in the first year of the NAFTA treaty, something to which we shall return below.

An important aspect of political corruption during PRI rule was the cosy relationship that politicians, police chiefs and military generals had enjoyed with centralised power. Loyalty to the PRI and, in particular, to the President himself often granted leaders throughout the country immunity to prosecution for involvement in criminal activities. The judiciary was the branch of government with least purchase to exercise its powers, and political interference often threatened its independence and integrity. The authoritarian democracy that had taken power following the Revolution was largely unaccountable. Corrupt officials and police chiefs were not so much answerable to the law as to the President himself (Dillon and Preston 2004: 325–6). Thus, during the seventy years of PRI rule, political ties, connections and bribes were more likely to achieve change than democratic and legislative processes. This was a context in which corruption bred quickly. In the 1990s, the strengthening of the neoliberal reforms – from which much of the formal work sector was essentially excluded – meant that the stakes became higher as profits became greater and corruption an easier route to empowerment and wealth. It also ensured and encouraged a climate of impunity for some of the country's worst human rights abusers and criminals. Against this backdrop of impunity and corruption, justice, as carried out by the state, was often highly selective and politically or commercially motivated.

In an apparent move finally to address the issue of drug trafficking and its links to power, in 1996 Zedillo appointed General Jesús Gutiérrez Rebollo to lead the anti-drug agency, the Instituto Nacional para el Combate a las Drogas. For Bill Clinton's top drug czar, General Barry McCaffrey, the choice of Gutiérrez Rebollo to lead Zedillo's fight against the scourge of drugs was beyond reproach; he was a man of 'unquestioned integrity' (*New York Times* 1997). The Pentagon offered $28 million in aid and agreed to train 1,100 Mexican troops – Mexicans accounted for the largest number of foreign soldiers to be trained in the United States. By 1997, funding had increased to $78 million and correlated with increased political repression in Mexico. Cockburn and St Clair note that the training of an Airmobile Special Forces (GAFE) squad at the School of the Americas in Fort Benning, Georgia, had by 1997 not led to one cocaine seizure nor the arrest of any major criminals in Mexico (Cockburn and St Clair 1998: 373–4). Instead, some of the new anti-narcotics trainees were in 1997 arrested for trafficking cocaine, while others still had been involved in the torture and murder of 'suspects', but were unable to provide evidence from their investigations of their victims' ties to trafficking organisations (*ibid.*). In a terrible irony, one which has become familiar to US planners, as we note in Chapter 5, some members of these elite anti-drug squads eventually defected and joined trafficking organisations like the Gulf cartel and formed the paramilitary death squad, *Los Zetas*. They took their arms and training in military precision with them and became the standard instrument for resolving conflicts with competitors (Bowden 2010a: 25).

It soon became apparent that increasing US involvement in anti-narcotics strategies during the Zedillo administration also had the aim of restraining and hampering the activities of oppositionary political forces, which were becoming better organised and more articulate. We discuss this further below.

Shortly after Gutiérrez Rebollo filled the post of head of Mexico's anti-drug agency, he was working with *El Señor de los Cielos*, Amado Carrillo Fuentes, leader of the Juárez cartel. Using his position within government and the military resources at his disposal, Gutiérrez was able to arrest or eliminate some of the Juárez cartel's competitors. Again, if Carrillo Fuentes was able to create the largest narcotics empire Mexico and Latin America had yet seen, it was partly because he had contacts within the political system who, like Gutiérrez, were willing to offer protection and immunity to prosecution.

Ironically perhaps, it was Gutiérrez Rebollo who had been in charge of Carrillo Fuentes's arrest in 1989, before he reached the pinnacle of his power. Carrillo Fuentes was subsequently released from the Reclusorio Sur prison in Mexico City in 1990 when the charges against him were dropped. Adrián Carrera, who had been director of the prison and was on Carrillo Fuentes's payroll soon after, became director of the PJF, the federal police. Carrera continued to receive payments (as much as one million dollars) in his new role, and appointed police commanders who could be trusted not to investigate the wrong traffickers. By 1998 Carrera had been arrested by the Mexican authorities, convicted and given the option to act as a witness in the 'war on drugs' rather than face a lengthy jail term. In one of his testimonies, taken in Houston as part of a bilateral initiative to investigate the ties between traffickers and Mexican officials, he claimed to have collected US$2 million and given it to Mario Ruiz Massieu, brother of the assassinated PRI Secretary General and Deputy Attorney General (Golden 1998a).

Carrillo Fuentes, a US government drug intelligence report alleged, also paid the governor of Sonora to ensure protection from state police. According to the same report, Jorge Carrillo Olea, who had been Deputy Secretary of the Interior (Subsecretario de Gobernación) under de la Madrid, and the top anti-drug czar under Salinas, became governor of the state of Morelos in 1994, and was Carrillo Fuentes's most 'influential associate in the Mexican government'. Furthermore, the same report claimed, it was Carrillo Olea who had guaranteed safe passage through Mexican airspace of the *Señor de los Cielos*'s Boeing 727s (Dillon and Preston 2004: 333–4). In 2000 the Mexican Federal Supreme Court ordered the Attorney General's office to place Carrillo Olea under house arrest for his alleged protection of drug traffickers (DEA 2000). Nonetheless, Carrillo Olea was never prosecuted for what the DEA alleged amounted to a protection racket involving politicians and Carrillo Fuentes.

An airforce lieutenant, Eduardo González Quirarte, whom Gutiérrez Rebollo had been investigating following an order from the Defence department, confessed that his secondary, unofficial employment was to act as an air traffic controller for Carrillo Fuentes. Staff were taken aback when they realised that rather than investigating González Quirarte, Gutiérrez Rebollo had chosen instead to collaborate with him, claiming González Quirarte was an 'informant'. These two were entrusted by Carrillo Fuentes to conduct investigations into the activities of the Arellano-Félix brothers with a view to staging their arrest, not in the public interest, of course, but on behalf of the Juárez cartel. Carrillo Fuentes covered the whole cost of the three-month operation, which involved police officers, soldiers and all their expenses (Dillon and Preston 2004: 336). The information about the Tijuana cartel that Gutiérrez Rebollo's access to the criminal underworld via Carrillo Fuentes provided allowed his anti-drug intelligence-gathering operations to appear successful, but in fact he was working for one cartel against another.

When a businessman living in the same building in which Amado Carillo Fuentes owned two apartments reported that Gutiérrez Rebollo, the Zedillo-appointed drug czar, was the tenant of Latin America's most notorious drug trafficker, it would not take long before a major scandal would develop, although the government did attempt to keep the story quiet, at least initially.

Having lost one of his best political contacts with the arrest of Gutiérrez Rebollo, Carrillo Fuentes eventually exiled his family to Chile. In 1997 Gutiérrez Rebollo was sentenced to 31 years for abusing his post and using military resources for criminal activities. A decade later he was detained for a further 40 years, having been convicted of using his position to work for Carrillo Fuentes.

Losing Gutiérrez Rebollo's protection was a setback for the Lord of the Skies. When he returned to Mexico City to have his appearance changed by plastic surgeons, he apparently died from the effects of the anaesthetic as a result of the toll taken on his heart by his extravagant lifestyle. Various reports claim that the dead body in the surgery was not in fact that of Carrillo Fuentes and that he had disappeared into hiding. Be that as it may, neither the apprehension of Gutiérrez Rebollo nor the death of the Lord of the Skies would put an end to the multi-billion-dollar business. Nor would its influence within the political sphere change significantly as a result. Amado's brother, Vicente Carrillo Fuentes, *El Viceroy*, took over leadership of the Juárez cartel, while Ismael El Mayo Zambada took over the Sinaloa cartel. Often the arrests of high-level traffickers or even officials were as much media spectacles as crackdowns on corrupt practices and did little, if anything, to alter the causes of the problem itself. For every *capo* or corrupt official arrested or assassinated, there was a new job opening at the top. Furthermore, as the United States government and the Pentagon were increasing military funds and training to Mexico, high-level busts like that of Gutiérrez Rebollo had the effect of convincing US patrons that the Zedillo government was serious about addressing corruption, particularly in the light of the US anti-drug certification for which Mexico was pushing and which was to be awarded only a few weeks later (Fazio 1998: 75–6). They should have known better: previous administrations had been characterised by high-level corruption; why would the Zedillo government be any different? The sacrifice of the occasional scapegoat and the media attention that followed allowed the corrupt PRI system to retain the appearance of legitimacy and a façade of political integrity. At a hearing into Gutiérrez Rebollo's trafficking activities, he implicated President Ernesto Zedillo, his family and his political supporters in drug trafficking. Zedillo's father and brothers-in-law, he claimed, had business links to the Amezcua brothers of the Colima cartel, who were major suppliers of methamphetamine to the US market (de la Vega 1997). Though Gutiérrez Rebollo did not offer evidence for his assertions, the idea that involvement in drug trafficking went to the top of the political hierarchy no longer seemed implausible.

'The Zapatistas Have to be Eliminated'

Clearly, if anti-drug policies were genuinely designed to combat the growth of the narcotics industry, they were an outright failure both in Mexico and the United States. After nearly a century of ostensible attempts to eliminate the smuggling of drugs into the United States, a reasonable person might ask why in the 1990s the US and Mexican governments opted for an increasingly militarised policy, when it was evident from past experience that this approach to control had not curbed the trade. Of course, many of the Mexican police and officials and their US counterparts in the DEA have conscientiously tried to enforce the law and bring the corrupt and the criminal to justice. But these individuals are working within large institutions and agencies, and are trying to implement policies in whose formulation they have little say and whose operation they are powerless to control. Instead, the context of widespread poverty, which neoliberalism and NAFTA had intensified, and the climate of impunity, lawlessness and official corruption were barriers to any genuine attempts to limit the power of organised crime.

But if the policy of militarisation was not particularly successful in its primary aim of stemming the drug trade, it had a secondary application now that the ideological crusade against 'Communism' had lost its *raison d'être* in the wake of the collapse of the Berlin Wall. If, as Fukuyama, Thomas Friedman and Washington Consensus intellectuals had maintained, post-1989 was the beginning of a historical period in which the obvious benefits of transnational capitalism had triumphed over all else, those groups and movements who argued for an alternative socio-economic order would simply disappear. These dissidents had clearly been proved wrong about the ills of capitalism and within time, the neoliberal market, with some fine tuning, would settle social conflict, just as Milton Friedman and his 'boys' from the Chicago School of Economics had promised.

Yet on the same day that NAFTA came into effect, 1 January 1994 – which should have been a day of jubilation for Carlos Salinas and Bill Clinton – an army of insurgents, who took their name from the anarchist Emiliano Zapata, who had fought for land rights during the Mexican Revolution, had risen up in protest against the NAFTA accord, the exploitation of their natural resources, the lack of infrastructure and terrible social inequalities, and, in armed resistance to the authorities, occupied four towns in the state of Chiapas. For the Zapatistas, the government and business elites were totally removed from the everyday lived experience of Mexico's impoverished majority. NAFTA, as they saw it, was the ultimate assault on the poor, the indigenous peoples and the natural environment. The state was thus, in their view, not a legitimate institution and the Zapatistas vowed to form their own autonomous communities in rebel areas.

The final year of Salinas's *sexenio* was thus characterised by events that intensified political instability, which in turn affected financial markets; developments which flatly contradicted the idea that NAFTA and the globalised market were a solution to social and economic grievances. The emergence in January 1994 of the EZLN (Zapatista Army of National Liberation), led by some of the poorest and most marginalised people in the country, and the assassination of the PRI presidential candidate, Luis Donaldo Colosio, during the campaign for the 1994 presidential election, provoked a massive departure of foreign financial capital that year.

One of the achievements of the Mexican Revolution had been to separate the military from civilian politics, a division which was widely credited as one of the reasons Mexico had been relatively stable, and practically the only Latin American republic not to have had a lasting military dictatorship throughout most of the twentieth century. But both the Mexican and US governments saw the Zapatista uprising as an opportunity to use the military, under the pretext of suppressing the drug trade, as a means of social control and repression. Increases in military funding and training were justified with an often rather confused rhetoric that conflated the EZLN with common delinquency, terrorism and narcotrafficking. In addition, the government claimed that the Zapatistas were receiving support from left-wing groups throughout the continent – these included former Argentine guerrillas, Nicaraguan Sandinistas, the FMLN in El Salvador and rebels in Guatemala. However, such claims were echoes of the now bankrupt rhetoric of the Cold War and anti-Communism, and were not supported by evidence. On the other hand, notes Kate Doyle, the Mexican army definitely was receiving assistance from the armed forces of Britain, Chile, Argentina, Guatemala, Israel and Spain (2004).

Both US and Mexican intelligence agencies had been monitoring political activity in Chiapas during the previous years and had claimed to find 'training camps' there. Three thousand troops had been dispatched to the Ocosingo Valley in 1993, equipped with light-armoured vehicles, helicopters and parachutes. Sometimes the army claimed that the soldiers were present in the area to carry out 'civic projects', to subvert Guatemalan guerrilla activities and as part of counternarcotics operations (*ibid.*). Just as Salinas and the Mexican proponents of the free market were about to bask in Washington's praise for having pushed through NAFTA while ignoring Mexican public opinion, it looked as if a group of indigenous peasants was trying to ruin the party.

According to US Defense Intelligence Agency (DIA) documents obtained by the National Security Archive at George Washington University, 'concern over the impact of political unrest on NAFTA led Salinas to downplay reports . . . of an incipient insurgency in the conflict-ridden state of Chiapas following the murders of several soldiers'. But behind closed doors, it appeared, the activities of the Zapatistas had caused anxiety 'at the highest level of government' (*ibid.*). Indeed, according to another DIA cable, the Zapatistas were jeopardising the success of NAFTA and the authority of the PRI that Carlos Salinas had tried so hard to maintain by attracting $750 million dollars from Mexico's most powerful billionaires: 'A stand-off with recurring violence could frighten foreign investors and embarrass the government, affecting presidential elections in August. The government will beef up security in the region, and could be tempted into repressive acts' (*ibid.*).

Given the importance of the shift in the government economic strategy of the preceding years, which was to accelerate under NAFTA, there was little reason to expect the government to allow the Zapatistas to form an alternative and autonomous social and economic organisation on *ejido* land that, under the new measures, was set to be privatised. The rebels were now affecting how foreign capital – the cornerstone of the export-driven economy – was investing. Investors were less likely to put money into regions that they viewed as politically unstable. To quell the threat to multinational capital and 'stability' posed by the peasants, the military strategy would be to wear people down in areas considered to be pro-Zapatista (Harvey 1998: 239–40). The Salinas government was now using US military equipment provided to Mexico under the rubric of drug enforcement pro-grammes to quell the insurgency in Chiapas.

As Carlos Fazio (1998: 85) has remarked, it was in the mid-

1990s that US funding of military supplies and training was stepped up considerably, so that the army had a presence outside its bases where it could take charge of internal conflicts. Crucially, this involved protecting the investments of multinationals, particularly in oil and sub-soil uranium. The development of an armed insurgency in Mexico, as Donald E. Schulz of the US Army War College put it, could endanger 'access to oil' and 'US investments'. Under such circumstances, he noted, the US would have to militarise Mexico's southern border. The vice-president of Chase Bank in the US was clear about how the Mexican military should act. He circulated a memo to staff in which he wrote, 'the Zapatistas have to be eliminated' (cited in Cockburn and St Clair 1998: 376). This in part might explain the US government's insistence on increasing arms exports and foreign military aid to Mexico. In 1996, the US State Department assured the Mexican government that the aircraft provided to Mexico did not necessarily have to be used to combat narcotrafficking and that they would not interfere unnecessarily in domestic operations, giving a green light for their use in Chiapas (*ibid.*: 378). Protection of the NAFTA economy, in the face of popular discontent and the prospect of a possible armed insurgency spreading beyond Chiapas meant that, as far as possible, US planners were intent on having a military influence throughout the country. Only a little more than two years after the Zapatista uprising, the Zedillo administration was concerned about qualifying for 'certification' from the US for its anti-narcotic programmes. Yet the detention and prosecution of Gutiérrez Rebollo, while it was a high-profile arrest and an apparent victory against corruption, demonstrated that the 'war on drugs' was not really working. The Zapatista uprising, however, gave both administrations cause for concern and a reason to work together to ensure 'security' and economic stability. The 'war on drugs' thus provided a mutually beneficial pretext for a crackdown on the insurgents.

The US/Mexican reaction to the uprising of Zapatista peasants threatening their mutual interests might have seemed shrill to outsiders, particularly against the backdrop of impunity often afforded to corrupt officials involved in drug trafficking. Yet this was perhaps the most significant peasant rebellion since the Mexican Revolution; the country's most marginalised were demanding to be heard and were demanding rights. Rights, however, were all very well, so long as they did not interfere with the accumulation of profit and power.

Thus the training and equipment apparently intended to crack down on the narco-industry's billionaires was diverted towards suppressing the rebellion of impoverished indigenous peasants demanding equal rights. In the years 1988 to 1992 Mexico received $214 million in arms from the US (*Proceso*, 12 December 1994), more than at any previous time in relations between the two countries. By 1994 Bill Clinton had increased arms programmes to Mexico, providing $64 million of surveillance equipment and satellite-guided UH-60 Blackhawk helicopters. Mexico purchased stealth aircraft – the Schweizer Condor plane for covert surveillance and the Aravas from Israel. US Secretary of Defense, William Perry, likewise pointed out that Mexican and US interests were inseparable, being united on issues relating to security, in particular as it affected NAFTA and narcotrafficking. But the satellite equipment and helicopters purchased from the United States, while used to monitor the cartels and spy on narco-traffickers, were all also used in Chiapas to subvert the development of Zapatista autonomy and influence (Fazio 1998: 93–4).

Although the increase in reports of systematic human rights abuses and assassinations correlated with the army's presence in Chiapas, the Mexican government did not withdraw its forces from the region, nor did it investigate any of the complaints. Nor did the US government reduce its military funding for the 'war on drugs'. Instead, by this time Mexico was the recipient of one of the US's largest military foreign aid programmes. Of the millions spent by the Zedillo and Clinton governments on anti-drug initiatives, there was little to show in terms of interdiction and seizures. On the other hand, hundreds of supposed Zapatista supporters had been killed by the army and paramilitary death squads. The most infamous of these attacks has to be the massacre at Acteal in 1997, when the *Máscara Roja*, a government-trained paramilitary group, massacred 49 people at a gathering of a Catholic pacifist group and sympathisers of the Zapatistas called *Las Abejas*. The victims included 21 women, 15 children, nine men, and four unborn babies (Ross 2007). Soldiers stationed nearby did nothing during the attack, which lasted several hours, but were on hand the following morning to destroy some of the most visible evidence by washing blood from the walls of the church while the police (who had in fact been ordered to burn the victims) stacked the bodies on to trucks before any media organisations could arrive.

Of the massacre, journalist John Ross wrote:

> After an hour, the shooters advanced downhill, firing their weapons as they pushed forward through the trees. At the bottom of the hill, the dead were spread around a wood plank chapel where they had been fasting and praying for several days. Most were women, their dead children still clinging to them. The shooters continued down the ravine, taking their time, killing their victims slowly, slicing them open with machetes. Four of the women were pregnant. Marcela Capote, the wife of the catechist, was nearly at full term and they hacked open her womb and yanked out the baby inside and dashed its skull against the rocks. They told each other that they had come to kill '*la semilla*' – the seed. (*Ibid.*)

The savagery and brutality of the punishments meted out against unarmed indigenous peasants were not random acts of terror. They were part of a much larger strategy of social control, of maintaining an order and stability that would keep in place the hierarchies and inequalities evident in Mexico since the Spanish conquest. Those who benefited most did not intend to allow change. Ross continues:

> Acteal was, indeed, the bitter fruit of the Chiapas Strategy Plan, a counter-insurgency plan cooked up for the Seventh Military Region in the Chiapas state capital of Tuxtla to combat the uprising in the 37 municipalities where the EZLN had influence,

by arming and training 'patriotic' paramilitary units. The Chiapas Strategy Plan was implemented by General Mario Renon Castillo, a graduate in counter-insurgency warfare of the Center for Special Forces at Fort Bragg, North Carolina. (*Ibid.*)

If the bilateral initiatives, money and wherewithal that ostensibly had been intended for combating narcotraffickers were instead used to safeguard profits and privilege for the NAFTA beneficiaries, this was because these were the higher priority. And if the human rights of Chiapas peasants suffered as a result, this was a mere 'externality' to the functioning of the neoliberal narco-state. The Zapatistas, in the words of the Chase Bank vice-president, had to be 'eliminated'. It is unlikely that Francis Fukuyama (1998: 107) had foreseen such events occurring, far less as contributing positively to 'the end point of mankind's ideological evolution'.

El Cambio (The Change) 5

In 2000, PRI rule – the longest of any political party in the world – eventually ended with the political transition to a government of the Partido Acción Nacional led by former Latin America Coca-Cola executive and ex-governor of Guanajuato, Vicente Fox. After seventy years of authoritarian rule, it seemed, a new era had truly begun with the dawn of the new millennium. Fox promised to clean up the corrupt and dictatorial practices that had come so naturally to a largely unaccountable PRI government, which had viewed itself as immortal. Just over a decade later, it is clear that the promises of the democratic transition remain unfulfilled. Evidently, despite the inflated rhetoric of the *políticos*, a democratic system in which citizens have a stake and can make a meaningful contribution to social and economic development does not accord with the priorities of Mexican and US elites.

For narcotraffickers, the new millennium brought with it massive opportunities for increasing and expanding their business interests. *Forbes* magazine, in its annual celebration of wealth and power, lists Joaquín *El Chapo* Guzmán Loera, *capo* of the Sinaloa cartel, as the sixtieth most powerful person on the planet. The death of the richest criminal in history (Pablo Escobar is ranked number two), Amado Carrillo Fuentes, *El Señor de los Cielos*, in 1997, allowed Guzmán Loera eventually to become Mexico's most important trafficker. *El Chapo* ranks number 1140 in terms of the world's richest people. Carlos Slim, meanwhile, with a net worth of $74 billion, still holds first place. Nonetheless, *El Chapo*'s status as one of the richest and most powerful people in the world is an enviable position for someone whose formal education ended after three years of primary school, who was incarcerated in 1993 on charges of murder and trafficking, and who mysteriously escaped from Mexico's maximum security prison, Puente Grande, in a laundry cart, according to the official story. For all the billions of dollars spent by the US and Mexican governments on the 'war on drugs' during this last decade, and with the thousands of soldiers patrolling Mexico's cities and pueblos, it does seem extraordinary that *El Chapo*, the uneducated and semi-literate peasant from Badiraguato, Sinaloa, should be so shrewd as to evade Mexican and US intelligence, the Mexican army and federal and state police forces for so long. *El Chapo* has been on the run since his escape from the prison in 2001, which, as investigative journalist Anabel Hernández (2010a) demonstrates in her exceptional account of official corruption and complicity with the cartels, *Los señores del narco*, he had effectively governed with complete impunity from the authorities. His 'escape', one month after the PAN took power, was facilitated, she claims, by a $20 million bribe offered to Vicente Fox when he was governor of the state of Guanajuato. For narcotraffickers, Hernández notes, the transition to 'democracy' and the supposed political disagreements between the two parties made little difference, other than the evident opportunities to increase and expand their activities which the *cambio* presented. It allowed *El Chapo* Guzmán to become the world's most powerful trafficker and a number of cartels to control the trade in narcotics, which has become one of the economy's principal sources of revenue. Perhaps the most significant change in narcotrafficking as the new millennium began was that the cartels now started to treat members of the army, police forces, bankers and political officials as their employees, a reversal of the relationship under the previous PRI rule and a turnaround which spelt the end of the cosy arrangements of the *plaza* system.

Here, therefore, we consider the consequences of the democratic transition of 2000, when the PRI was defeated by a triumphant PAN led by Vicente Fox. We argue that the so-called 'democratisation' contributed to the escalation of a crisis in the 'war on drugs' as the PRI finally surrendered its dominance over the drug trade. It is fair to assume that, just because the PRI was defeated in the 2000 and 2006 elections, official complicity in the drugs trade did not suddenly disappear, as we discuss below.

Democratisation

The intensification of narcotrafficking and its related problems in the twenty-first century can be understood better if we consider three interrelated factors that transformed the political system and the ruling elite in the last two decades of the twentieth century. First, political liberalisation, initiated in the late 1980s and resulting in the democratisation of 2000, eroded the hegemony of the official party – which, as noted earlier, was one of the principal features of the strategy that had enabled it to maintain control over the drug cartels. Second, as a result, the regulation of organised crime by the state diminished within the political-institutional system. Finally, the implementation of a set of governmental initiatives, designed by the technocratic elite that had gained ascendancy within the PRI government, particularly during the administrations of de la Madrid, Salinas and Zedillo, was not enough to contain the advance of drug cartels. During the 2000s, under the presidencies of Fox and Calderón, the cartels gained greater dominance, in part because they seized opportunities provided inadvertently by a weak federal government.

Democratisation is widely understood as the replacement of an authoritarian government by one that has been democratically elected (Huntington 1991: 9), but also requires the removal of authoritarian social practices (Grugel 2002: 31). According to this view, a democratic regime implies the protection of civil liberties underpinned by free and fair elections with no interference from the military or other actors (Hagopian and Mainwaring 2005: 3).

Yet democratisation in Mexico did not deliver its anticipated outcomes. Aside from an electoral defeat of the PRI by the PAN in the 2000 elections, the democratic transition failed to deliver on areas of key concern to the majority of voters, not least those relating to public security, a central component of policy since 2000. Shannon O'Neil (2009: 72) has commented that,

> The decline of the PRI and the onset of electoral competition transformed the workings of the executive and legislative branches quite quickly, but the changes have had much less influence over the judicial branch or over law enforcement more generally. Instead, even after the transition to democracy, accountability mechanisms remain either non-existent or defunct. Most of Mexico's various police forces continue to be largely incapable of objective and thorough investigations, having never received adequate resources or training. Impunity reigns: the chance of being prosecuted, much less convicted, of a crime is extremely low. As a result, Mexicans place little faith in their law enforcement and judicial systems. And as today's democratic government struggles to overcome this history through legislative reform, funding new programs for vetting and training and creating more avenues for citizen involvement, it faces a new threat: increasingly sophisticated, well-funded, and autonomous criminal organizations intent on manipulating the rule of law for their own benefit.

Dissatisfaction with the democratic transition's inability – or unwillingness – to combat the climate of impunity is also reflected in its comparable refusal to redress flagrant economic inequalities. As the polling agency Corporación Latinobarómetro has recorded over the past decade, there has been widespread disenchantment with democracy in Mexico and throughout Latin America. More than 50 per cent of citizens polled said they would prefer an authoritarian or military government if it were capable of creating economic prosperity (UNDP 2004). Clearly, citizens viewed a greater degree of economic equality as vital to the development of a vibrant democratic system. Similarly, mainstream political parties and other political institutions have lost credibility in recent decades and, perhaps partly in reaction, important social movements – like that of the Zapatistas – have emerged.

Latin America has remained 'democratic' so far, but there is more poverty in the region today than there was twenty years ago. The same applies to inequality; the region still has the highest levels in the world, while the political institutions are mired in corruption (Philip 2003). The obvious question that arises is to what extent democracy can have any meaning within a context in which the levels of economic inequality are so extreme. Carlos Slim, the world's richest man, acquires on average $27 million every day, while around half the population (50 million) must survive on less than two dollars per day. Political power is bestowed on those who can pay most. And if they have earned their billions via corruption and criminal activities, if the law is not applied and there are few regulations to hinder such massive accumulations of wealth, the political system is unlikely to reform itself. Democracy in Mexico post-2000 has thus proved illusory for the country's poor majority.

By contrast with other Latin American countries, political 'democratisation' in Mexico arrived belatedly, taking place *after* the onset of neoliberal reforms. Neoliberal policies did not necessarily entail the democratisation of the country, but successful integration into the world economy and membership of international institutions now required at least a façade of democratic pluralism. The process of democratisation begun in the late 1980s was consolidated in the late 1990s, when the Partido Acción Nacional (PAN) opposition won provincial elections to governorships and a number of positions in the Congress and the Senate. From its creation in 1929 up until 1988 the PRI had occupied all the governorships in the country but in 1989 the PAN won its first governorship in Baja California and by 2000 there were eleven states governed by parties other than the PRI. Furthermore, during the Zedillo administration the PRI lost its majority in Congress (in 1997) and then the presidency in 2000 (Woldenberg 2002). This political transition to greater power sharing was also evident in the political makeup of municipal governments. In 1983, opposition parties had governed in only 1.7 per cent of the 2,378 municipalities in the country, a proportion that, by 1986, had risen to 2.4 per cent. In 1990 it increased to 5 per cent (Castañeda 1993: 366). By 2006, however, around 60 per cent of municipal governments were ruled by political parties other than the PRI (IFE 2009).

In this context, the escalation of narco-related violence emerged first in the states and municipalities that had become 'democratic' and where opposition parties had defeated the PRI. For instance, disputes between cartels vying for control of territory became more common in Baja California and Chihuahua in the early 1990s, and in municipalities such as Ciudad Juárez towards the end of the 1990s (O'Neil 2009).

Fearing the possibility of having to give up some of their influence, the political elite successfully controlled and restrained the extent to which democratisation in the 1980s and 1990s was allowed to develop (Cook, Middlebrook and Horcasitas 1994: 5). The changes taking place in Mexico from the 1980s onwards are better described not as democratisation so much as a kind of political liberalisation, a process which in fact steadfastly retained the power of the governing class. Soledad Loaeza puts it this way:

liberalisation can be an option for authoritarian elites who want to remain in power and who respond to the demands for political liberalisation by broadening spaces for the free action of individuals and groups. Hence, liberalisation enlarges the social bases of the regime. For those in power, this type of limited change is attractive for at least two reasons. First, the elite does not abdicate its power to direct change and it retains the possibility of reversing the process – which is a powerful negotiating card *vis-à-vis* mobilised groups or individuals. Second, to the extent that liberalisation is seen as a transitional formula, it offers a wide margin for pragmatic and ad hoc solutions. Both the group in power and those who are mobilised can make use of this margin for manoeuvre. (Loaeza 1994: 108)

Yet what made Mexico different from other states that had undergone a similar process was how slowly Mexican liberalisation took effect. There had been a democratic opening at the societal level, the emergence of a politicised civil society, the birth of new social movements making demands for greater participation in the political sphere, the founding of human rights organisations, and openings in the press which extended back to the late 1970s. Indeed, many state and local governments were demanding greater resources and autonomy from centralised power and members of Congress were increasingly challenging the validity of the one-party system (Levy and Bruhn 2006: 67). All of these factors indicated that an important shift in the distribution of power was likely to oust the PRI dinosaur, owing to changes in the electorate's political attitudes.

But the kind of democracy permitted by the process of political liberalisation controlled by elites did not go much beyond holding freer elections with the participation of opposition parties. The PAN, a conservative right-wing party, had comprised the opposition since the late 1930s but had never gained political power until the 2000 elections. Meanwhile, the PRD, the centre-left party, which had emerged after the 1988 presidential elections, increased its presence and influence throughout the 1990s.

With Fox's election in 2000, the previous corporatist arrangements of the PRI all but disappeared. This transition modified the relationship between organised criminal gangs and the state. A new era had begun, which, for the business of the narco-cartels, heralded a new momentum and a lucrative investment opportunity. This was the result in large part of the disappearance of the PRI's authoritarian rule and, consequently, of its dominance of the drug trade. The PAN government formed in 2000 was weakened by the fact that, although it controlled the federal government, it did not have an absolute majority (more than 50 per cent of the total) of congressional seats. Besides, by 2009, the PAN had under its control only seven, a mere 22 per cent, of provincial states. By contrast, the PRI governed the majority of provincial state governments (19 out of 32 states, or 59 per cent of the total). PRD governors at the time of writing, in 2011, rule in six states, including Mexico City (the capital and the most important region in political and economic terms) and its number of congressional seats has been increasing. The map

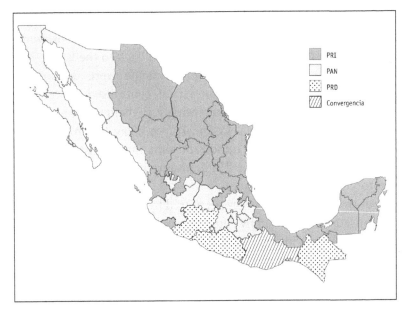

Figure 5.1 Governorship in Mexico by political party, 2011

Figure 5.1 illustrates the weakness of the present PAN government and demonstrates that the rival PRI is still a considerable force in Mexican politics.

When the PAN won the presidency in 2000, many predicted that the much-hyped *cambio*, or 'change', would see the dawn of a new democratic regime committed to altering the authoritarian features of the PRI beyond recognition. In actual fact, despite the political plastic surgery, from the point of view of the mass of Mexicans the character beneath, as with the 'Lord of the Skies', remained all too recognisable. Indeed, the results were a massive disappointment. 'Mexico's so-called democratic opening', explains Howard Campbell (2011: 21), 'was mainly an opening for Mexican venture capitalists and international investors. Democracy neither improved the conditions of the poor nor allowed them more access to political decision making.'

Venture capitalists and international investors aside, for most Mexicans the Fox administration came to be viewed as the lost *sexenio* (Pastor and Wise 2005) because opportunities to consolidate the democratic transition were wasted and the economy failed to expand. Indeed, the economy's position in the world ranking descended from ninth to fourteenth under the Fox regime. Neither did the boom in oil prices generate high rates of economic growth, as was the case in other oil-exporting countries during the early 2000s (Venezuela, Russia and others). The absence of advances during this period was a consequence of an incomplete transition from authoritarian rule to an authentic democracy which extended beyond the electoral realm. As Luis Rubio (2004: 27) has observed,

> [the] Fox victory took place in an institutional and legal vacuum. While the party wielding power had changed, the old institutional structures remained the same. But instead of the traditional system of PRI rule, where the executive and legislature operated as one, Mexico now had to rely on constitutional provisions that were inadequate to bring about effective cooperation between the two branches of government. The creation of new institutional arrangements would require two-thirds majorities in Congress (because most of these would involve constitutional amendments), something difficult to achieve with a relatively even split in congressional seats between the PRI and the PAN.

Likewise, democratisation in Mexico weakened the formerly strong presidency, or executive power, something which has contributed to the stagnation of the political agenda. In this context, problems like corruption, violence, and criminal excesses, already present in the country in previous decades, intensified. It can also be seen that the influence of the PRI in the drawing up of legislation and formulation of public policy is still a determining factor. Indeed, the authoritarian features of the PRI era that had prevailed at the national level remain intact in the many states still ruled by that party. Consequently, the two federal PAN governments since 2000 have faced PRI opposition, not only in the legislature, but also in the negotiation and agreement of policies that require legislative approval; for instance, labour, energy and fiscal reforms, among others. On the results of the *cambio*, George Philip (2003: 176) comments that 'democratization did not lead to the immediate collapse of the PRI, which, even after its defeat in the elections of 2000, continues to be an influential force in Mexican politics' (see Tables 5.1 and 5.2).

For Luis Astorga,[5] the absence of political agreements and consensus in the Chamber of Deputies and the Senate, mainly between the PRI and PAN, has hindered the design and implementation of national legislation and the drawing up of a security agenda to combat criminal activities and drug trafficking. Similarly, there has been little cooperation with the national government in terms of state and municipal governments sharing narco-related information, especially where the respective ruling parties are different. The failure of elements of the political and security structures to work together has also contributed to the authorities' loss of control over the *plaza*. Through the *plaza*, they had been able to eliminate any competition from outsiders which threatened the monopoly of their favoured cartel. The collapse of the *plaza* system has in turn led to more turf wars among rival cartels, resulting in even more gang-related violence and more murders than heretofore. These disagreements and changes, spawned by the new 'democratic' environment, have hindered a strong government response to organised crime and drug trafficking. In consequence the multi-party system in Mexico has been hijacked by criminal organisations to increase their influence and control and their ability to engage in illicit activities without major constraints. As Levy and Bruhn (2006: 223) argue, 'the drug trade brings wealth so vast that it creates alternatives to central power'. Further, 'there is money to buy weapons, to bribe officials, to intimidate people. As with corruption in general, the drug trade brings benefits (economic reward and enhanced political

---

5 Interview with the authors, 4 August 2011, UNAM, Mexico City.

Table 5.1 Composition of the Senate by political party, 1982–2006

	1982	1988	1991	1994	1997	2000	2006
PAN	0	0	1	25	33	47	52
PRI	64	60	61	95	77	58	32
PRD	0	4	2	8	15	17	26
Others	0	0	0	0	3	6	18
Total	64	64	64	128	128	128	128

Sources: 1982–2000, Fox (2006); 2006, Cámara de Senadores, www.senado.gob.mx (consulted 10 July 2008).

Table 5.2 Composition of the Chamber of Deputies by political party, 1988–2006

	1988	1991	1994	1997	2000	2003	2006	1988–2006 (% change)
PRI	262	320	300	239	208	222	106	−60%
PAN	101	89	119	121	207	151	206	104%
PRD	22	41	71	125	53	95	126	473%
Others	115	50	10	15	32	32	69	−46%
Total	500	500	500	500	500	500	500	

Source: Cámara de Diputados, www.diputados.gob.mx (consulted 8 July 2008).

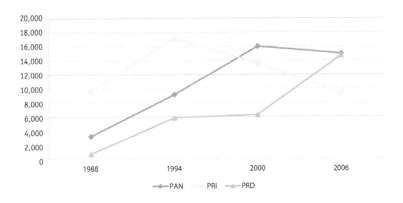

Figure 5.2 Number of votes by party in the presidential elections, 1988–2006 (in 000s)

Source: Prepared by the authors from figures from the Federal Electoral Institute (IFE 2009).

influence) to individuals in government while, for the system, the destabilizing impacts far outweigh the benefits.'

The escalation of narco-related and criminal violence during the democratic environment of the 2000s should be understood in this context. Control of social groups and political stability during post-war PRI rule relied on a corporatist structure, but during the 1980s and 1990s, neoliberal governments radically reversed this model of governance.

Recognising that after 2000 political infighting had resulted in a power vacuum that could now be occupied by criminals, Luis Astorga argues that the consolidation of drug cartels in Mexico has been a long process, going back several decades. From the beginnings of drug trafficking, the PRI had imposed the rules of the game on criminal groups. As soon as the hegemonic party began losing ground as the dominant political force, drug-trafficking organisations began to achieve a greater autonomy, freeing themselves from those institutions of national security that had functioned as intermediaries between the two spheres of politics and crime. Astorga claims that the heightened violence of recent years is the result of disputes over the control of the official security institutions at their different levels, as mediators between these two fields. In the absence of strong, coherent government, drug cartels are contending with one another for the manipulation of federal security institutions, which are crucial for the territorial operations of criminal organisations.[6] The closure of the corrupt Direccion Federal de Seguridad (DFS) in 1985 and its replacement by other, less effective official institutions also contributed to a relaxation of the federal government's grip on criminal organisations. Consequently, the drug cartels became more independent of government and more powerful.

The consolidation of narcotrafficking in Mexico is the reflection of profound problems in the absence of a national state able or willing to protect its citizens. For Porfirio Muñoz Ledo, Mexico is quickly becoming a 'failed state' in its inability to control all economic and political activities, being in some cases subordinate to those very groups whose activities it is supposed to regulate. There are now entire communities, zones and regions in which criminal groups maintain control and not only run checkpoints but even decide who walks the streets (Muñoz Ledo 2010). Throughout Mexico, a weak political authority is further undermined by corrupt officials, while political pluralism has served to remove the few controls exercised by the former hegemonic authority, allowing corrupt practices to multiply (Albarran de Alba 2010).

As we have seen, the *cambio* effectively ended the PRI's domination of the drug trade and allowed actors outside government control to get a stronger foothold and act more autonomously. Shannon O'Neil (2009) adopts a similar argument, suggesting that 'drug-trafficking organisations took advantage of the political opening to gain autonomy, ending their subordination to the government. They focused instead on buying off or intimidating local authorities in order to ensure the safe transit of their goods.'

Yet the effects of political democratisation were contradictory.

---

6 Interview with the authors, 5 August 2011, UNAM, Mexico City.

On the one hand, it did enable the citizens to appoint their political leaders through credible elections (at least in 2000). On the other hand, it undermined the political 'stability' achieved during the PRI era so that, paradoxically, the democratic *cambio* did not generate the outcomes desired by an electorate voting for change, in particular where social and economic reform and crime and corruption were concerned.

The fact that the PRI had been defeated at the federal level but still maintained control of a majority of state governorships meant that the leaders of the political class were constantly submerged in partisan conflict when they could have been developing cross-party strategies to counter the violence being unleashed daily. Furthermore, as Howard Campbell (2011: 21) observes, federal, state and municipal police forces in places like Juárez often view themselves as mutual enemies and have at times ended up fighting each other instead of the cartels.

Raúl Benítez Manaut (2011) argues that social and political stability, indeed, the democratic transition itself, are endangered by a number of regressive factors, the most important among them the increasing influence of drug trafficking and organised crime. Intense competition between criminal organisations, combined with the massive deployment of the armed forces and police on the streets, has contributed to an environment of violence and has led to a serious deterioration in civilian life and protection of human rights. Furthermore, notes Benítez Manaut, the present crisis stimulates governmental corruption across the political spectrum and erodes democratic practices. Just over a decade since the *cambio*, the Mexican state is ever more reliant on the army and police to implement policy and strategy, a status quo that seems increasingly authoritarian.

As a result, Mexicans today live in a society characterised by ever-rising levels of insecurity and crime. The democratic transition failed because it was not negotiated; in other countries, such as Spain and Chile, that have experienced a similar process of democratisation, political pacts, or negotiated transition, permitted them to maintain political stability and a relatively democratic form of government.

Economic Factors

Economic growth in Latin America slowed in the last two decades of the twentieth century. This period of economic slowdown coincides with the implementation of structural adjustment policies, but the outcomes in different countries have been divergent. Although Mexico has presented rates of economic growth in the last decades broadly similar to those of others in the region, it is very obvious that in recent years, in the 2000s, the economic expansion of Mexico has been slower than that of most Latin American countries (see Table 5.3). Nonetheless, it cannot be affirmed that neoliberal policies have propelled poor economic performance in the region, since, as shown by statistical data, countries such as Chile have recorded growth in the period 1980–2005 above the average for the region. Therefore, it is necessary to analyse the national context in which the economic policies were implemented. Certainly, what is not anomalous is that labour markets today in Latin America are increasingly characterised by a majority of jobs in the informal sector, a lack of social security provision, lower salaries than before and low-skill occupations.

Despite the fact that the economy in Mexico experienced periods of growth between 1980 and 2007, it is clear that the general performance was poor in relation to that of other countries in the area. Furthermore, economic growth did not increase, on average, beyond 3 per cent in the period 1980–2000. Mexico's economy not only suffered two striking shocks in the 1980s (1982 and 1986), but endured yet another collapse in the mid-1990s, producing negative effects for the working class. However, it quickly recovered during the period 1996–2000, displaying constant rates of growth ranging between 3.7 and 6.8 per cent. Notwithstanding this, the momentum failed as Mexico entered into recession in the early 2000s; the GDP growth rate registered

Table 5.3 GDP growth rates in selected Latin American countries, 1980–2005

	1981–90	*1991–2000*	*2000–05*
Chile	3.0	6.6	4.2
Colombia	3.7	2.6	3.5
Bolivia	0.2	3.8	3.0
Ecuador	1.7	1.7	5.3
Mexico	1.9	3.5	1.9
Paraguay	3.0	2.2	2.6
Brazil	1.6	2.6	2.8
Uruguay	0.0	3.0	0.9
Argentina	-0.7	4.2	2.2
Peru	-1.2	4.2	4.3
Venezuela	-0.7	2.0	1.5

Sources: 1981–90 and 1991–2000, CEPAL (2000); 2000–05, UNCTAD (2009).

at 0.3 per cent in 2001, thanks mainly to its heavy dependence on the United States economy. Indeed, during the Fox administration (2000–06), the overall economic growth was only 2.3 per cent. In short, in comparison with its trade partners, the United States and Canada, economic performance in Mexico over the period 1980–2000 was weak.

In fact, during the first decade of the twenty-first century, Mexico's economic performance was among the poorest in Latin America. According to Economic Cooperation in Latin American Countries (UN ECLAC 2010), Mexico reached an economic growth of 1.4 per cent on average during the 2000s. The lowest rate was in 2009 with a decline of 6.5 per cent. As the *Financial*

Times (Rachman 2010) observed: 'Mexico might be able to cope better with the drugs issue if it were not also suffering from other ailments', and '2009 was an economic disaster for the country; while China and India grew strongly and Brazil barely lost ground, the Mexican economy tanked, shrinking by almost 7 per cent'.

The poor living conditions of the working class and rural inhabitants in Mexico are evident in the low incomes as measured by GDP per capita. In contrast with most countries of the developed world, Mexico was showing poor indicators in terms of economic development and worker well-being by the mid-2000s. For instance, during the period 1980–2003, Mexico's GDP per capita remained the lowest in North America. While this indicator improved considerably in the USA (up 57 per cent) and Canada (up 45 per cent), by comparison it hardly moved in the case of Mexico during the period (up 12 per cent). Furthermore, despite widespread economic reforms, Mexico's per capita output grew by only 0.45 per cent per year between 1980 and 1999 (Lustig 2001: 86). Indeed, GDP per capita continued its decline in the last years of the first decade of the 2000s.

To encourage growth the neoliberal economic model has relied heavily on a group of prescriptions consisting of foreign investment, export-oriented industry, and public policies designed to control inflation and restrain public expenditures. However, these stimulants have not created the jobs required by an emerging labour force, but have produced a precarious labour market characterised by low salaries and minimal social security, which has become a breeding ground for the emergence and development of other dynamics such as crime and drug trafficking. Jorge Carpizo McGregor, former rector of the National Autonomous University of Mexico (UNAM), has argued that, in order to achieve security and democracy, the Mexican government must address the poverty in which more than half of Mexicans live. Likewise, the high levels of social inequality and social and political privileges must be tackled (Olivares Alonso 2011).

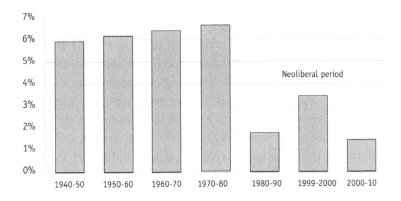

Figure 5.3 GDP growth by decades in Mexico, 1940–2010
Source: Calculated from INEGI (1999; 2011).

Maquiladoras

Maquiladoras are foreign-owned plants located mainly along the northern border between Mexico and the United States. Mexico's *maquiladora* industry, established in 1965 by the Border Industrialisation Program, is made up of assembly plants that use imported components to make goods for export to the US market (Milberg 2004: 68). Initially, the *maquiladora* plants assembled electronics and clothing. In recent years, however, they have begun to assemble more complex products, including electrical control equipment, electronics, and auto and aircraft parts (Ramírez de la O 2002: 9).

Mainstream economists suggest that the employment generated by the *maquiladora* industry is a favourable outcome of neoliberal policies and the NAFTA agreement. However, although these jobs have made a significant contribution, they have not been numerous enough to employ a total labour force of 43 million, which every year rises by around 1 million. Employment in the sector is not more than 1.5 million, accounting for less than 5 per cent of the employed labour force. Moreover, a notable share of *maquiladora* jobs shifted to other countries during the first half of the decade.

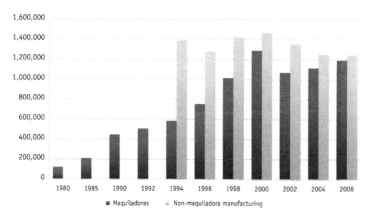

Figure 5.4 Maquiladora and non-*maquiladora* jobs in Mexico, 1980–2006   Source: Calculated from Calderón (2007); STPS (2008a).

China, with a cheaper and even more flexible labour force than that of Mexico, has seen its share of sweatshop labour increase dramatically. The employment evolution in the *maquiladora* industry exhibited diverse patterns in the last three decades. In 1980, the total number of jobs in the *maquiladora* belt was around 120,000, but by 1990 this had risen to around 450,000. This trend continued throughout the 1990s and by 2000 reached its peak at almost 1.3 million jobs. However, during the Fox administration, employment in the sector began to decline. By 2002 it had fallen to just over 1 million, and by 2006 it accounted for almost 1.2 million jobs: around 100,000 fewer than in 2000.

On the other hand, the growth of *maquiladoras* 'has had only a limited impact on the wider economy because Mexican companies are not required to supply the machinery for the factories or the materials for the finished products, except in a few cases of very low-value inputs' (Livingstone 2009: 204). Although the *maquila* sector has provided jobs, it has been detrimental to the living standards of Mexico's skilled workers, because jobs in the *maquila* industry require fewer skills and are lower paid than those in the rest of manufacturing industry (*ibid.*).

The growth of the *maquila* industry in the 1990s and the relative decline in the 2000s are important to understanding the growth of narcotrafficking. As thousands of workers migrated to the *maquiladora* belt in northern Mexico throughout the 1990s in search of work (for reasons we have considered in Chapter 4), the labour pool available to cartels increased. Moreover, many of the *maquila* employers in the apparel and electronics industries preferred female labour, presumably because their smaller hands were better suited to the work. In many cases, this left a large surplus of the male population unemployed. Besides, as narcotrafficking organisations offered superior wages, it is not difficult to see why they came to recruit so many young men in search of work.

Companies setting up shop provided little for workers outside the factory, while neoliberal ideology demanded that the state should retreat from the provision of public services and let the market take care of infrastructure. As a result, the expansion of *maquila* factories did not see a corresponding investment in parks, schools, hospitals or housing – most workers ended up living in precarious and squalid *barrios* with almost no protections or adequate services from the state (Campbell 2011: 21). In Juárez, for example, bus services taking people to the factories were provided, but, even then, these tended to make people's lives difficult. Bus routes all went into and out from the city centre, meaning that a worker going to and from a factory, even one in a neighbouring area, would have to take a bus to the city centre first before taking another to her workplace.

It also happened that some of the major drug trafficking routes went through the same places that had a concentration of *maquila* factories. Tijuana, Ciudad Juárez, Nuevo Laredo and Matamoros on the Mexican side were inextricably linked to San Diego, El Paso, Laredo and Brownsville on the US side. What's more, the infrastructure (rail and highways) necessary to transport the products of Mexican *maquila* labour to the United States had been improved as a result of NAFTA. Likewise, the traffic increased – in Tijuana alone, for example, 65,000 cars cross into the United States every single day. For trafficking organisations, NAFTA had provided both the infrastructure and the labour pool to facilitate smuggling, especially during the Fox administration when much of the demand for cheap labour was transferred to Chinese sweatshops. The growth in the population of Mexico's border states as a result of migration from rural areas, as Tony Wood (2011: 131–2) has written, created 'a large pool of cheap labour that, in the event of any downturn or market tightening, would be thrown onto the streets in search of survival; this has meant a generous supply of foot-soldiers for the cartels'.

Unemployment

Data taken at face value suggest that unemployment in Mexico has been relatively low, although there have been some fluctuations during the period 1980–2007. This may be attributable to various factors. First, a crucial consideration is that Mexico does not have any programme of unemployment compensation, an obvious explanation for the low level of officially recorded unemployment rates. Furthermore, workers do not report themselves as unemployed, because of the absence of unemployment insurance schemes. Second, the methodology used to measure unemployment rates does not provide a satisfactory assessment of the actual employment environment. For instance, household surveys performed by INEGI (National Institute of Statistics and Geography) use the term *occupation*, instead of *employment*. In this sense, every person who is *occupied* is regarded as employed. Many people do not have wage-earning jobs, but they are *occupied* in performing a great variety of activities, even though they are not necessarily receiving remuneration in return. Accordingly, in official statistics, these people are neither registered nor recognised as unemployed, significantly reducing published unemployment rates.

The economy in the last two decades has not been able to generate enough jobs for the emerging labour force, which annually increases by around 1.2 million. In the period 2000–06 the number of formal jobs created represented around 500,000. In other words, there was a deficit of more than 5 million jobs in this period alone, which has contributed to the significant increase of recent years in informal employment, crime (mainly drug trafficking) and migration. In addition, Mexico's domestic industrial sector has shrunk and recently the economy has depended, to a great extent, on incomes from two main sectors: first, natural resources, mainly petroleum, and second, the remittances sent from the USA by Mexican emigrants.

Another result of the population increase in the last few decades has been the destabilisation of the labour market. The total population climbed from 67 million in 1980 to around 81 million in 1990; but it went up to 97 million in 2000; indeed, by 2005, Mexico's population had increased to slightly more than 103 million. There was therefore a population increase of around 56 per cent in the period 1980–2005, more than 2 per cent annually. The rapid increase in the population has generated an available labour force many times larger than the number of vacant jobs in the labour market. When the demand for labour is lower than the supply, average wages and fringe benefits for workers tend to be reduced and unemployment rises. This has been one factor that, along with many others, has exacerbated conditions faced by workers and labour unions in recent periods, and made so many workers turn to the informal market.

This situation has led many individuals to seek alternative options such as self-employment (workers who are in the streets offering services such as plumbing, brickwork, gardening, among others), informal employment (street vendors in small-scale commerce) or, as extreme cases, illegal activities (from stealing to drug trafficking). Neoliberal policies contributed radically to the growth of the informal sector between the 1980s and 2005. Although reliable data from past decades are scarce, we know that around 60 per cent of the labour force or 'economically active population' (EAP) is located in the informal sector. According to official statistics (see www.inegi.gob.mx), the unemployment rate during 2007–11 averaged 4 per cent, but this figure hides a reality in which more than half of the employed labour force is working outside the formal economy.

In June 2011, the number of informal workers rose to 13.4 million, which represented 2 million more than in December 2006, adding considerably to the increase of 17.4 per cent over the period mentioned (2006–11), according to statistics released by INEGI in August 2011 (Yutzil González 2011).

The average income of Mexican households had deteriorated markedly by the end of 2010 as a result of the recent financial and economic crises, producing the lowest income levels since the *cambio* in 2000. According to the survey conducted by INEGI, normal incomes fell 12.3 per cent between 2008 and 2010. During the administration of Calderón, from 2006 to 2010, the overall incomes of Mexican families fell by some 13.7 per cent. Julio Boltnivik, of the Colegio de México, comments that 'this decline in income represents a net loss in household incomes equivalent to 1 out of every 8 pesos' (quoted in *ibid.*). According to the same survey Mexican households registered an average income of 34,936 pesos per quarter, which represents 11,645 pesos monthly. This represents the lowest registered in the country since the democratic transition in 2000.

Around 6 million workers survive on less than or at most one minimum wage daily. Almost 7.5 million do not receive any remuneration at all. Additionally, real wages have eroded drastically, by around 70 per cent during the period 1980–2000 (Salas and Zepeda 2003). The proportion of wage earners in the employed labour force decreased by 9 to 15 per cent in all age groups between 1991 and 1998. Furthermore, most industries experienced a decrease in waged employment during the 1990s (*ibid.*: 529).

In northern cities like Ciudad Juárez, where illegal migration to the United States is becoming more difficult, many young people have been pushed into working for organised crime. Howard Campbell observes that the laid-off border workers were left with nothing to fall back on as the US militarised its southern border with fences, walls, more Border Patrol agents, and a general crackdown on undocumented migrants. Crossing into the United States to find work was no longer an option for most poor Juarenses. Crime became the main economic opportunity for unemployed youth. (Campbell 2011: 21)

These economic developments are crucial to understanding the recent parallel developments in narcotrafficking in Mexico. They indicate that people are virtually forced to become involved in the industry because of an absence of viable alternative methods of making a living. Some estimates suggest that around half a million people now work in the drug trade, though again, this is difficult to measure. Nonetheless, as Viridiana Ríos (2007: 8) points out, 'assuming this . . . is accurate, the approximate number of drug employees in Mexico is 468,000, a figure equivalent to almost three times the number of employees of PEMEX, the largest state-owned company in Mexico and the fourth most important oil company in the world' and almost double the number of soldiers enlisted in the Mexican army. 'Comparing the drug industry to other Mexican industries,' notes Ríos, 'drug smugglers employ five times more people than the whole timber industry of the country, and between 50,000 and 100,000 more people than the paper and editing industry, the basic-metals industry and the non-metallic industry.' As more people are pushed into the informal market, it should come as no surprise that many opt to obtain employment (and considerably better wages) in the informal sector's fastest-growing industry.

Migration
Seeking work in the United Sates, Mexicans and Central Americans take what some now call the 'most dangerous journey on Earth'. Riding upon freight trains through the states of Chiapas, Oaxaca, Tabasco, Veracruz and Tamaulipas, migrants heading towards the United States face arrest, deportation and violent attacks. Drugs cartels have seen in the migrants an opportunity to diversify their

business by preying on some of the most vulnerable people in the world. Attacks often involve migrants being robbed and at times being held for ransom. Criminal gangs will demand payment of ransoms by family members of the kidnapped victims, often of sums so high that they are impossible to pay. When the payments are not received, the victims are murdered, and sometimes they are murdered even if the victim's families have paid the ransom. There has been an explosion in kidnapping and extortion as drug cartels have expanded and diversified. Numerous incidents see criminal gangs working with the police to round up as many as a hundred people, get the telephone numbers of relatives in the USA or Central America and demand a ransom. If the relatives fail to pay, the captives are tortured, beaten, raped and often killed. In August 2010, on a ranch in San Fernando, Tamaulipas, 72 migrants (from South and Central America and Mexico) were found executed. *Los Zetas*, the gang which was originally formed by elite anti-drug squads, some of whom had been trained by US forces as part of the 'war on drugs', and who left the security forces to work for the Gulf cartel, were thought to be responsible. This was one of the worst massacres in Mexico since Díaz Ordaz and Echeverría ordered the attack on students in 1968. More people were killed in this episode than in the massacre in Acteal in Chiapas in 1997 or in Aguas Blancas in Guerrero in 1995. And yet the massacre of migrants in Tamaulipas appears to be part of what is becoming a terrifying norm in which the police and criminals cooperate in extorting money from people they treat as disposable.

Cases like that of Ediño Martínez are becoming quite common. Martínez, a Honduran migrant living in Los Angeles, was travelling across Chiapas atop a freight train heading back towards the United States when a gang, apparently working in collusion with the police, attacked him with machetes. As human rights and political activist Fionn O'Sullivan, who lives in San Cristóbal de las Casas, told us, Martínez had

> got attacked by a criminal gang last year when crossing Mexico en route from a trip to see his parents in Honduras. Instead of helping

him, the police got him to put his finger prints to a document that he wasn't allowed to read, that he found out later to be a confession to being a member of the Zetas, and to murder.[7]

One has to ask why the police would be interested in rounding up impoverished economic migrants and forcing them to sign unread confessions that they are members of Mexico's most notorious death squad. Could it be that it helps the authorities appear to be winning the war against the cartels?

The boom in Mexico's migration in the last ten years has been so remarkable that currently the remittances sent by migrants in the United States are among Mexico's main sources of income, exceeded only by oil revenues. According to the World Bank (2007), Mexico was positioned in third place (after India and China) in a list of top remittance-recipient countries. In 2007 alone, this income amounted to US$25 billion, a figure that has been climbing steadily in recent years. For instance, in 2002 the remittances sent by Mexican workers in the USA to their families in Mexico accounted for US$9.8 billion; however, by 2004 it had risen to US$16.6 billion and to US$20 billion in 2005 (Banco de México 2007). By 2004 one in every five households relied on remittances to survive, while in some states this rose to one in every two (Delgado-Wise 2004: 596–7).

This rise in the number of migrants in part reflected the increase in population, but was also a direct result of policies that made it harder for farmers to obtain returns on their crops, given that the NAFTA economy imported cheap subsidised foodstuffs with which Mexicans could not compete, as we discussed in Chapter 4. Unlike corn, coffee and beans, illicit drugs like heroin, marijuana and methamphetamines are much less subject to price fluctuation and consistently fetch a high price, while demand remains steady. By 2007, for example, a kilo of illicit drugs fetched 300 times more than one of maize and a kilo of marijuana or poppy was worth more than a ton of beans. Producers of marijuana and poppies

---

7 Personal communication with the authors, 4 March 2011.

could earn sixteen times more per kilo than their counterparts producing vanilla and fifty times more than almond growers. One study by the Universidad Michoacana de San Nicolás de Hidalgo suggested that of the 31 million hectares of Mexico's arable land, as many as nine million were devoted to growing illegal drugs, while 8.2 million produced the most ancient Mexican staple, maize (Méndez 2007). Under such circumstances, it is not difficult to account for the massive expansion and cultivation of illegal crops since the 1980s. In areas such as the drug-producing regions of the *triángulo dorado*, so great is the importance of marijuana and poppy production to people's livelihoods that children aged six and seven are often required to help harvest their parents' crops. This was *Chapo* Guzmán's introduction to the business and the reason why he never made it past year three of primary school, hardly an untypical plight in an area afflicted by poverty. In fact, most of the major Mexican traffickers, with the exception of Amado Carrillo Fuentes, came from similar backgrounds and were introduced to trafficking as children.

Although narcotics have been prevalent in Mexico since the nineteenth century, the level of illicit drug production and trafficking has now reached unprecedented proportions. For example, around 90 per cent of cocaine consumed in the USA has been trafficked through Mexico (Hanson 2008). As farmers abandon their plots to head north, migration has had the effect of opening up more land for the cultivation of marijuana and poppies. Proponents of NAFTA thus bear no small responsibility for the growth of drug production in Mexico and, ironically, are often the very same individuals behind the 'war on drugs'.

Throughout the first decade of the twenty-first century, the export of methamphetamine to the United States increased dramatically, at least if we take the number of seizures of the product at border crossings as a guide. From 2002 to 2003, for example, there was a 75 per cent increase in confiscated methamphetamine at Mexico–US border crossings. As US domestic production of the substance waned (owing largely to increasing restrictions on the sale of chemicals used to make the drug), Mexican producers progressively found a favourable market for the product. A crackdown in the United States on methamphetamine thus had the effect of displacing production to clandestine laboratories in Mexico, making it much harder for US drug enforcement agents to control. Distribution networks of meth had been confined mainly to the western and south-western states of the USA but, by the 2000s, had pushed eastward into almost every region in the country. In rural areas of the mid-west, for example, consumption of the substance increased by some 126 per cent in the first half of the 2000s (Lyman and Potter 2010: 82–3).

A variety of estimates exist for the scale of contemporary drug trafficking in Mexico – anything between 20 and 50 billion dollars per annum, though given that it is an illegal black market activity, it is almost impossible to generate reliable statistics (Gibler 2009a: 53). This could mean that drug trafficking may be worth more to the Mexican economy in terms of incoming revenue than the national oil industry and remittances sent by migrants living in the United States. The free market's genuine triumphs, then, have been to increase the number of economic refugees (up to half a million annually) heading towards the United States, to create an economy heavily reliant on remittances from those same migrants, and to contribute to the growth of a parasitic economy based on extortion and illegal drug trafficking.

'We All Seem to Know This Except for the Authorities'

In 1993 Joaquín *El Chapo* Guzmán Loera was arrested in Guate-mala and taken across the border into Mexico. To a loud media fanfare, the arrest of *El Chapo* ('Shorty') – coordinated by Jorge Carrillo Olea, appointed by Salinas to lead the newly created *Lucha contra el Narcotráfico* ('war on drugs') – was proclaimed a triumph over organised crime in the fight against narcotrafficking. *El Chapo* Guzmán was a relative newcomer to the Guadalajara cartel (now Sinaloa) and had come from very humble beginnings. Earlier on, he was far from being one of the country's top *capos*. He had started out as a chauffeur for Miguel Ángel Félix Gallardo (also known as *El Jefe de los Jefes*) when Ernesto Fonseca Carrillo (Amado Carrillo Fuentes's uncle), Manuel Salcido (*El Cochiloco*), Pedro Avilés (who pioneered trafficking massive quantities of Colombian cocaine by aeroplane), and Rafael Caro Quintero were the cartel's leaders and innovators. Guzmán Loera, it seems, was inventive, constantly developing new methods of trafficking narcotics – so goes the story (Hernández 2010a: 58).

During his interrogation on board the aeroplane to Toluca, *El Chapo* spoke quite freely about his criminal activities and admitted responsibility for various assassinations in which he had been involved. The first transcript of the interview was not made public, however. A subsequent declaration, which glossed over some of *El Chapo*'s most potentially destabilising claims, was subsequently released by the authorities. The first version of his confession on board the flight to Mexico was obtained by the magazine *Milenio* in 2002.

El Chapo acknowledged responsibility for various killings in his attempts to liquidate the Arellano-Félix brothers. He himself had been the target of an assassination attempt by the latter in 1992, but survived – an incident which spurred on a war between the two rival cartels. Two revenge attacks, carried out by *El Chapo* and his associate, Hector *El Güero* Palma, were a shoot-out in a nightclub in Puerto Vallarta, an attempt to kill the Arellano-Félix brothers which left eight people dead, and another in Iguala, Guerrero, where nine associates of his former boss, Miguel Ángel Félix Gallardo, were found dead with signs of torture. Guzmán Loera also spoke freely about how he had worked for both the Cali and Medellín cartels in Colombia, facts that a high-level criminal might ordinarily want to keep secret. Yet in this first declaration, *El Chapo* was effusive.

However, his answers contradicted the official account of the assassination of Cardinal Juan Jesús Posadas Ocampo at Guadalajara airport. The cardinal's outspoken claims about the links between politicians and drug traffickers had drawn attention from Carlos Salinas himself, who requested Posadas Ocampo visit the presidential office, where he was warned to be more cautious in his public statements. The official story claimed that the cardinal had been caught in a shoot-out between the Arellano-Félix brothers and Guzmán Loera's men as *El Chapo* was about to board a plane to Puerto Vallarta, one of his favourite recreational haunts. But according to *El Chapo*'s initial statement, none of his men was armed because their guns were in the cases that had already been checked in. Most of them were killed at the airport; *El Chapo* survived, having thrown himself to the ground and crawled into the terminal (Hernández 2010a: 51–3). This was not the version of events that *Televisa* had reported and that politicians had carefully scripted.

El Chapo explained that after the attack he had hidden out in Mexico City and contacted an associate in the army, a Commander Gómez, who agreed to take him to Chiapas whence he would cross the border into Guatemala. In order to prevent his arrest, he was furnished with a false passport. In Cuauhtémoc, Chiapas, *El Chapo* claimed, he met up with Manuel Castro Meza, the link with a lieutenant colonel of the Guatemalan army, Carlos Humberto Rosales. Humberto Rosales had assured Guzmán Loera and his colleagues that they would be helped once they crossed the border, for a fee of 1,200,000 dollars. The magazine *Milenio* alleged that, instead, the Guatemalan lieutenant colonel took the money (though this was never proven) *and* told the Mexican authorities that he had detained a high-level Mexican drug trafficker and was ready to hand him over (*Milenio* 2002). For Jorge Carrillo Olea – the man Salinas had chosen as his captain in the 'war on drugs', and to found and lead CISEN, the intelligence-gathering replacement of the DFS – this sting against a major cartel would be a great media and public relations opportunity.

One is struck by Guzmán Loera's candour in admitting to various killings and to working for Colombia's largest and most violent criminal organisations, though he denied involvement in the slaying of the cardinal. He also explained – dangerously closer to home

– that he and his business were protected by the highest levels of the Attorney General's Office (PGR). In his first declaration, *El Chapo* Guzmán claimed to have paid Federico Ponce Rojas, then Deputy Attorney General under Salinas – and who later worked as Banamex's and CEO Roberto Hernández's top lawyer – one and a half million dollars every two months in exchange for 'protection' every time he made a major shipment. Again, these were only *El Chapo*'s words, and these connections were never proven.

In another casually tossed verbal grenade, *El Chapo* declared that the Arellano-Félix brothers of the rival Tijuana cartel in turn received protection from the politician Ernesto Ruffo Appel – although this has never been proven, either. According to *El Chapo*, they had also been provided with federal police badges to allow them to operate with impunity. When Ruffo Appel was elected governor of Baja California in 1989, he became the first politician to take office in opposition to the PRI. Ernesto's brother, Claudio Ruffo Appel, was a business partner of the Arellano-Félix brothers, according to the declaration.

Although practically all of *El Chapo*'s statement remains unproven, it is worth noting the official reaction when two Tijuana journalists of the *Diario Frontera* – Ernesto Álvarez and Gonzalo González – reported that Claudio Ruffo Appel had opened fire on them. Although the car was riddled with bullet holes, apparently a lack of evidence prevented the police from charging Ruffo Appel with attempted murder. Similarly, the newspaper owners refused to file charges on behalf of the journalists. Ruffo Appel was charged with having activated a firearm and sentenced to pay 6,000 pesos for the repair of the car.

El Chapo stated that he had paid millions of dollars to federal police commanders of the PJF throughout the country in exchange for protection. He claimed that he had regularly bribed José Luis Larrazolo in Sonora; Cristian Peralta in Mexicali; and Guillermo Salazar in Guadalajara. Salazar later became a director of the PJF (Federal Judicial Police), a position in which he worked closely with Jorge Carrillo Olea.

On various occasions *El Chapo* said he made payments of $500,000 to high-level police officials so that they would let him 'cultivate a plantation of marijuana', and so that he could export 700 kilos of cocaine to the United States. Following his revelations, José Luis Larrazolo, the federal police chief from Sonora, was murdered, while Cristian Peralta from Mexicali was arrested though never charged. Perhaps these events gave some credence to Guzmán Loera's disclosures, although the only evidence available is *El Chapo*'s initial statement (*ibid.*).

Soon after the Department of National Defence (SEDENA) passed on *El Chapo*'s declarations to the presidential office, the detainee was visited by a high-level functionary who explained that were he not to cooperate with the authorities by changing his declaration, he would be killed. His initial statements sat rather uneasily with the version of history that the government intended to present publicly. Unsurprisingly, *El Chapo*'s redacted confession differed radically from the original. According to the new version, all suggestions of official complicity disappeared. He had never met Larrazolo, Peralta or Salazar. He had heard about the terrible shoot-outs in Puerto Vallarta and Iguala, but only because he read the newspapers avidly. Similarly, he had never met Hector *El Güero* Palma but knew of him. He made no mention of the PAN governor of Baja California, Ruffo Appel, nor the protection he afforded to *El Chapo*'s rivals of the Tijuana cartel. *El Chapo*, according to the version which the government made public, claimed he was a humble farmer from Sinaloa who made a living from his produce (which did not include marijuana and poppies) (Hernández 2010a: 53–61). No mentions either, of the extensive and numerous laboratories for processing methamphetamine. Regarding the attack against him by the Tijuana cartel and the murder of Cardinal Posadas Ocampo at Guadalajara airport, however, *El Chapo* deferred to the authority of *Televisa* and the PGR (Attorney General's Office) in order to establish the sanitised record of events for public consumption: 'Everything that I declared about the shoot-out at the airport was exactly how they presented it on television when the PGR explained it' (*ibid.*: 63).

El Chapo's first declaration had touched on a major taboo; it acknowledged that narcotrafficking in Mexico is as much white-collar crime as it is the province of semi-literate delinquents like Guzmán Loera. For obvious reasons, officialdom is intent on maintaining the imaginary barrier between blue-collar criminals and the respectable milieu of the political elites. In holding this line, major television stations like *Televisa*, owned by the Azcárraga family, play a fundamental role.

Yet these taboos were broken again in 1996 by Miguel Ángel Segoviano Berbera, *El Chapo*'s accountant, following his detention by the DEA in California, for whom he acted as an informant and witness. *El Chapo*, it appeared, had been exporting drugs via underground tunnels 25 metres deep and 300 metres long into California and Arizona. His inventiveness also found him disguising shipments of cocaine in cans of jalapeños which crossed the border by rail, while cases full of millions of dollars frequently arrived by plane in Mexico City. In order to carry out these activities successfully, it was necessary to bribe police and officials (*ibid.*: 171–2). Such business operations required some very creative and efficient accounting, and Segoviano was the man entrusted to manage *El Chapo*'s financial affairs. He tesitified to the DEA that *El Chapo* made regular payments to the office of the Procurador General de la Nación (Office of the Attorney General) (Lunhow and De Córdoba 2009).

As fate would have it, by an extraordinary coincidence, investigators discovered in 1992 that Segoviano happened to live, not only in the house next door to the man who became one of Vicente Fox's closest friends and advisers, Luis Echeverría Álvarez, but that the ex-President was also his landlord. Echeverría stated that he and the family knew nothing of the activities of their tenant – something which, as Anabel Hernández (2010a: 174–5) comments, was 'barely credible given that in the house of the ex-President there is an entourage of the Presidential Guard [of the Mexican Army] large enough to hear movements in the next room'. Furthermore, as one might expect of the residence of an important dignitary, the profile of everyone who visits gets thoroughly checked and the house is protected by armed guards. When investigators and federal agents arrived looking for Segoviano, they arrived too late.

The resulting investigation and search of the Echeverría residence took place on 2 October, the twenty-fourth anniversary of the 1968 Tlatelolco massacre overseen by President Gustavo Díaz Ordaz and Luis Echeverría, then Secretario de Gobernación, the crime for which he was placed under house arrest in 2006 and subsequently acquitted in 2009.

When the PRI was defeated in 2000, and the democratic transition appeared imminent, Echeverría became one of Fox's closest advisers. Fox was not ready to allow partisan politics to interfere with the new government and appointed many of Echeverría's loyal supporters to his presidential circle. Among them was Rafael Macedo de la Concha, one of Luis Echeverría's military generals from the *guerra sucia* (dirty war) against left-wing opposition movements, who became Attorney General. Another of Echeverría's closest associates was Juan José Bremer, whom Fox made Mexican ambassador to the United States. During the days of the dirty war, Echeverría had appointed Adolfo Aguilar, an ex-Marxist scholar, to run the Centre for Economic and Social Studies of the Third World. Fox appointed him national security adviser. Perhaps the most controversial appointment was that of a close colleague of Echeverría, Alejandro Gertz Manero, whom Fox appointed as head of the federal police, the Secretaría de Seguridad Pública (SSP). In 1972, Gertz Manero had been an agent of the PGR and had been involved in the death of the historian, Miguel Malo Zozoya (*El Heraldo de Chihuahua*, 6 April 2006).

Gertz Manero's involvement in the death of the historian was linked to a dispute over some pre-Hispanic artefacts collected by Malo Zozoya. A number of federal agents accompanying Gertz Manero appeared on Malo Zozoya's doorstep in 1972 and demanded he hand over his entire collection. It happened that a new law, the *Ley Federal sobre Monumentos y Zonas Arqueológicas*, required collectors to register historical artefacts with the National Institute of Archaeology and History (INAH) and now the historian was required to relinquish his collection. Malo Zozoya was aware that, whatever the requirements of the new law, President Echeverría himself was a keen collector of pre-Hispanic artefacts and had his own private collection. When Gertz Manero later returned to collect the items, Malo Zozoya (who had hidden the artfefacts) claimed he had destroyed everything. According to Malo Zozoya's wife, Gertz Manero had entered the house and had been pressing the historian to surrender his collection. From an adjoining room, she heard a shot. Malo Zozoya, according to the official story, had shot himself in the head while in the presence of Gertz Manero and federal agents (*ibid.*). The official cause of death was suicide.

Gertz Manero also stood out as one of Echeverría's most important assets – he had chosen him to head one of the country's first campaigns against narcotrafficking, the ill-fated Operation Condor in 1976, which we discussed in Chapter 2. Still, Vicente Fox evidently saw no incongruity in appointing Gertz Manero to head the federal police. Fox had promised that, with the *cambio*, he would crack down on corruption and clean up old practices. However, his appointments of PRI politicians from the *ancien régime* seemed to signal the exact opposite.

After Fox had been only a month in power and had appointed Gertz Manero to run the federal police, *El Chapo* Guzmán realised he would have to leave his prison in order to avoid extradition to the United States following a ruling by the Mexican Supreme Court which now made this a real possibility. On the other side of the border, unlike in Mexico, he would miss the privileges (prostitutes, expensive restaurant meals, alcohol) to which imprisoned traffickers were accustomed. He managed to escape from one of Mexico's maximum security prisons, equipped with heat sensors, camera surveillance, several sets of security doors and a security perimeter. According to the official account, he hid inside a laundry cart and somehow managed to bypass the heat sensors. In other accounts recorded by Hernández, he walked out in broad daylight dressed in police uniform.

Anabel Hernández's claim that *El Chapo* had offered a $20 million bribe to Vicente Fox is taken from an interview with an ex-DEA agent who managed to infiltrate Guzmán Loera's organisation. Because revealing the name of the agent would jeopardise the safety of her source, she says she is obliged to keep it secret. She has been criticised by the powerful – including Vicente Fox himself, who sent outraged messages on Twitter – for engaging in inflammatory conspiracy theories.

The claim that the Sinaloa cartel's power following *El Chapo*'s escape resulted from an official preference for the organisation over others merits some scrutiny, as Tony Wood (2011: 132) explains:

> Government officials made much public fuss about pursuing Guzmán, but kept conveniently losing his trail; he remains at large ten years later. In the meantime, Guzmán's fortunes advanced at the expense of his rivals: in 2002, the Tijuana cartel all but dissolved after the death or arrest of its heads, the Arellano-Félix brothers; in 2003, the leader of the Gulf cartel, Osiel Cárdenas Guillén, was captured. The DEA, meanwhile, had opened an investigation against the President and his family.

In 2003, offices of the anti-drug agency, FEADS, created by ex-President Zedillo in 1997, were raided by soldiers in eleven states following the arrest of seven agents in Tijuana for complicity with drug traffickers. FEADS agents had apparently been making seizures of illegal drugs, and failing to declare the confiscated goods before selling them. In this one raid, soldiers discovered five tons of undeclared marijuana held by FEADS (Murray 2003). FEADS had had some successes, however. Their agents, who were also trafficking drugs, had killed Benjamin and Ramón Arellano-Félix, among *El Chapo*'s major rivals and competitors. Clearly, the integrity of these stings on the cartels by the FEADS was compromised by the fact that they were trafficking themselves. Similarly, a number of high-ranking officials had been arrested as part of the transition government's crackdown, spearheaded by Attorney General Rafael Macedo de la Concha, a cold warrior general from Echeverría's dirty war.

Al Giordano (2000), writing for the *Narco News Bulletin*, comments on the striking presence of the authorities in patrolling highways and border crossings in Mexico:

> Passing through Mexico, for business or pleasure, one directly encounters so many police and soldiers that one wonders: Is there a ratio of police to citizens that adds up to define a Police State? . . . There's a cop or soldier for every 165 Mexicans. Along the smuggler's path there are FEADS agents, Federal Judicial Police, the Federal Highway Patrol, immigration checkpoints at the borders and in the bowels of the country.

In this context, it seemed odd that there were not in fact many more seizures and arrests than those that the authorities released to the media. For Giordano (*ibid.*), the problem arose from corruption, which was rife among the state authorities: 'The Public Security police of 32 Mexican states, the local cops in every city and town, and the soldiers and sailors of the military all want a piece of the drug trafficker's action.'

Perhaps the authorities will capture the world's most wanted drug trafficker in the coming years. To others, his whereabouts are less of a secret. The Archbishop of Durango, Héctor González Martínez, told reporters of the common knowledge of Guzmán Loera's place of residence: 'just up the road from [the town of] Guanacevi, that's where he lives, but, well, we all seem to know this except for the authorities' (Lunhow and De Córdoba 2009).

◆

A combination of processes seems to have determined the escalation of narcotrafficking and violence that has beset some areas of the country since the dawn of the new millennium. Democratisation led to the break-up of the PRI's dominance of the trade, and the fragmentation of its monopoly created space for the cartels to grow. In addition, neoliberal trade accords facilitated cross-border smuggling thanks to the increased traffic moving north as a result of an improved infrastructure of highways and railroads. These accords also aggravated poverty and unemployment, pushing ever more people to work in the informal economy in a country where unemployment benefits are virtually non-existent. Similarly, the decrease in opportunities in the *maquiladora* belt, as China became the preferred choice for cheap and flexible labour, meant there was a massive, cheap and flexible workforce in the very cities conveniently located on major drug-trafficking routes. Combined with corruption of the state security forces, bribable police and officials, and a general climate of lawlessness, traffickers found compelling investment opportunities after the *cambio*. Fox's appointment to the government of 'change' of politicians who had worked within the PRI system for decades seemed more a statement of continuity than anything else. Moreover, if it were true that the government's strategy to privilege *El Chapo*'s Sinaloa cartel was intended to create a monopoly of the trade and a *Pax Mafiosa*, as there had been under the PRI, the coming years were likely to provoke severe levels of violence as the diverse cartels competed with him and the security forces for control of the market. Rather than easing a transition to democracy, the Fox government of the new millennium heralded a perfect storm, which we examine in Chapter 6.

War is Peace

In the town of Tancítaro, in the state of Michoacán, 2009 ended with a bizarre turn of events. In a letter addressed to the state governor, Leonel Godoy Rangel, and the Mexican president, Felipe Calderón Hinojosa, the municipal authorities of Tancítaro announced their resignation *en masse*. As the troubled decade closed, the town faced the prospect of entering the New Year without a local government (Lemus 2009).

Despite the heavy presence of federal, state and municipal police and soldiers, local political leaders and functionaries cited the increasing power of organised crime and threats to their personal safety as the cause of their resignation and took a cross-partisan vote to 'disappear' the local authority. Those who resigned said their decision was 'irrevocable', identifying the growing occurrence of executions, kidnappings and forced disappearances in recent years as having made their work increasingly and intolerably dangerous (Martínez Elorriaga 2009).

The case of Tancítaro is representative of many towns in Mexico whose local authorities and civic life are suffering from the escalating power of organised crime. According to *Reforma*, since Felipe Calderón assumed the presidency in December 2006, there have been 39,000 deaths related to drug cartel violence. In addition, between 2006 and (2 April) 2011 alone, the National Human Rights Commission in Mexico (Comisión Nacional de Derechos Humanos – CNDH), registered more than five thousand files of missing or disappeared persons. Furthermore, the CNDH reported that around 9,000 corpses were yet to be identified (CNDH 2011). The inescapable conclusion is that the total number of people killed during the Calderón administration may be much higher than the number of reported murders and executions.

Concurrent with the wave of violence resulting from the influence of drug cartels has been a massive deployment of military personnel throughout Mexico, ostensibly designed to limit or destroy the power of narcotrafficking organisations. In a significant strengthening of a bilateral strategy to take on the cartels, US President Barack Obama in 2009 signed off $1.4 billion of US taxpayer money under the Mérida Initiative, which, according to the White House, 'aims to strengthen regional security cooperation' (White House 2010). Around half of these funds were intended for Central America, the Dominican Republic and Haiti, the rest for Mexico. In 2010, a further $450 million was allotted to Mexico for military training and equipment, although none of the money for the Initiative is allowed to leave the United States. As financial 'aid', the money is awarded to booming US security and defence contractors and to the US military for training their Mexican counterparts.

US/Mexican policy under the rubric of the Mérida Initiative has a two-pronged approach: to arm and secure unpopular neoliberal policies, investor rights and US geopolitical interests while quashing and punishing dissent and popular protest. The illegal trade in drugs had found conditions favourable to expansion under neoliberal governments post-1982 and post-NAFTA in 1994, and has continued to benefit from the similar policies of a weak Partido de Acción Nacional (PAN) government post-2000.

In this chapter we examine some of the key developments that we believe have contributed to the alarming escalation of violence and breakdown of security in various parts of the country. Clearly, there are multiple factors involved, and we do not pretend to account for all of them. Nonetheless, there are some salient features that we hope will facilitate a better understanding of the problem.

Only by taking into account the historical contexts and

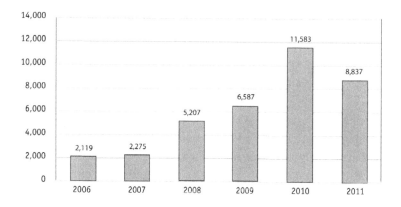

Figure 6.1 Number of homicides related to narcotrafficking in Mexico, 2006–2011
Source: prepared by the authors with the database of *Reforma* newspaper. Data comprise the period 1 December 2006 to November 2011.

consequences of the current breakdown in Mexico can one hope to find possible alternative solutions to the crisis that has unfolded since 2000. None of this can be understood, of course, without considering the impact of free-trade policies, poverty, migration and unemployment, which together have produced a massive pool of cheap labour for narcotic capitalism. Undoubtedly, the profound economic problems that intensified during the neoliberal period and the militarisation of parts of Mexico are unsustainable and unacceptable. So too are the frequent abuses of human rights and miscarriages of justice committed by the authorities using the pretext of the *Guerra al narco*. These current ills did not come out of the blue and in some senses were quite predictable, as a number of both US and Mexican politicians knew well before they sketched out an economic plan that would benefit only a tiny minority.

One of the foreseeable results of the *Guerra al narco* has been the creation of favourable conditions for a huge increase in the rate of violent crime, particularly since 2006 when President Felipe Calderón initiated a new phase in the 'war on drugs' by expanding the use of military intervention. This in turn has contributed to an escalation of human rights abuses; intimidation of, and attacks on, journalists; violent acts committed against police officers and politicians who refuse to adhere to the demands of the cartels; and the criminalisation of social protest and dissent. In all, the picture is extremely bleak, but we believe that the first step in proposing ways of ameliorating Mexico's current crisis is to attempt to understand it.

A major contributor to the terrible violence witnessed every day, particularly in towns and cities and in northern Mexico, has been the increased military presence. The apparent contradiction of anti-drug squads – charged with maintaining security – in fact largely contributing to the escalating violence was one of the most scalding accusations levelled against the government's anti-drug policies in the mass protest movement led by the poet Javier Sicilia in 2011. The protesters identified the Calderón government's insistence on militarisation of the problem as the major obstacle to creating peace. Another accusation has it that in fact the PAN government was actually using the military to allow *Chapo* Guzmán's Sinaloa cartel to establish a monopoly of the trade, and is therefore attacking rival organisations and arresting their leaders to this end. Given past history, this seems plausible; indeed its advantage, according to proponents of this view, is that it would re-establish the *Pax Mafiosa* of the PRI years. As the drugs industry is unlikely to disappear within the foreseeable future, protecting the most powerful cartel and allowing it to dominate the market means that the state could negotiate with – and ultimately control – one cartel instead of trying to engage with several in ferocious competition with each other (Hernández 2010a: 17).

'A Danger for Mexico'

It is a paradox that, of the last three presidential elections in Mexico (1994, 2000 and 2006), the most controversial was that of 2006, following the supposed transition to democracy. A vicious public relations campaign against the PRD's centre-left candidate, Andrés Manuel López Obrador (also known as AMLO) had not seemed to dent his popularity; there was the real possibility that, following six years of widespread disillusionment with Vicente Fox's PAN government of the *cambio*, a left-leaning party would win the general election. In fact, even after the propaganda campaign that declared 'López Obrador: a danger for Mexico', and compared him to Mussolini, Hitler and, interestingly, Hugo Chávez, he still led Felipe Calderón in the polls. When the Federal Electoral Institute (IFE) refused to release an exit poll on 2 July, widespread suspicions of electoral fraud began to emerge. Memories of the PRI fixing the elections – particularly those of 1988 – now found parallels post-transition. An annulment, rerun or re-count of the ballot sheets would have dispelled widespread misgivings about a fraudulent election, but the IFE ruled this out and announced that Calderón and PAN had won by just 0.58 per cent over AMLO. Reports of missing votes turning up in rubbish dumps and in rivers emerged immediately after the election. It was, to much of the electorate, very familiar.

Following the election, the sense of outrage and indignation at the course of events was palpable and frequent rallies in the Zócalo in the centre of Mexico City, organised by AMLO, attracted between one and two million demonstrators. In the months following the election AMLO formed a parallel government. The inauguration of the new government, in December 2006, saw PRD and PAN representatives involved in a punch-up in the Chamber of Deputies. Calderón himself was forced to use the back entrance to the Chamber to avoid protesters. At the podium, he was met with jeers and heckling. Widespread discontent and frustration with what many saw as a flagrant disregard for the democratic process was matched by the massive police and army presence on the streets and around the presidential residence in Los Pinos. On Calderón's takeover of power, John Gibler (2009a: 17) has commented that 'the election's outcome was a message to the underdogs of Mexico: you cannot win, even if you follow all the rules and participate in the game of electoral democracy; we will take power, just as we have for centuries, by tricks, chicanery, and, if necessary, imposition of violence. In 2006, the short-lived myth of the Great Transition came to an end.' Ten days after his inauguration, Calderón began his militarisation of the country and increased the number of troops on the streets to 50,000, more than Tony Blair had sent to invade and occupy Iraq in 2003. Five years into Calderón's war on the narcos, around 40,000 Mexicans have been killed but narcotrafficking has continued to flourish.

In March 2010 in the Chamber of Deputies, one PRI deputy, Ruben Moreira, claimed that 'the Calderón government is already finished because it does not rule anymore, because he is confined in Los Pinos, surrounded by security guards, because Calderón became the leader of his party but not the state'. 'Calderón stole the presidency in 2006,' he declared.[8] One day before the session, PRI federal deputy, César Augusto Santiago, had revealed that the only reason Felipe Calderón was President was because – when it had become clear the PRI would not win the election – he had formed a pact with senior PRI officials prior to the election. In order to safeguard the established political and economic order, Mexico's ruling class were not about to risk a programme of reform and wealth redistribution instituted by a popular left-of-centre candidate, as AMLO had promised.

Calderón's 'war on drugs' was a strategy designed to gain legitimacy for his presidency and to distract public attention and media scrutiny from the elections. Popular support for the new government was weak; a 'war' based on fear, soaked in a political rhetoric of nationalism and vacuous slogans, was intended to win popular backing. Like so many politicians justifying military spending and violence against civilians, Calderón insisted that a period of instability, insecurity and hardship was a necessary evil in order to ensure eventual peace. 'Restoring public safety will not be a simple or quick task', pronounced Calderón to the US

---

8 Transcript of session in the Chamber of Deputies, 10 March 2010.

Congress in May 2010. 'It will cost time and money and, sadly, to our great regret, it will also cost human lives. This is a battle which must be fought because what is at stake is the future of our families. But as I said, you can be sure of one thing: this is a battle which, united as Mexicans, we will win.'[9]

The fact is that, if this was genuinely a war on the narcos, it employed a strategy that could not succeed, as can be seen in the rise of narco disputes over the control of national territory and the traffic of narcotics in the country, the number of violent deaths, and increasing insecurity in the streets. As the Calderón presidency draws to an end, opinion polls in national newspapers suggest that PAN will be defeated in the 2012 elections by the PRI. Five years into the war, the public seems to find even the authoritarian corruption of the PRI preferable to government by PAN, which is now placed third in the polls behind the PRD.

Violent Crime and Human Rights

Over the last five years from 1 December 2006 to the time of writing (November 2011), the outcomes of the 'war on drugs' launched by the Calderón administration (2006–12) are hardly encouraging. Perhaps one of the most insidious and self-justifying insinuations of Mexican political discourse is to associate all those who have been killed in the past five years with improper activities. Most of the violence, however, seems to have been directed towards civil society in order to create a climate of fear and terror. How else do we explain the very public displays of violence and killing, now prevalent in places like Ciudad Juárez? Howard Campbell (2011), an anthropologist who studies the drug war, summarises a few of the more extreme incidents since 2008:

- Eighteen recovering drug addicts massacred by a death squad at a drug rehabilitation centre in the Colonia Bellavista;

---

9 Speech delivered to US Congress, May 2010.

- Fifteen teenagers, mistaken for gang members, gunned down in Colonia Villas de Salvárcar;
- Several Juárez journalists murdered, including legendary crime reporter Armando Rodríguez;
- Three people associated with the US Consulate assassinated;
- Thousands of quartered, duct-taped, beheaded, burned, sexually mutilated, or otherwise desecrated cadavers dumped in the streets;
- A car bomb, killing a Juárez policeman and a respected paramedic;
- One hundred and forty-nine policemen murdered in Juárez in 2010;
- Three hundred and four women murdered in 2010;
- Dozens of mass killings in bars, homes, drug rehab centres, private parties, shopping centres, restaurants, used car lots, junk yards, car repair shops and other businesses; and
- An estimated 20 per cent of the homicides during the Mexican 'drug war' have occurred in Juárez.

Were this not grim enough, the government's 'security' budget has climbed dramatically during the Calderón administration and seems to be one of the key factors contributing to the escalation of violence. Between 2007 and 2011, the funds provided to the four institutions dedicated to fighting narcotrafficking (SEDENA, SEMAR, SSP and PGR) grew by 77 per cent (see Table 6.1). The institution to benefit most was the Secretaría de Seguridad Pública (SSP – Department of Public Security). The SSP budget almost tripled, going from 13 to 35 million pesos. The Secretaría de la Defensa Nacional (SEDENA – Department of National Defence) saw an increase of 55 per cent; while the budget for the Navy, the Secretaría de la Marina (SEMAR), rose by some 67 per cent. The institution to receive the smallest increase, though it was still significant, was the Attorney General's Office (PGR – Procuradoría General de la República), with an increase of 32 per cent between 2007 and 2011. The number of federal police, a body within the SSP, saw a notable increase: there had been 12,907 personnel in 2006

Table 6.1 Government spending on security-related institutions (millions of pesos)

Institution	2007	2008	2009	2010	2011	2012*	% of change 2007–11
SEDENA	32,196	34,851	43,623	43,632	50,039	55,611	55%
SSP	13,324	18,890	32,917	32,438	35,519	40,536	167%
SEMAR	10,941	13,372	16,059	15,992	18,270	19,677	67%
PGR	9,077	9,028	12,310	11,781	11,998	15,385	32%
Total	65,538	76,141	104,909	103,843	115,826	131,209	77%

SEDENA Department of National Defence
SSP Department of Public Security
SEMAR Department of the Navy
PGR Attorney General's Office
* Projected budget

Source: Secretría de Hacienda y Crédito Público, www.shcp.gob.mx (consulted July 2011).

but this figure was boosted to 35,450 in 2011, an increase of 174 per cent. In contrast, the organisation created by Vicente Fox, ostensibly to investigate corruption and organised crime, the Agencia Federal de Investigacion (AFI – Federal Agency of Investigation),[10] saw its numbers reduced by almost 40 per cent (Zermeño 2011b), perhaps because of public revelations of its involvement in the drug trade.

Nonetheless, increased spending on 'security' has not reduced the level of crime and violence – quite the opposite. Despite the implementation of operations in half of the states of the Mexican Republic, narco-related deaths or executions have intensified and accelerated. Nor did the traffic in narcotics shrink significantly between 2006 and 2010. Impunity for the killers remained

10 The agency became the Policía Federal Ministerial (PFM – Federal Ministerial Police) in 2009.

unaffected, with the federal government investigating less than 5 per cent of drug war murders (Gibler 2011a: 32). Furthermore, less than 1 per cent of the cases of criminal investigation were related to the trade in narcotics.

In July 2011, the federal government claimed that during the Calderón administration more than half of the most dangerous narco *capos* in the country had been arrested or killed (Zermeño 2011b) (see Table 6. 2).

While the elimination of major *capos* may seem like a victory for the government's security strategy, it is one seriously undermined by the fact that the policy of militarisation has done nothing to affect the profits and assets – the motor of the industry – of major organised criminal organisations.

At the same time, there has been a lack of coordination among the diverse institutions charged with maintaining security and combating narcotrafficking. For example, the Mexican Army, the PGR, the SSP, and the Navy are all dependent on the federal government, but the absence of mutual cooperation and the rivalry between them has prevented an effective strategy from developing. Furthermore, competition between these institutions has also meant that they have frequently refused to share important information and intelligence on organised crime. This also reflected a weak presidential leadership unable to discipline the federal cabinet and concentrate on a common objective, and whose only response to the illegal drugs trade was to dispatch more and more troops to fight a so-called war which has become an unmitigated disaster.

Far from establishing security, the strengthening of a police and military presence has clearly coincided with a drastic deterioration in the security situation. For instance, in 2007 there were 438 kidnappings in Mexico, but in 2010 alone 1,262 cases of this kind were registered, an increase of 188 per cent. The same trend can be seen for other offences, such as car theft, extortion, homicide and theft with violence (see Table 6.3). The number of cars stolen in 2010 was 60,592 while there were 6,235 cases of extortion reported. There

Table 6.2   List of the most wanted narcotraffickers in Mexico (released in March 2009), with data of captures to November 2011

Leaders for whom the PGR offered a reward of 30 million pesos in total ($2.1 million per head)	
Golfo-Zetas Cartel	
Heriberto Lazcano Lazcano, *'El Lazca'*; *'Z-14'*; *'Z-3'*; *'El Verdugo'*	Free
Jorge Eduardo Costilla Sánchez, *'El Coss'*	Free
Ezequiel Cárdenas Guillén, *'Tony Tormenta'*	Captured
Miguel Angel Treviño Morales, *'L-40'*; *'Comandante 40'*; *'La Mona'*	Free
Omar Treviño Morales, *'L-42'*	Free
Iván Velázquez Caballero, *'El Talibán'*; *'L-50'*	Free
Gregorio Sauceda Gamboa, *'El Goyo'*; *'Metro-2'*; *'Caramuela'*	Captured
Sinaloa / Pacífico Cartel	
Joaquín Guzmán Loera/Joaquín Archivaldo Guzmán Loera, *'El Chapo'*	Free
Ismael Zambada García, *'El Mayo Zambada'*	Free
Ignacio Coronel Villarreal, *'El Nacho Coronel'*	Executed
Juan José Esparragoza Moreno, *'El Azul'*	Free
Vicente Zambada Niebla, *'El Vicentillo'*	Captured
Beltrán Leyva Cartel	
Arturo Beltrán Leyva, *'El Barbas'*	Executed
Mario Alberto Beltrán Leyva and/or Héctor Beltrán Leyva, *'El General'*	Free
Sergio Villarreal Barragán, *'El Grande'*	Captured
Edgar Valdez Villareal, *'La Barbie'*	Captured
Carrillo Fuentes Cartel	
Vicente Carrillo Fuentes, *'El Viceroy'*; *'El General'*	Free
Vicente Carrillo Leyva	Captured

(*continued*)

Table 6.2 (cont.)

'La Familia' Cartel

Nazario Moreno González, *'El Chayo'*	Captured
Servando Gómez Martínez, *'El Profe'*; *'El Tuta'*	Free
José de Jesús Méndez Vargas, *'El Chango'*	Captured
Dionicio Loya Plancarte, *'El Tío'*	Free

Arellano Félix Cartel

Teodoro García Simental, *'El Teo'*; *'El Lalo'*; *'El 68'*; *'El K-1'*; *'El Alamo 6'*	Captured
Fernando Sánchez Arellano, *'El Ingeniero'*	Free

Lieutenants of drug cartels for whom the PGR offered 15 million pesos (1 million per head)

Golfo-Zetas Cartel

Sigifredo Nájera Talamantes, *'El Canicón'*	Captured
Ricardo Almanza Morales, *'El Gori'*	Captured
Eduardo Almanza Morales	Captured
Raymundo Almanza Morales, *'El Gori'*	Captured
Flavio Méndez Santiago, *'El Amarillo'*	Captured
Sergio Peña Solís/René Solís Carlos, *'El Concord'*; *'El Colosio'*	Captured
Raúl Lucio Fernández Lechuga, *'El Lucky'*	Free
Sergio Enrique Ruiz Tlapanco, *'El Tlapa'*	Captured

Beltrán Leyva Cartel

Francisco Hernández García, *'El 2000'*; *'El Panchillo'*	Captured
Alberto Pineda Villa, *'El Borrado'*	Captured
Marco Antonio Pineda Villa, *'El MP'*	Captured
Héctor Huerta Ríos, *'La Burra'*; *'El Junior'*	Captured

Juárez and/or Carrillo Fuentes Cartel

Juan Pablo Ledesma/Eduardo Ledesma, *'El JL'.*	Free

were 20,127 homicides in 2010 alone (cartel-related and other); and theft with violence accounted for 228,499 cases, the crime with the highest incidence in that year. Edna Jaime, director of the NGO México Evalúa (Mexico Evaluates) noted that, in the last four years, the homicide rate has increased by 96 per cent, incidents of extortion by 101 per cent, theft with violence by 42 per cent and car theft by 123 per cent. Figures prepared by México Evalúa based on official statistics also suggest that all states in Mexico experienced an increase in the frequency of at least one of these crimes, implying that the presence of federal troops has spectacularly failed to reduce violence and crime (de la Luz González 2011; Notimex 2011a; *El Economista* 2011; Baranda 2011). All this occurs in a country in which around one in ten crimes is reported and in which there is a prosecution rate of around 1 per cent.

On the growth of the power of organised crime, writer, historian and analyst Paco Ignacio Taibo (2011) comments:

> Today the Narco is not only a dozen armed groups that control one of the most important economic activities of the country. They are companies that charge for protection, for example to all Cancún merchants. They control all street vendors in Monterrey. They represent justice in entire zones of Michoacán. ... They are the controllers on federal roads that charge tolls. They are the ones that offer (and deliver) protection to a restaurateur in Ciudad Juárez if he pays, and no more health inspectors or Treasury requirements. They are the controllers of the largest human trafficking and kidnapping network on the planet. They are the ones who offer gainful employment to thousands of youths in border gangs. They are in a large part of our country, a new state. A state that replaces another state based on abuse and corruption.

Half a million people now work directly or indirectly in organised crime, and, as Juan Ramón de la Fuente (2009: 70) writes of the current context, 'we are confronted by a brutal and very sophisticated force, which has submarines, helicopters, airplanes, and sophisticated weaponry'. In 2011 narco-gangs operated with an annual budget of approximately $25 billion, but, if we include

Table 6.3 Rise in crime, 2007 and 2010

	2007	*2010*	*Intensification*
Kidnapping	438	1,262	188%
Car theft	27,173	60,592	123%
Extortion	3,123	6,235	101%
Homicides	10,253	20,127	96%
Theft with violence	161,014	228,499	42%

Source: *Reforma*, 23 August 2011.

money laundering, this reached a staggering $40 billion per annum (*ibid.*).

Between December 2006 and July 2010, 963 public confrontations occurred in the streets and highways of Mexico, equivalent to almost one confrontation per day during the period (Ramos Pérez 2010). In April 2011 alone, more than 300 dead bodies, presumably victims of the narcotraffickers, were found in Tamaulipas, Durango, Sonora and Chihuahua. In San Fernando, Tamaulipas, almost 200 corpses were found in 40 *narco-fosas* (mass graves). In August 2010, in the same place, 72 Central American migrants were found executed. In Durango, 103 corpses were discovered in clandestine *narco-fosas*. Twelve executed bodies were found in Sinaloa and four in Sonora, in April 2011 alone (*El Universal*, 28 April 2011). According to the confidential testimony of one *sicario* (assassin), by 2011 there could have been at least a hundred clandestine *narco-fosas* throughout the country, containing thousands of executed bodies yet to be discovered (Esquivel 2011). The number of dead already found by that date indicates the extent of the impunity afforded to criminals and the military forces involved in such killings. The bare statistics point to a policy not just of failure, but of outright disaster and tragedy.

According to Human Rights Watch (2011), security strategies

in Mexico have failed in two respects. Their report, following two years of investigation in the states of Baja California, Guerrero, Chihuahua, Nuevo León and Tabasco, which have the highest number of reported violations, establishes the participation of the military and police in 170 cases of torture, 39 forced disappearances and 24 extra-judicial executions. Not only has government policy been unable to reduce levels of violence, but it has also generated a dramatic increase of human rights violations, which are rarely prosecuted adequately. Rather than strengthening public security in Mexico, Calderon's 'war' has worsened and intensified the climate of violence.

Dead bodies with signs of gruesome torture, accompanied by *narco-mantas* (messages written by the killers on banners) have become ever more frequent. The public display of violence and terror seemingly has no limits. Videos posted on YouTube of the torture and killings of employees of rival cartels reveal a sickening and unrestricted climate of impunity and societal breakdown. Given the government's own refusal to recognise the fact that the Calderón administration's policy is the problem, not the solution, and the continued support for the same policy by the US government, the grim picture that emerges is that this kind of violence is set to continue for the foreseeable future.

The Mérida Initiative

Originally termed Plan Mexico, the three-year Mérida Initiative, initiated in 2007, and renewed in 2010, is an outgrowth and replacement of the Security and Prosperity Partnership (SPP). The SPP, agreed by signatories of the 1994 North American Free Trade Agreement (NAFTA) in 2005, was, according to the White House, an 'initiative among the United States and Canada and Mexico to increase security and to enhance prosperity' (US State Department 2009). The SPP was neither a treaty nor a legal agreement but an understanding between the governments of the three countries on how to protect NAFTA from supposed security threats to the three economies. Because the plan was never signed into law, it was never debated publicly and, in line with 'anti-terror' measures taken in the USA following the 9/11 attacks, the SPP was an attempt to extend 'Homeland Security' to Canada and Mexico. Public documents about the SPP merge the language of protecting economic security with 'terror' threats, emphasising the policing and militarisation of borders.

The Mérida Initiative thus brought into law the basic outlines of the SPP. The latter was scrapped in August 2009 and the Mérida Initiative essentially took its place. Perhaps because the Initiative had to go through the US Congress and was therefore much more exposed to public scrutiny, the language of protecting economic interests like the NAFTA gave way to a rhetoric that emphasised combating organised crime, particularly Mexican drug cartels.

Sceptics regard the programme as a process of *colombianización*, a version of Plan Colombia in Mexico. As a policy of drug control, Plan Colombia's critics regard it as a failure, given that during its enforcement cocaine production and export continued at the same level or at times increased (O'Shaughnessy and Branford 2005: 2). However, as a means of maintaining political and military dominance in the country and securing investor rights, it can be viewed as something of a success.

Under the Mérida Initiative, the USA has provided Mexico with high-tech assistance in the war against organised crime cartels, yet has made no attempt to tackle the support systems and white-collar corruption that have allowed them to expand in the last two decades. Washington's approach to the problem has focused primarily on supporting military means of combating social problems that it played no small part in exacerbating with the implementation of NAFTA in 1994.

According to the US Department of State, the Initiative assures:

- Non-intrusive inspection equipment, ion scanners and canine units for Mexico and Central America to interdict trafficked drugs, arms, cash, and persons.

- Technologies to improve and secure communications systems that collect criminal information in Mexico.
- Technical advice and training to strengthen the institutions of justice – vetting for the new police force, case management software to track investigations through the system, new offices of citizen complaints and professional responsibility, and witness protection programmes in Mexico.
- Helicopters and surveillance aircraft to support interdiction activities and rapid response of law enforcement agencies in Mexico.
- Equipment, training, and community action programmes in Central American countries to implement anti-gang measures and expand the reach of these measures. (Bureau of International Narcotics and Law Enforcement Affairs 2009)

Celebrating the extension of cooperation between the two governments in the 'war on drugs', President Obama stated in August 2009 at the North American Summit that, 'I would not be committed to dealing with this if I wasn't convinced that President Calderón had the will and the desire to protect his people from narcotraffickers' (White House 2010). Similarly, Obama had 'great confidence in President Calderón's administration applying the law enforcement techniques that are necessary to curb the power of the cartels, but doing so in a way that's consistent with human rights . . . . [As] the national police are trained, as the coordination between the military and local police officials is improved, there is going to be increased transparency and accountability and ... human rights will be observed' (*Democracy Now*, 11 August 2009).

Such pledges are unlikely to comfort the residents of Tancítaro, its former public servants, and indeed the majority of Mexicans, who have witnessed a marked increase in violence since President Calderón dispatched 20,000 troops, increasing the nationwide total to around 49,000, to the areas worst affected by violent crime associated with narcotrafficking (Gibler 2009a: 52–3;

O'Shaughnessy 2010). In a country whose government's own figures indicate that the number of people living in poverty and unable to satisfy basic needs has risen to 47 per cent (CONEVAL 2010), the Mexican government's budget for counternarcotics had reached $5 billion by 2006. Yet the gloomy picture which emerges suggests that such spending has failed to reduce the influence of the cartels and has contributed to the intensification of violence. As the US Department of State Mérida Initiative webpage acknowledges, a contributing factor to the escalation of violence has been the very deployment of troops to the streets: 'Criminal organizations, under great pressure by law enforcement agencies, are behaving in increasingly violent ways.' Thus, while US funding for the Mérida Initiative is supposed to make 'our streets safe once again from drug and gang-related crime', the same document concedes that Mexican streets have become much more dangerous thanks to American 'aid' (Bureau of International Narcotics and Law Enforcement Affairs 2009).

Despite this, advocates of the Mérida Initiative claim that the violence does in fact represent progress. They explain that the crackdown on the cartels squeezed their capacity to operate relatively unhindered. As a result, they compete with one another more fiercely and therefore more violently. According to this view, the rise in executions, forced disappearances, threats to personal safety and the continued breakdown in places like Ciudad Juárez and Tijuana are a sign of success, for it means that the cartels have been truly feeling the heat (USGAO 2007: 11).

Whether we can judge the 'success' of the government's strategy by the death toll, as Mexico's ex-Attorney General, Eduardo Medina Mora once suggested, depends on the value one places on human life. There is scarcely any doubt, however, that the drug war is among the principal contributory factors to the escalation of violence. The authors of a Global Commission on Drug Policy report (*ibid.*: 15) suggest that

> poorly designed drug law enforcement practices can actually increase the level of violence, intimidation and corruption associated with drug

markets. Law enforcement agencies and drug trafficking organisations can become embroiled in a kind of 'arms race', in which greater enforcement efforts lead to a similar increase in the strength and violence of the traffickers. In this scenario, the conditions are created in which the most ruthless and violent trafficking organisations thrive. Unfortunately, this seems to be what we are currently witnessing in Mexico and many other parts of the world.

Furthermore, while it may be true that the cartels have experienced some disruption to their operations from the authorities, the production and trafficking of illicit substances has continued to thrive in Mexico. As a United States Government Accountability Office report has admitted, Calderón's strategy of disrupting and hindering the trade 'does not appear to have significantly reduced drug trafficking' (*ibid.*: 11).

The 'increasingly violent ways' in which cartels operated were facilitated to a great extent by activities on America's own soil that undermined official US policy. Given that the arms used by cartels, including many assault weapons, have overwhelmingly originated in the USA, one might expect an initiative whose declared goals were to combat narcotrafficking and reduce violence would lead to unstinting efforts to tackle the problem of illegal arms smuggling into Mexico. One source has it that some 90 per cent of illegal arms seized by the authorities over the decade had originated in the United States (O'Shaughnessy 2010). Towards the end of the same decade, in a country of 105 million inhabitants, some 15 million arms were in illegal circulation. A report by three US senators in June 2011 ('Halting US firearms trafficking to Mexico'), suggested that 70 per cent of illegal arms confiscated in Mexico could probably be traced to legal US suppliers (Feinstein 2011). Table 6.4 may indicate that the Mexican security forces were more successful from 2008 onwards in taking the weapons used by cartels out of circulation, but it may also reflect an enormous increase in the supply of such weapons from the USA over the same period.

Table 6.4 Seizures of arms in Mexico, 1994–2011

Year	Arms
1994	4,026
1995	11,589
1996	12,237
1997	9,743
1998	9,002
1999	7,271
2000	7,494
2001	8,466
2002	8,381
2003	5,626
2004	5,577
2005	5,115
2006	4,220
2007	9,576
2008	21,047
2009	32,588
2010	33,545
2011	22,158

Source: Calderón (2011).

Colombianización

The most notable precursor of current US policy and military aid to Mexico is Plan Colombia, initiated ostensibly to combat the production of illegal narcotics. Colombia, like Mexico, is a major US ally in a Latin America where electorates are increasingly rejecting the neoliberal model and US imperialism. Creating highly militarised allies in a region whose future (and dependence on the USA) is increasingly uncertain is one way of securing investment rights and access to resources for multinational companies. As with Plan Colombia, behind the declared goals of the Initiative would seem to be a strategy designed less to combat narcotrafficking and more to maintain secure access to markets while stifling political dissent and protest with the potential to damage business interests (Carlsen 2008).

In their book, *Chemical Warfare in Colombia*, Hugh O'Shaughnessy and Sue Branford (2005) argue that Plan Colombia failed to reduce the production of illegal crops (particularly cocaine). Indeed, levels of cultivation either stabilised or actually increased. In the interim, however, millions of Colombians were displaced, making it the country with the highest number of displaced people after Sudan. Militarisation of the countryside and the growth of paramilitary organisations were used as methods of social control, again ensuring that elite interests were protected from the population, while opening vacated lands to further exploitation of natural resources. Additionally, with increases in US military 'aid' to Colombia, the human rights situation worsened, making it the most dangerous country in which to be a dissident, unionist or journalist in the western hemisphere. O'Shaughnessy and Branford note that if the reduction of coca production were the intended goal of Plan Colombia, it was clearly a failure.

In the post-Cold War world in which the ideological currency of the battle against 'Communism' has become virtually worthless, military spending to protect, enhance and promote the interests of free trade and the geopolitical interests of the US government would have been altogether unpalatable. Accordingly, the 'war on drugs' and the 'war on terror' have provided conveniently timed cover for the suppression of organised dissent.

Plan Colombia responded to the perceived threat of guerrilla insurgency posed by the Revolutionary Armed Forces of Colombia (FARC), but also to the US desire to bolster its dominance in the region. With the election of several left-leaning governments and the political mobilisation and organisation of marginalised groups from El Salvador to Uruguay, President Obama's funding of seven military bases in Colombia is a significant step in attempting to rein in and intimidate Latin America's more progressive forces. As the USA's closest ally, Mexico has become the latest battleground in assuring US hegemony throughout the hemisphere. The possibility of AMLO's victory for the PRD over

Calderón in the 2006 elections was enough to cause alarm among Mexican elites (who engaged in a bitter and vicious propaganda campaign to discredit him), to say nothing of arousing concern in the US government, even though his programme was a relatively mild one of left-of-centre reform.

Strengthening Institutions of Justice?

Obama's declaration that 'enforcement techniques' should be 'consistent with human rights' is exposed as worthless by Mexican and foreign human rights organisations, which have recorded a strong correlation between a military presence and violence against civilians (Human Rights Watch 2009; Bricker 2009). They are virtually unanimous in their scepticism about the value of increased military spending in the 'war on drugs', highlighting the differences between declared goals and the failure to eradicate the production and export of illicit substances. In May 2009, over seventy Mexican human rights and civil rights groups petitioned both governments not to push through the Mérida Initiative. They cited institutionalised corruption within the military, and the sharp rise in executions, torture, arbitrary detention and sexual abuse reported by the National Human Rights Commission since Felipe Calderón had assumed the presidency and begun a crackdown on organised crime (Centro Prodh 2010: 90).

The Mexican state has a history of guaranteeing impunity to the military and politicians, and failing to investigate human rights violations. Often, those individuals and groups pressing for investigation into alleged abuses are met with indifference and contempt; there is little recourse for anyone seeking restitution, as the burden of proof usually lies with the complainant. For example, in a country where the poorest people (who usually bear the brunt of the worst violations) are those with the least education and most likely to be illiterate, there are in practice few systems in place for registering a complaint. Complainants themselves are expected to present legal evidence against the state and the military, but when they do, both local and national governments unite to place hurdles in their path.

In an unprecedented ruling in December 2009, the Inter-American Court of Human Rights found the Mexican state guilty of the crimes of forced disappearance, extra-judicial execution and torture. The Court ruled that the present administration is, like its predecessors, guilty of human rights violations because it fails or refuses to investigate complaints made against its own security forces. It recommended that the government scrap Article 57 of the military code which guarantees legal immunity to violations committed by military personnel (Watt 2010: 51).

Human Rights Watch (2009) similarly observes that the increased military and police presence has multiplied human rights violations and that immunity for the perpetrators continues. Meanwhile, Centro Prodh, the human rights organisation based in Mexico City, notes that between early 2007 and early 2009 – in step with President Calderón's deployment of troops throughout the country – human rights violations committed by the military rose by 472 per cent. According to the same report, 'the rise in abuses by the military against the population owes itself to the increase in the number of military personnel spread throughout the country as well as to impunity, thanks to the fact that the military know they can commit them without suffering any consequences'. The authors also observe that violations by the military are becoming increasingly normalised and that, 'within this logic and in light of the above we can suppose that during the next three years of the government of Felipe Calderón, abuses by the military against the population will continue to rise in the "war against organised crime"' (Centro Prodh 2010: 49).

As a result, President Obama's optimism that 'enforcement techniques' will be 'consistent with human rights' is barely credible. If the crackdown on organised crime was intended to increase security on the streets, funding a military whose human rights abuses were already well-documented made little sense.

Vetting the New Police Force

Between 1993 and 2009, some 217,000 low-paid soldiers deserted the Mexican army, many of them taking their weapons with them (Reyez 2009). Among these are former members of special elite forces and anti-drug squads trained in the same methods as those specialists from whom the now notorious mercenary army, *Los Zetas*, was formed. Having previously trained, funded and armed many *Zetas*, the US government has now declared war on them and increased military funding under the Mérida Initiative to that end (Miller 2009).

Likewise, the bilateral strategy does little to account for military and police corruption. Elements of the police forces that resist working with the cartels are frequently compromised by the criminal gangs' sheer power. Refusing to cooperate with a cartel in control of the local or regional *plaza* can prove fatal for non-corrupt officers and their families. Those who enter the police because they have few or no qualifications and who pursue a career in the profession very often encounter the quandary of whose interests they should serve (Campbell 2009: 200–14). A 2008 report by the United Nations, for example, estimated that between 50 and 60 per cent of municipal government offices have been 'feudalised' by the cartels, partly because soldiers and police officers can supplement or replace low pay with money from the drug trade (Castillo García 2008). In recognition of this, Calderón increased the basic soldier's salary by 46 per cent in 2007, in spite of which soldiers continued to desert (Herrera and Aranda Enviados 2007). Other estimates by Mexican Intelligence indicated that the majority of police forces – some 62 per cent – throughout the country were either linked to or controlled by narcotrafficking cartels, and that 57 per cent of the arms given to the police were used in illegal activities (Castillo García 2008). Likewise, reports of cooperation and mutual support between the military and narcotrafficking organisations have become more common, with the army at times opting not to destroy plantations of poppies and marijuana, or working actively for narcotraffickers by protecting these crops.

For organised crime, recruiting soldiers and police officers to their ranks to work as *sicarios*, or assassins, makes good business sense. In the film, *El sicario, un documental proscrito en México* (2010), an ex-*sicario* interviewed by journalist of the drug war Charles Bowden revealed that police and military training courses teach them everything they need to know before joining criminal organisations. As a result, when cartels recruit police officers and soldiers, they do not need to spend resources and time providing them with adequate training. The new recruits to criminal organisations have been trained in how to use firearms, are disciplined and physically fit, and are prepared to kill if ordered to do so. The *sicario*, covered by a black hood in order to disguise his identity, claims that, at the end of his training in the police academy, at least fifty of his 200 companions joined criminal organisations after graduation. In another strange perversion, the taxpayer and the state find themselves providing the training of future *sicarios*.

Such statistics cast doubt on the effectiveness of a binational policy which regularly increases spending on the military and the police in order to combat the cartels. The Mexican military – with little threat of foreign invasion and a history of repressing dissent and rebellion at home – has traditionally viewed civil society as an internal enemy. Now, however, the army carries out civilian tasks previously performed by the police. In some states, like Coahuila and Nuevo León, which have among the highest number of reports of human rights violations by the military, military officers command some municipal police forces and have taken charge of public security. In fact, military generals and soldiers have access to posts within the police at municipal, state and national level (Centro Prodh 2010: 51–2).

The US training of elite Latin American military and police squads has numerous precedents, constituting a bloody history of violence and repression. The notorious School of the Americas, located in Fort Benning, Georgia, now renamed – following negative publicity in connection with its training of Latin American military officers in 'counterinsurgency' and torture techniques – the Western Hemisphere Institute for Security Cooperation, is an ominous indication of what may lie in store for Mexico. Under the Mérida Initiative, explains a press release issued by the US Embassy in Mexico, Mexican federal police investigators will be trained by a 'cadre' of US and Colombian instructors (US Embassy in Mexico 2010). Given Colombia's recent history, in which the security forces, in collaboration with paramilitary organisations, won the country the accolade of the worst violators of human rights in the Western hemisphere, a reasonable person might ask what military 'training' entails.

With the US military overstretched in the Middle East, the Obama administration has invested heavily in training Mexican military Special Forces. Deployment of US troops to the country would be massively unpopular on both sides of the border, and, besides, legally US troops cannot serve on Mexican soil, although many FBI and DEA agents are stationed there while others cross the border to carry out investigations. Also, Mexico was one of twelve Latin American and Caribbean governments not to grant US military personnel immunity from a decision by the International Criminal Court which could make them vulnerable to international law (Livingstone 2009: 120). Training Mexican troops to fight a war planned by the American government, supposedly to curb the supply of illegal narcotics into the USA, has the further advantage of allowing Washington to be seen as having no involvement in human rights violations.

Criminalising Dissent

Neoliberal policies, the 'free market' and the version of 'democracy' that have prevailed in Mexico in the last two decades are becoming increasingly unpopular. For US and Mexican planners, 'armouring NAFTA', and thus furthering the interests of investors and US geopolitical ambitions, makes sense in a Latin America in which civil society support for the Washington Consensus has been shrinking visibly. The emergence of the Mercosur treaty of regional economic integration and the more recent formation, spearheaded by Venezuela, of the Bolivarian Alliance for the Americas (ALBA), with the prospect of a new common currency and bank for ALBA members, are signals that US hegemony in the region is waning.

In this context, Colombia and Mexico have received the largest amount of US aid of all the Latin American countries, and are also its strongest political allies. President Obama's programme for seven military bases in Colombia reflects concerns that US political and business interests are increasingly vulnerable to new and populist civilian governments. General John Craddock, Commander of US Southern Command (South Com) articulated preoccupations about a democratic opening in Latin America in 2006, noting that 'An election can present an opportunity for those with extremist views to exploit themes of nationalism, patriotism and anti-elite or anti-establishment rhetoric to win popular support', leading to a 'distrust and loss of faith in failed institutions [which] have also fuelled the emergence of anti-globalisation and anti-free trade elements that incite violence against their own governments and their own people' (*ibid.*: 120). In short, the concern of US planners seems as much, if not more, about threats from economic nationalism and a rejection of the neoliberal order in Mexico and Latin America than about organised crime.

With this background, the militarisation of Mexico under the rubric of 'the war on drugs' can be seen as a tool with which to maintain control of an unpredictable political climate. López Obrador's near-victory in the elections in 2006 was a fitting indicator of the public mood, and the unpopular Calderón government has sought to reinforce its authority through strengthened military capabilities. However, its power to control events has been weakened by its minority share of seats in the Congress and state governorships, the majority of which were held by the PRI.

Since the attacks on the Twin Towers in New York in 2001, the rhetoric and justifications for sending millions of dollars in military aid to Colombia and Mexico have become increasingly murky. 'Security' and 'terror' have become so ambiguous and fluid in their meanings as to connote practically any challenge to the dominant order. Dissent and political action which oppose elite political and economic interests are frequently presented as 'terror' threats, regardless of their legitimacy. Duncan Hunter, Chair of the House Armed Services Committee, underlined the US government's fear of 'unconventional threats' in Latin America, expressing alarm over 'extremist groups and supporters of Islamic terrorist groups' and adding that the US government is 'also concerned about the possible shipment of weapons of mass destruction' (Livingstone 2009: 120). In a similar vein, South Com General John Craddock associated the 'war on drugs' with the 'war on terror', grouping together alleged threats to US security as diverse as, 'The transnational terrorist, the narco terrorist, the Islamic radical fundraiser and recruiter, the illicit trafficker, the money launderer, the kidnapper and the gang member' (*ibid*.: 122). From the perspective of US geopolitical interests, such statements have the advantage of delegitimising left-of-centre challenges to the Washington Consensus by creating the impression of a hugely dangerous conspiracy between drug traffickers, leftists, Islamic terrorists and smugglers of WMD, all bent on the destruction of the United States.

In practical terms, there are signs that the ambiguous definitions of 'terrorism' and 'narcotrafficking' are leading to a criminalisation of public protest. For example, in 2009, during Operation Chihuahua, spawned by the Mérida Initiative, in which the military replaced the local police force and occupied entire towns, soldiers targeted peasant and indigenous leaders using three-year-old warrants related to their leadership of anti-NAFTA protests, under the pretext of eradicating drug trafficking. Similar charges have been brought against groups protesting against the expansion of transnational mining operations in the Sierra Madre (Carlsen

2009). Mexico does not have an insurgency on the scale of the FARC in Colombia, but dissidents and leaders of social movements and activist groups find themselves increasingly threatened and intimidated by the armed forces.

Recent attacks on Zapatista communities in Chiapas have also been justified by using the vocabulary of the drug war. In June 2008, when the army raided the Zapatista communities of La Garrucha, Hermenegildo Galeana and San Alejandro in an attempt to regain land taken by activists following the 1994 uprising, they issued public statements defending their incursions by claiming they were searching for illegal drugs (Carlsen 2008: 21). Such statements strained credibility, not least because they failed to present any evidence that the Zapatistas were involved in drug trafficking, but also because both alcohol and drugs are strictly banned in those communities. Furthermore, in a country in which over 11,000 people were killed in incidents associated with narcotrafficking in 2010, the Zapatista-controlled territory must be one of the few corners of Mexico not to be subjected to the current explosion of cartel violence (Gibler 2009b: 41).

This focus on virtually non-existent drug trafficking in autonomous Zapatista territories is peculiar, given that Ciudad Juárez, on Mexico's northern border, now the world's most violent city, witnessed almost 3,000 drug-related executions in 2010. In Juárez alone, the number of femicides (*feminicidios*) reached unprecedented levels in 2009 and 2010, a 50 per cent increase on all those committed in the previous 16 years (Villalpando and Castillo García 2011). Around 10 per cent of these *feminicidios* were committed against children and female teenagers. Additionally, according to the Attorney General of Chihuahua, there has been a dramatic rise in homicides against females there. In 2010 alone, almost 600 females were executed or killed, around 10 per cent of the total executions in the state (Notimex 2011b).

At the same time as these murders were occurring, President Calderón's crackdown on drug-related crime was manifested in a new wave of attacks on communities in Chiapas. Military attacks in

Zapatista rebel territory in recent years have intensified, threatening around 800 families and 12,000 hectares of rebel-controlled land. According to Ernesto Ledesma, director of the Centre for Political Analysis and Social and Economic Investigation in San Cristóbal de las Casas, 'we haven't seen an offensive this intense for at least ten years' (Gibler 2009a: 214). A greater military presence in Chiapas has brought with it allied paramilitary organisations, which, according to Ledesma, the state has 'reactivated'. 'They are doing what the Spaniards did during the Conquest and what the ranchers and local mafias did after the Mexican Revolution', he notes, 'dispossessing the indigenous people once again from their lands, from their territory' (*ibid.*) It may not be coincidental that much of the land controlled by Zapatista communities is rich in biodiversity and natural resources, and that developers interested in expanding ecotourism and mineral and timber extraction have for some years focused on Chiapas as a potential market to be unlocked.

Unlocking and developing those markets is likely to lead to further conflicts with the communities already inhabiting those areas. Thus, by 2011, the army maintained 79 bases in the state, 56 of which were in Zapatista territory (*ibid.*: 216). Such bases were occupied by special elite units whose presence served a double function. Some surrounded Zapatista communities and acted as effective tools of counterinsurgency and spying. A secondary function of the military presence in Chiapas was to act as an immigration and security barrier as part of Plan Sur, which was implemented at the behest of the US government in order to prevent Central American economic asylum seekers heading north through Mexico to the US border (Delgado-Wise 2004: 593).

In this context current Mexico/US policy would appear to prioritise protecting and developing unpopular economic interests, while employing heavy-handed military and police methods to deter challenges from social movements and civil society, using the convenient pretext of the drug war.

'Armouring NAFTA'

While the SPP was a plan to enhance economic prosperity for the beneficiaries of NAFTA, the introduction of neoliberal policies had a detrimental effect on the livelihoods of ordinary Mexicans. Ironically, the cartels were among the prime beneficiaries of NAFTA, and, like the *maquiladora* plants of transnational corporations, exploited the cheap and readily available labour force and lax implementation of labour laws, at the same time capitalising on the widespread corruption within governmental institutions, the police and the military and, like other moneyed interests, financing the campaigns of candidates in elections (Alvarado Álvarez 2009).

One of Barack Obama's presidential campaign pledges had been to renegotiate NAFTA, but, soon after assuming power, it was clear that he would renege on such promises and thus, at the North American Summit in August 2009, the President cited the recent economic crisis as a reason for strengthening the agreement as the Mérida Initiative was implemented.

Although the rhetoric of the SPP and, latterly, of the Mérida Initiative emphasises combating organised crime, neither has addressed the profound inequalities in Mexico that have allowed narcotrafficking to flourish in the NAFTA-driven economy, which, while beneficial to investors, has weakened the country's social fabric by pauperising whole sections of the population, thus rendering them vulnerable to a host of social ills, including criminality.

Faced with the burgeoning unpopularity of neoliberal policies in Mexico, confirmed by the massive protests following the elections in 2006, the business leaders and politicians of both countries were faced with an enduring dilemma: how to maintain the status quo of Mexico's dependency on its northern neighbour, in which 85 per cent of exports were destined for the USA, whence the majority of imports also originated (Carlsen 2008: 18). The problem was how to make the mass of people accept the economic inequalities and disparities necessary to neoliberal capitalism without a heavy investment in infrastructure and social programmes. The answer to this difficulty has had many precedents in Latin America over the course of this and the preceding century and has been found in increased military spending. It is ironic that Mexico, virtually alone in Latin America in never having experienced military rule since 1911, has moved progressively towards militarisation since democratisation in 2000. Yet, in a climate in which the neoliberal model is becoming increasingly unpopular, free trade and militarism go hand in hand. 'To an extent,' noted the unusually candid Thomas Shannon, US Assistant Secretary of State under the Bush administration, 'we're armouring NAFTA' (*ibid*.: 17).

Money Laundering

The government crackdown on organised crime would be more effective in combating the power of Mexican drug traffickers were it to target the banks responsible for housing their profits. Matteo Dean, the Italo-Mexican journalist killed in June 2011, reported that Banco Santander's Mexican operations were being investigated for laundering millions of dollars on behalf of Mexican crime syndicates. Yet Banco Santander was not the only one on the list of institutions being investigated for profiting from Mexican drug money. In addition, Wachovia, part of the Wells Fargo group, Bank of America, Citigroup (which owns Banamex), American Express, Western Union and HSBC were all being investigated by the US Drug Enforcement Administration and the Internal Revenue Service (Dean 2010). Wachovia was fined $50 million although no individual faced prosecution. The investigation also found that Wachovia had not applied anti-laundering measures to *casas de cambio* (*bureaux de change*) accounts for the transfer of $378.4 billion, a figure roughly equivalent to a third of Mexico's GDP (Vulliamy 2011). Wachovia was given a fine that represented less than 2 per cent of its $12.3 billion profit in 2009. As journalist of the Mexican drug war, Ed Vulliamy, commented:

The conclusion to the case [of Wachovia] was only the tip of an iceberg, demonstrating the role of the legal banking sector in swilling hundreds of billions of dollars – the blood money from the murderous drug trade in Mexico . . . – around their global operations, now bailed out by the taxpayer. (*ibid.*)

In the economic crisis that deepened in 2007 and 2008, and for which banks were largely responsible, the US government bailed out Wells Fargo, Wachovia's parent company, to the tune of $25 billion of American taxpayers' money (*ibid.*). Mexicans could have warned them from bitter experience that a characteristic of the neoliberal economy is that profits are privatised, while costs are socialised.

As Martin Woods, the ex-Money Laundering Reporting Officer at Wachovia Bank in London, who blew the whistle on his company's profiteering from the drug trade, has repeatedly argued, it is simply not credible that major international banking institutions do not know the origins of dirty money. Drug money cannot launder itself; it is the individuals working in those same institutions who are directly responsible for laundering illegally earned cash, in this case, billions of dollars. Aside from the obvious advantage of increasing profits, hard cash from criminal syndicates and bailouts from government give banks liquidity that, during the frequent economic crises that the neoliberal period has provoked, keeps them afloat.

According to Woods, interviewed by Vulliamy for *Observer* (*ibid.*), the money-laundering practices of the banks have real and very serious consequences in Mexico:

These are the proceeds of murder and misery in Mexico, and of drugs sold around the world. All the law enforcement people wanted to see this come to trial. But no one goes to jail. What does the settlement do to fight the cartels? Nothing – it doesn't make the job of law enforcement easier and it encourages the cartels and anyone who wants to make money by laundering their blood dollars. Where's the risk? There is none.

Genuine attempts to limit the power and influence of Mexican cartels would address the issue of the banks. The Sinaloa cartel, for example, which is thought to control between 45 to 48 per cent of all narcotics destined for the United States, would suffer a serious blow were the banks to cease accepting narcodollars. Equally, however, the international banking system would suffer a blow were drug traffickers to stop providing them with liquid assets. Woods claims that the majority of criminal money is nowadays laundered through New York and London (*ibid.*). Yet following the 2007–08 crisis during which national governments bailed out the international banking system with taxpayer money, it has become very clear that powerful governments do not view cracking down on the white-collar criminals within them as a worthwhile option.

The protection afforded to trafficking organisations is set to continue with the support of the international banking system, thanks to pacts between big business and politics. Politicians are also unlikely to launch investigations into companies and banks that benefit from and even support the drug trade, when these same institutions lend their financial support to election campaigns. If this seems exaggerated, recall Carlos Salinas's PRI fundraising dinner in 1993, which earned his party three quarters of a billion dollars in one evening from Mexico's top billionaires (Chapter 4).

Calderón's campaign of militarisation leaves intact the financial structures through which organised crime prospers. Without intervening in major corporations and without regulating illegal financial practices via audits, and prosecuting white-collar criminals, the 'war on drugs' is doing little to touch illicit money. The strategy of militarisation is a reaction only to the escalation of violent conflict but does nothing to prevent the accumulation of capital by organised crime, which is, after all, what motivates the whole business. Were the crackdown to begin with a thoroughgoing investigation of fraud and money laundering, prosecuting the individuals involved and confiscating assets and property, it would have a huge impact on the power of criminal organisations.

The Favoured Cartel

Following the scandal of 2003 that engulfed FEADS, the federal agency responsible for investigating organised crime and corruption – with the revelation that high-ranking officials within it were in fact working *for* drug traffickers – the Vicente Fox government created its replacement, the Assistant Attorney General's Office for Special Investigations on Organised Crime (SIEDO – Subprocuraduría de Investigación Especializada en Delincuencia Organizada). Yet less than two years into the drug war, serious allegations of corruption and complicity with organised crime in the SIEDO emerged when Noé Ramírez Mandujano, the agency director, was found to be on the payroll of *El Chapo* Guzmán's Sinaloa cartel. Shortly before, Ramírez had resigned because of the agency's failure to produce satisfactory results in terms of the number of arrests of cartel members. As often occurs with disgraced officials, the government sent Ramírez abroad, appointing him as Mexican representative to the United Nations Office on Drugs and Crime in Vienna (Ellingwood 2008).

For a fee of $450,000 dollars, from the very outset of Calderón's war on the narcos in 2006, Ramírez had been providing the Sinaloa cartel with information about anti-drug efforts and stings to enable it to avoid prosecutions, an activity for which he was convicted and incarcerated in 2009 (*ibid.*). Not since the arrest and conviction of drug czar Jesús Gutiérrez Rebollo in 1997 had such a high-ranking official been implicated in working with organised crime. In addition, six other senior members of the FEADS organisation were arrested for drugs and arms smuggling, kidnapping and leaking information to the Sinaloa cartel. Thirty-five officials and agents, including the senior intelligence officer and the general technical coordinator, were also arrested or fired. Around the same time, Mexico's chief liaison officer with Interpol and two senior federal police commanders were arrested for leaking information to criminal organisations (*ibid.*)

For Edgardo Buscaglia (2010), legal scholar and an analyst of organised crime for the United Nations, diverse criminal organisations are competing for control of the state in a relationship that threatens to become the opposite of that prevailing during the PRI years. In part, he explains, this accounts for the surge in violence since the transition to democracy in 2000. At times, the loyalties of different police and military forces to various criminal organisations have resulted in shoot-outs between them. As the monopolistic grip of PRI state power began to decline towards the end of the twentieth century, different parts of the state authority began to work for and with different criminal organisations. The more competing organisations tried to capture control of elements of the state, the more violence there was.

Since 2006, the rate of violent crime has soared, in close correlation with the militarisation of the anti-drug policy, as criminal organisations have defended their economic interests and investments. Meanwhile their ongoing, mundane pursuit of the same end – bribing officials, the police and elements of the military to obtain their loyalty, and intimidating or killing those who refuse to be bribed or are on the payroll of competing organisations – has also contributed to the increase in violence.

Organised crime has executed dozens of politicians and former governmental officials, presumably either for refusing to be bribed or because they have offered protection to rival cartels. Other officials have been arrested by state authorities (and many subsequently released) for their alleged involvement with organised crime. The following is a selection of events from the last two years which illustrates these facts:[11]

- 26 May 2009. The army and the Federal Police (PFP) detained 28 governmental officials in the state of Michoacán (from both state and municipal governments), accused of links with

---

11 Prepared by the authors with information from the newspaper *Reforma*.

the drug cartel *La Familia*. A further seven officials were arrested in different police-military operations. Nonetheless, the federal government was unable to provide satisfactory evidence to support the accusations and all of the detained officials were released.

- 14 July 2009. The SSP (Secretariat of Public Security) accused federal deputy Julio Cesar Godoy of the PRD of connections with organised crime. During 15 months Godoy avoided justice and in September 2010 appealed for legal protection. He was released on bail on 14 December 2010 pending further investigation, but subsequently disappeared.

- 25 May 2010. Greg Sánchez, the PRD candidate for the state of Quintana Roo, was accused of organised crime, narco-trafficking, and money laundering. In June 2010 he was incarcerated in the Penal del Rincón, in Tepic, Nayarit. However, he was exonerated of all charges by a federal judge and released in August 2011.

- 28 June 2010. The PRI candidate for the government of Tamaulipas was executed by organised crime elements while campaigning in the midst of his delegation.

- 21 November 2010. The former governor of Colima, Silverio Cavazos Ceballos, was executed, presumably by organised crime elements.

- 4 June 2011. Jorge Hank Rhon, former mayor of Tijuana, was detained by the army at his farm. He was freed ten days later, after his lawyers demonstrated inconsistencies in the version of the arrest given by the military. Official authorities were unable to keep him in prison to answer an accusation of homicide.

- 15 June 2011. Discovery of the mutilated bodies of two members of the security staff of the governor of Nuevo León, Rodrigo Medina.

During the period December 2006–August 2011, 174 police, officials and politicians were murdered. Most of the victims were individuals in high to mid-level positions: 83 police chiefs, 32 municipal presidents and 5 political candidates for elected positions, all apparently killed by organised crime. Michoacán is the state with most murders in this category, with 21 homicides, including both officials of the public administration and members of police bodies. In Veracruz, the slaughter of police directors has been substantial, with 14 killings. In Hidalgo, Sinaloa and Tamaulipas four police chiefs were executed. One of the leaders of the SSP, Edgar Eusebio Millan Gómez, a senior official in the federal offensive against drug cartels, has been one of the most significant casualties among high-ranking members of the government apparatus (*Excélsior*, 31 August 2011).

During the Calderón administration, there have been at least thirty murders of municipal presidents in various states, contributing to a grisly league table. Durango is the state with most mayors assassinated (six); next come Chihuahua and Michoacán (four each); Guerrero with three executions; the State of Mexico, Nuevo León, Oaxaca and Tamaulipas (two each); and other states such as Coahuila, Morelos, Puebla, San Luis Potosí, Veracruz and Zacatecas (one each) (Grande 2011).

The states where most politicians have been executed, apparently by organised crime, are: Michoacán (twelve), Tamaulipas (ten), Chihuahua (eight), and Durango, Guerrero and Sinaloa, each with six murders of this type. The politicians killed included the PRI candidate for the governorship of Tamaulipas, Rodolfo Torre, and the ex-governor of Colima, Silverio Cavazos Ceballos.

Anabel Hernández (2010a) has noted that the escalation of violence in recent years also sprang from the fact that control of some *plazas* had been sold to two rival bidders. For example, control of the *plaza* for the Estado de México had been assured to the Beltrán-Leyva cartel (which had split from Guzmán Loera's organisation) and also to the Sinaloa organisation, which has led competing organisations to fight fiercely for control and to execute officials, police and politicians working for their opponents.

Clearly, the state has lost much of its political authority and control over the last decade, particularly since 2006. Now that violent crime is affecting not only civil society but mayors and police chiefs as well, competition for control of *plazas* has become fiercer. This ferocity is also a matter of deep concern to the political class, who have seen their ability to rein in and control organised crime diminish since the onset of neoliberalism and the democratic transition. An obvious way to re-establish some measure of control and order, then, as Edgardo Buscaglia (2010), Diego Enrique Osorno (2009) and Anabel Hernández (2010a) have suggested, is to favour one group – in this case the Sinaloa cartel – over others. In support of the argument, Buscaglia cites the prosecution figures for arrested cartel members. Of the 53,174 detained during the Calderón government's crackdown, only 941 belonged to the Sinaloa organisation, despite its being the largest drug-trafficking association in the world (*Economist* 2010). Figures compiled by investigative journalists at National Public Radio, using releases from the PGR in Mexico City, suggest a larger proportion, some 12 per cent of arrests. Yet if the Sinaloa cartel controls around 45 per cent of all Mexico's drug trade, one would expect both figures to be substantially higher than they are.

Many more stings have been made against the rival Gulf-Zeta organisation and account for around 44 per cent of arrests of its employees, as well as against the Tijuana, *La Familia*, and Beltrán-Leyva cartels. Figure 6.2 indicates some estimates of the territory controlled by competing cartels. The Sinaloa association clearly dominates, particularly owing to its command of a number of large urban centres where there are concentrations of population.

In addition, the official protection afforded to *El Chapo*'s organisation, originating in the SIEDO itself, suggests that its power has infiltrated the top levels of government. One Mexican intelligence report obtained by the *Wall Street Journal* noted that *El Chapo*, who, following the death of Osama bin Laden, lays claim to being the world's most wanted man, travelled with a caravan usually comprising at least six vehicles, and was often escorted by the Mexican army (Lunhow and De Córdoba 2009).

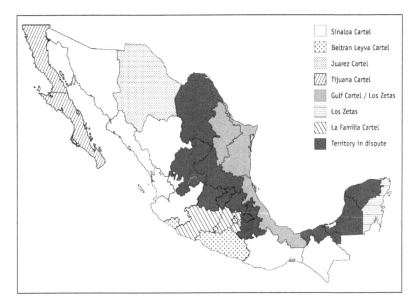

Figure 6.2 Territories controlled by crime organisations, 2011

Calderón's favoured choice to lead the war on organised crime also raises questions about the integrity of his government's policy. Eduardo Medina Mora, the current ambassador to the UK, had headed the SSP in the last year of the Fox administration and, before becoming Attorney General, had promised to address the issue of intervention in the financial assets of organised crime. Yet until he resigned in 2009, before being dispatched to the UK, Medina Mora's strategy had concentrated largely on militarisation. 'Success is measured by deaths' ('*El éxito se mide con muertos*'), he noted of Calderón's drug war, displaying a level of cynicism and doublethink that even Orwell might have failed to capture (Osorno 2009: 304). Medina Mora's comment nonetheless reflects the dominant rhetoric of the Calderón administration, one which ceaselessly attempts to justify the deaths of thousands of civilians by associating *all* victims of shootings, torture and forced disappearance with delinquency and organised crime. According to this view, the higher the number of civilians – or criminals – liquidated, the greater the signs of success in the war on crime. In short, war is peace.

It seems even less likely, given his past record, that Genaro García Luna, Medina Mora's successor to lead the SSP, will design an effective strategy to combat the corruption and financial power of organised crime, particularly in the case of the Sinaloa association. García Luna had headed the Federal Agency of Investigation (AFI), the federal police agency created by Vicente Fox in 2001 to replace the Federal Judicial Police. It was disbanded by the government in 2009 following charges of corruption and accusations that it had been infiltrated by organised crime. By 2005, almost 1,500 of the 7,000 agents working for the AFI were under investigation by the PGR, and 457 had been charged with colluding with criminal organisations (Cook 2007: 9). Nonetheless, the same person who had founded and directed the AFI was given the most senior policing role in the country, and was charged with enforcing the war on crime. Senior officials from SEDENA expressed serious concerns about Calderón's appointment of García Luna in the light of speculation about alleged but unproven links to the Sinaloa cartel. In 2008 a number of federal police agents drafted a letter to Congress detailing the results of an investigation in which they declared that García Luna was closely linked to high-level traffickers in Mexico, particularly Ismael *El Mayo* Zambada of the Sinaloa cartel. Furthermore, they contended that the SSP itself was infiltrated by organised criminal syndicates (Ravelo 2008).

Although García Luna's involvement with organised crime remains a matter of speculation, it needs to be explained how Calderón's replacement drugs czar was able to afford his numerous vehicles, restaurants, country retreats and luxury homes on the salary of a public servant. By 2009, for example, he had acquired several buildings with a total value of 42.5 million pesos but never declared his ownership, as public officials are obliged to do by law.

In less than three years as Secretary of Public Security, García Luna's acquisitions totalled seventeen times his salary (*Vanguardia* 2010). According to Anabel Hernández (2010a), government policy is not one of a war on drugs but *for* drugs; institutions of the state – led by the likes of García Luna and Calderón – are as inextricably involved in organised crime as the cartels themselves.

It is notable that the ex-commissioner of the federal police Gerardo Garay Cadena – who was accused of, and incarcerated for, protecting Ismael *El Mayo* Zambada's cell of the Sinaloa cartel – continued on the SSP payroll long after the allegations surfaced in 2008. During an investigation into corruption within the AFI that focused on one of its most senior officials, Domingo González Díaz, a PGR report suggested that, within the organisation, García Luna and his closest group of agents were protecting the Beltrán-Leyva brothers (then allied to *El Chapo* Guzmán but later at war with his organisation) – though, again, this was never proved. González Díaz subsequently disappeared completely and is still wanted by the Attorney General's Office. One of many payments made to the AFI in Mexico City, the same investigation claimed, was made by drug lord Edgar Valdez Villareal, also known as *La Barbie* (arrested in August 2010), on behalf of the Beltrán-Leyva brothers, a payoff in 2003 amounting to 1.5 million dollars (Hernández 2010b).

For the Sinaloa cartel, having AFI agents like González Díaz, who were under the command of García Luna, protecting their interests in the territory of the Gulf cartel gave them a strategic advantage, and was one of the factors that allowed the organisation continuously to expand. According to one Mexican intelligence report obtained by Anabel Hernández, on one occasion González Díaz received a payment of four million dollars from the Sinaloa cartel, 'for him and his bosses' (*ibid*.).

Assuming this is the case, the expansion of the alliance of organisations that is the Sinaloa cartel has taken on proportions that extend well beyond Mexico and the United States. Just as 'legitimate' capitalist enterprises have outsourced their operations abroad, so too, it seems, has the Sinaloa cartel, acting as a distributor for imported heroin, most of which appears to have originated in Turkey and Afghanistan, with the latter dominating the lion's share of production. There is also an increasing presence of armaments purchased (often in exchange for narcotics) from Russia and Albania (Gómora 2011).

In addition, both the Sinaloa and Gulf-Zeta cartels are thought to have extended their operations to South America, particularly northern regions of Argentina – Chaco, Formosa and Misiones – with bases for the production of synthetic drugs and cocaine to be distributed via Buenos Aires (Cuéllar Ramírez 2011). Thus, what seems to be a strategy to allow the Sinaloa cartel to create a monopoly of the market in Mexico has allowed it to extend its operations to countries where it finds a climate favourable to investment, with the apparent assistance of those charged with curtailing its influence.

Despite García Luna's questionable background, Felipe Calderón could, it appears, think of no one better to lead the battle which has defined his administration. In fact, García Luna was held in such esteem that in 2010 he was appointed to head the inter-American police agency, Ameripol, for a period of three years.

As a result of her investigations, Hernández claims, García Luna issued her with a death threat for which she filed a complaint with the National Human Rights Commission (CNDH) and a lawsuit with the Attorney General. In the five years up to 2011, Calderón's drug war made Mexico more dangerous than Iraq and the most dangerous country in the Americas in which to be a journalist.

In a parallel development, militarisation of the border turned places like Ciudad Juárez into some of the world's most hazardous cities. With no end to the violence in sight and a government which seemed to be complicit in the trade that it was supposedly combating, only a coordinated response by civil society organisations could have offered any hope of making a difference.

◆

One government claim underpinning the current war on drugs is that, in addition to the high levels of violent crime at the time Calderón took office, there was an urgent need to protect the young from the destructive effects of consuming narcotics. However, this looks like another excuse for using violence to suppress opposition when one considers that Mexico's position with regard to consumption looks much less bleak than that of other countries in the region, and positively healthy when compared to the United States. The 2008 National Survey on Addiction, produced by the National Institute for Public Health (INSP 2009), a federal government bureau, for example, notes that addiction to illegal drugs (marijuana, cocaine and its derivatives, heroin, methamphetamines, hallucinogens and inhalants) among Mexicans between 12 and 65 years of age rose by just over half a per cent between 2002 and 2008. Although consumption of cocaine and methamphetamines increased after having dipped at the end of the 1990s, levels of use and addiction are still lower than in neighbouring countries. So even with an increase in addiction, this represents 0.4 per cent of the population, while in the United States, addicts account for 3 per cent of the population, which means there are around five times as many addicts there per capita as in Mexico. For comparison, 2.1 per cent of the German population is classified as addicted to illegal drugs, while the corresponding figure in the Netherlands is 1.8 per cent.

As Rubén Aguilar and Jorge Castañeda note, citing the same study, 'The figures expose the nonexistence of a direct relation between official discourse – which assures us that the problem is getting worse – and what the same statistics actually indicate' (Aguilar and Castañeda 2009: 19). Again, if it were true that the *guerra al narco* has as its priority protecting public health, at a time when consumption and addiction in Mexico were, and still are, low by comparison with other nations, the huge investment of resources in the war seems totally disproportionate. Furthermore, the fact that there has clearly been an increase in rates of drug addiction following 2006 suggests that government strategy has been unsuccessful in its supposed aims.

With an annual increase in the homicide rate since 2006, there is little indication that the government's strategy is anywhere near achieving any of its stated goals. According to the government's own agency, the Sistema Nacional de Seguridad Pública, the murder rate had in fact declined in the years immediately preceding Calderón's presidency. For example, in 1997, there was a total of 16,867 reported homicides in Mexico. This figure had dropped to 11,775 in 2006 but has risen sharply since. By 2010, the national homicide rate had increased by some 8,000 to around 20,000; this after four years of intense crackdown on organised crime intended, if we believe the rhetoric, to reduce violent crime in Mexico. Violent crime is concentrated primarily in the regions where crime syndicates fight for control of territory or *plazas*. In Chihuahua, according to the same figures, there were 3,514 murders in 2010, while in Sinaloa, there were 2,251 reported homicides in the same year. Yet between 1997 and 2006, the murder rate had not risen but dropped in those same two regions, which had been specifically targeted by the Calderón government as part of the crackdown on the cartels. In 2006, the year Calderón's crackdown began, in Chihuahua and Sinaloa there were 593 and 602 reported homicides respectively (Secretaría Ejecutiva del Sistema Nacional de Seguridad Pública 2010).

Statistics compiled by the newspaper *Reforma*, which focus on deaths related to narcotrafficking alone, suggest similar trends and correlate the general rise in homicides with the intensification of military presence on the streets. The total number of homicides (according to the government's own figures) is higher than those attributed to narcotrafficking compiled by *Reforma*, but, assuming the figures are accurate, the majority of homicides are related to the drug war. It would be difficult to find a more damning illustration of the complete failure of the government's policy to improve public security, assuming indeed that that is the policy's genuine goal. Table 6.5 demonstrates that in the areas where the military

Table 6.5 Number of deaths related to narcotrafficking in Mexico, by state, 2006–2011

State	2006	2007	2008	2009	2010	2011	Total
Chihuahua	130	148	1,652	2,082	3,185	1,823	9,020
Sinaloa	350	346	686	767	2,028	1,287	5,464
Guerrero	186	253	294	638	984	1,511	3,866
Durango	64	126	272	637	777	885	2,761
Nuevo León	50	107	79	99	610	1,641	2,586
Michoacàn	543	238	233	371	259	308	1,952
Tamaulipas	181	89	110	49	725	647	1,801
Estado de México	31	111	360	354	464	428	1,748
Jalisco	45	93	148	212	545	699	1,742
Baja California	163	154	617	320	315	134	1,703
Distrito Federal	137	145	138	173	197	163	953
Coahuila	17	29	53	151	199	500	949
Sonora	61	125	137	152	249	132	856
Veracruz	25	48	30	55	52	306	516
Morelos	10	17	28	77	251	109	492
Nayarit	1	2	5	22	211	215	456
Guanajuato	25	40	61	146	50	35	357
San Luis Potosi	1	13	40	7	102	142	305
Zacatecas	12	13	24	30	21	141	241
Oaxaca	17	33	49	6	48	54	207
Tabasco	19	24	20	54	30	54	201
Hidalgo	16	37	37	36	28	34	188
Quintana Roo	9	34	18	27	52	35	175
Colima	2	0	5	12	72	82	173
Aguascalientes	2	27	38	34	21	29	151
Chiapas	14	12	30	30	37	26	149
Puebla	4	2	15	26	36	48	131
Queretaro	0	4	7	14	23	16	64
Yucatan	0	1	17	0	0	2	20
Baja California Sur	1	1	0	1	6	10	19
Campeche	3	2	3	2	2	4	16
Tlaxcala	0	1	1	3	4	3	12
Total	2,119	2,275	5,207	6,587	11,583	11,503	39,274

Source: Prepared by the authors with data from *Reforma* during the period 1 December 2006–25 November 2011.

has had a greater presence – like Chihuahua, Sinaloa and Guerrero – there has been a radical increase in drug war violence. Either the military is failing to combat the violent tactics of organised crime or, as Human Rights Watch (2011) has demonstrated, it is involved in committing atrocities itself. Another interpretation could be that the activities of both organised crime and state forces are contributing to the overall escalation of violence.

As Peter Reuter, Professor at the School of Public Policy and the Department of Criminology at the University of Maryland, has noted, illegal markets are not necessarily inherently violent, even though they function outside the protection of the civil court system. Further, Reuter suggests, illegal drug markets are generally peaceable, although, without legal protection, conflicts of interest must be resolved through extra-judicial measures, which can result in acts of violence. For example, in the case of Mexican crime syndicates, contracts are agreed orally and often in very ambiguous terms. Disciplinary measures within crime syndicates can tend toward violence simply because legal avenues are unavailable. High-level managers can also use violence as a disincentive to potential low-level employees to act as informants for other criminal organisations and the authorities (Reuter 2009). If this is so, the violence witnessed at present in Mexico is not necessarily the result of the existence of a major illegal market *per se*, but due to other factors specific to the country. Other illicit markets, like illegal gambling and prostitution, do not necessarily generate high levels of violence, though they operate outside the protection of the civilian courts and the state.

Traffic of contraband across the Mexico/US border is hardly a recent phenomenon and dates back to the late nineteenth century. Increasing restrictions on smuggling on both sides of the border have meant that the illicit trade has had an ever more confrontational relationship with the authorities. In the 1980s and 1990s, with a growing demand from the US market for narcotics – particularly cocaine and marijuana – and consequent mounting pressure from the US government's DEA, powerful trafficking organisations turned to violent measures to defend their competing business interests. Yet none of this compares with the eruption of extreme violence in the last few years, which seems to correlate with an intensified militarisation of the country and a concomitant increase in enforcement activities by both the Mexican and US governments.

Clearly, if the war on the narcos is intended to improve security for Mexican citizens, it has been an outright failure. In fact, if we take the government's own statistics as a guide, the war has had exactly the reverse effect to the one officials have declared publicly. Though violent crime in Mexico preceding 2006 was lamentably high, compared to other countries in the region Mexico's homicide rate was relatively low and had fallen significantly in the ten preceding years. Figures collected by the 2004 Geneva Declaration on Armed Violence and Development suggested that Brazil, Venezuela, El Salvador and Honduras had homicide rates much higher than those of Mexico, forcing us to ponder whether the *guerra al narco* is genuinely about increasing security and reducing crime or whether the officially declared goals are designed to resist scrutiny of its real aims (Geneva Declaration on Armed Violence and Development 2004).

Significant numbers of Mexicans have begun to ask that same question and public discontent with the *guerra al narco* has become more vocal. In May 2011, some tens of thousands of people took part in the first major demonstration against Calderón's drug war, presenting a citizen's pact of six key demands. The new movement, *No Más Sangre,* had as its spokesperson the poet Javier Sicilia, whose son was kidnapped, tortured and murdered in March 2011. The demonstrators demanded the resignation of Genaro García Luna, Secretary of Public Safety, accusing him of allowing large numbers of civilians to be caught up in the supposed war between the state and the cartels. Their representations also included demands that the war be terminated; that the government deal with impunity and official corruption; and that it redress economic disparities by prioritising budget allocations towards education, health care and jobs. The birth of a movement that challenged the legitimacy of the war on the narcos was a significant development and pointed to a profound sense of political frustration with the Calderón administration and a deep-seated scepticism about its good faith. Further, the calls for broader democratic participation in the political sphere and a restructuring of economic priorities suggest that disillusionment was directed not only at the government, but at the entire neoliberal political and economic system that has provoked ever wider disparities and inequalities, and has benefited Mexico's wealthy elite and foreign investors at the expense of most of the population.

Given the Mexican government's focus on issues of public security and a crackdown on organised crime, what of the conviction rates for reported crimes? A 2008 report by the National Human Rights Commission (CNDH) estimated that throughout Mexico, only one of every ten violent crimes was reported. The authors note that, of all the crimes committed in Mexico, slightly more than 1 per cent were punished, leaving a margin of impunity of 98.76 per cent (CNDH 2009). Thus, according to the CNDH figures, 99 of every 100 crimes committed in Mexico go unpunished. Among those who are convicted of a crime, there are clearly many who are innocent, as Mexico's judicial system is in need of serious reform, as has been documented frequently in reports published by Amnesty International and Human Rights Watch. This is a topic which Roberto Hernández tackled recently in the documentary, *Presunto Culpable* (Presumed Guilty), a film which made such an impact in exposing corruption in the judicial system that one Mexico City judge had it censored.

Article 57 of Mexico's military code, the *fuero militar*, stipulates that human rights abuses allegedly committed by soldiers are to be investigated by military, not civil, courts. Perhaps unsurprisingly, as an institution the Mexican military has a past of protecting itself from the public exposure of abuses and atrocities it has committed. In 2009, the Inter-American Court of Human Rights (IACoHR) condemned the Mexican state, ordering it to reform its military code and to investigate crimes committed by military personnel, in this case the disappearance of folk singer and community activist, Rosendo Radilla Pacheco, in 1974 (Watt 2010). The reluctance of the Mexican state and military to investigate alleged crimes is systemic. More recently, the state has been in the dock and sentenced again by the IACoHR, notably for refusing to investigate the rape and beatings of Valentina Rosendo Cantú and Inés Fernández Ortega by soldiers in Guerrero. While the case has received recognition and coverage internationally, the Calderón government's refusal to investigate and punish the perpetrators indicates where its real priorities lie in relation to human rights. Perhaps more telling, as recorded in one 2011 Amnesty International report, is that 1,600 complaints of human rights abuses committed by military personnel were received by the Mexican authorities in 2010. Considering the difficulties put in the way of reporting such abuses, and the fact that complainants are very often subjected to further acts of intimidation and violence, it is likely that the total number of abuses committed by the military is much higher than the recorded instances suggest. It is a measure of the administration's commitment to justice that during the entire presidency of Calderón there was just one conviction of a military official (Amnesty International 2011).

From the evidence above, it would seem that the *guerra al narco* is neither about achieving security and stability, nor about bringing those guilty of violent crime – whether delinquents or soldiers – to justice. Nor does the war seem to be a temporary measure, as Calderón stated, a claim that is contradicted by evidence on the ground and the absence of a termination date for US funding via the Mérida Initiative.

Another Century of Drug War? 7

Ciudad Juárez, on Mexico's northern border, has become more violent than Baghdad: indeed, it can now claim to be the world's most violent city. The Global Peace Index study of 2011 ranks Mexico 121 of the 153 countries studied, eight places below Haiti.

Narco-cartels have prospered in Mexico; especially since the year 2000, their violent tactics have generated a climate of terror among the population. Narcotraffickers resolve their internal and inter-cartel disputes by using indiscriminate violence and shootings, by executing rivals mercilessly and publicly, by hanging their victims' bodies from bridges. Their robberies and extortions from individuals and businesses are carried out in broad daylight. Cartels now perpetrate what amount to terrorist outrages in public places with seeming impunity; the attack at the Casino Royale in Monterrey in August 2011, which killed 52 people, is but one example of many. Violence arising from the battle for control of the narco trade, far from being directed at the legal authorities by criminals (the distinction between the two is often blurred), has its greatest impact on the lives of ordinary and innocent citizens.

According to a United Nations report, around 60 per cent of all the municipalities in Mexico have either been infiltrated or are controlled by narcotrafficking cartels (there are 2,440 municipal governments in the country). The paradigmatic cases of narco infiltration in politics are in the states of Chihuahua, Baja California, Sonora, Sinaloa, Michoacán, Morelos and Oaxaca, but the problem appears to be endemic in all states in the country (Ballinas and

Becerril 2009). Indeed, Edgardo Buscaglia noted that, by the end of 2010, a total of 982 municipalities in Mexico were similarly controlled by narcotrafficking organisations. He commented that 'The narco controls territories, promotes and funds candidates for deputies and mayors and has kidnapped the municipal structure of the country.' According to Buscaglia, who acts as an adviser to the UN on matters of organised crime in Mexico, in 2007 there were 353 municipalities dominated by narcos; by 2009, there were 650 and, by October 2010, 982 (Ravelo 2010).

Perhaps one way to undermine rule by drug cartels would be to change the environment in which they operate, but this would mean restructuring the economy in favour of a more protectionist and egalitarian model, one which could invest in the amelioration of poverty and in the infrastructure, addressing the woeful economic disparities in a Mexico where the world's richest man, Carlos Slim, acquires on average another million dollars every hour, while the majority live on less than two dollars a day (Gibler 2009a: 98; Osorno 2009: 45). Improving living conditions will not be easy in a country governed by billionaires who have little interest in change. Furthermore, the United States government is unlikely to allow its key strategic ally in the region to go further towards genuine democracy than granting its citizens electoral participation.

One obvious reason for the violent tactics of the cartels arises from the prohibition of marijuana, heroin and cocaine. Because narcotrafficking has to operate illegally and clandestinely, criminal organisations must compete for control of *plazas* outside the framework of the law. And cartels compete with each other aggressively for *plazas* precisely because the industry provides such enviable profit margins. Illegality means heightened risk for the chain of producers, runners, traffickers and dealers alike, which translates into higher prices on the streets. If the illegal narcotics were decriminalised and stringently controlled, it is likely that cartel profits would be severely constrained. Such a move would have some heavyweight backing: three Latin

American ex-presidents – Ernesto Zedillo of Mexico, Fernando Enrique Cardoso of Brazil and César Gaviria of Colombia, all executive members of the Latin American Commission on Drugs and Democracy – have argued that cannabis at least should be decriminalised. In 2009, even Vicente Fox had joined groups arguing for the relaxation of legislation relating to the drug.

The legalisation of narcotics seems a distant dream, however. Polls conducted to test Mexican public opinion suggest that only 15 per cent of the population favour the legalisation of arguably the least harmful illegal drug, cannabis. In contrast, in the United States, where consumption is far more widespread, around 46 per cent favour legalisation (Campos 2011). In any case, so long as the Mexican political and business elites can make money from the trade, they are unlikely to appreciate the potential benefits of ending the prohibition of even a comparatively harmless drug. From the perspective of narcotraffickers, prohibition, while problematic, is in fact extremely profitable, with the illegal industry now among the country's most significant exporters, providing the economy with a key source of revenue. Little wonder, when colossal fortunes are there to be made, that the scramble to control the drug trade has become so violent.

Nonetheless, it seems that the legalisation of some, if not all, drugs, which could potentially reduce the huge profits involved, would not necessarily on its own present a long-term answer to the institutional corruption and the eruption of violence of the last few years. In fact, drug trafficking accounts for 40–48 per cent of the activities of organised crime. In the pitiless neoliberal economy, criminal organisations have been able to diversify and have sought new business opportunities. Kidnapping, human trafficking, extortion, piracy and counterfeiting are by now all massively profitable enterprises of the informal economy (Buscaglia 2010). The required infrastructure, networks, distribution lists and contacts are all readily available to those already involved in drug trafficking; the legalisation of narcotics could be a massive setback for organised crime, but, so long as the climate of impunity, corruption and lawlessness exists, and while there is such an extreme inequality in the distribution of wealth, there is little reason to believe that these same organisations would not expand further into other areas of criminality; indeed, such a process has already begun.

In April 2009, the Senate passed a law – *Ley Federal de Extinción de Dominio* – which granted the authorities legal powers to confiscate the goods and assets of criminals or businesses associated with organised crime. Were the law to be enforced systematically, it could be used as a weapon against traffickers, corrupt officials and bankers involved in money laundering. In countries like Italy and Colombia, where there have been serious and concerted efforts to tackle the support network of organised crime, legislators, politicians and bankers were investigated and subsequently prosecuted, revenues seized, assets confiscated and storage facilities containing contraband destroyed (*ibid.*). In Mexico, however, the financial and political structure that allows drug trafficking to flourish has remained all but untouched. Without serious blows to the substructure of organised crime, it is unreasonable to expect a campaign focused almost entirely on policing conducted by the army to combat powerful drug trafficking organisations. As we have attempted to show throughout this book, drug trafficking in Mexico has been, for a long time, facilitated by official complicity, by white-collar crime. It should be clear by now that narcotrafficking over the last century has been a component part of the state apparatus. It is not that *every* politician, soldier or police chief participates in the narcoeconomy. Nonetheless, corruption among low-level police officers, and right up to high-level politicians, has been sufficient to allow cooperation between criminals and members of the state apparatus to expand narcotrafficking into a massive cancerous growth on the social body. And so long as the demand for narcotics in the United States exists, it does not seem unreasonable to conclude that the country on its southern border, where the majority live in poverty, will continue to satisfy that demand.

As the strategy of the Calderón administration has shown, organised crime responds to violent attacks with increasingly defensive and intimidatory measures in order to defend its assets and control of territory. Without serious reforms to the judicial and police systems and an application of the law, it is difficult to see how the political class can even pretend to be serious about curbing organised crime. The militarisation of cities like Ciudad Juárez, Tamaulipas, Tijuana and Culiacán is in fact the one strategy that, as amply demonstrated by Calderón's government, simply does not work.

Nor are attempts to combat violent crime aided by the ease with which Mexican traffickers can buy powerful firearms and weaponry in the United States and smuggle them back across the border. How many of the thousands killed in recent years would still be alive, one wonders, if access to guns at arms fairs and gun stores in California, Arizona, New Mexico and Texas, for example, were denied to the cartels?

In terms of addiction, addicts should ideally have access to rehabilitation programmes that treat what is, after all, an issue of public health, in much the same way as alcoholics should not be incarcerated but treated for their addiction. Although studies demonstrate that drug prevention and treatment programmes for addicts are twenty times more successful than interdiction, bilateral initiatives invest only tiny amounts in rehabilitation. In fact, the Bush administration, rather than extend funding to rehabilitation programmes, slashed them at the same time as the Mérida Initiative was being drafted (Carlsen 2008).

Government investment in social programmes like education, health care and infrastructure would be one way of spending taxpayer money to improve people's lives and alleviate some of the unrewarding toil, misery and other social problems that push people into the illegal economy. In a country in which there exist few employment opportunities for young people, it is not surprising that many end up working for criminal organisations. One way to address youth unemployment is by investing in infrastructure, services and social programmes. Nor should financial investment be designed solely to benefit foreign multinational corporations and the rich. Neoliberalism in Mexico has encouraged a programme of selling off the country – its land, resources and infrastructure – to the highest bidders. Creating the semblance of a healthy democracy in Mexico – as indeed elsewhere – should involve enabling a popular and more equitable control of resources and wealth, a thought that terrifies economists, bankers, politicians and drug traffickers.

Those concerned with a dignified future for Mexico, one in which human rights and social stability are vigorously protected, should understand the conditions that allowed the illegal market in drugs to thrive. Bilateral policy addresses neither institutionalised corruption nor the socio-economic problems that have empowered drug cartels, and it is doubtful whether spending on Blackhawk helicopters, surveillance equipment and training by the Colombian military will guarantee the security Obama and Calderón have promised in public pronouncements.

In 2011, extraordinary events took place in areas of the globe in which it had seemed that democratic openings were equally, perhaps even more hopeless. The Arab Spring toppled several dictators supported by the West – including Egypt's Mubarak, no less, supported by the EU, the USA and Israel. In the United States the birth of the Occupy Wall Street movement both responded to and seeded popular protests globally. These are signs that things can begin to change and improve, despite the selfish rhetoric of those with a vested interest in the status quo, including drug traffickers, who try to convince us that alternatives to the dominant global order – which they coincidentally control and profit from – are impossible. The Mexican political and business elites have proved over the first decade of this century, and throughout the entirety of its predecessor, that they are too corrupt, too enslaved to the international money market and too concerned with their own self-interest to be trusted to create policies that are genuinely in the public interest. They cannot be expected to provide a solution to problems they themselves created, and by which they have been so spectacularly rewarded.

Thankfully, there exists in Mexico a colourful array of vibrant and creative social justice movements composed of courageous individuals who, often risking their lives, fight back against a system of injustice, inequality and repression as they seek a better future. We should also look to those who participated in the *No Más Sangre* and *Indignados* movements, and those who refuse to believe that the current crisis was somehow inevitable and beyond explanation. Their outrage at daily injustice and a corrupt and seemingly untouchable political and business class could be a powerful weapon if wielded carefully and with reason and justice. The odds against these fragmented and often disparate movements are overwhelming, but must – and can – be overcome nonetheless.

Bibliography

Agee, P. (1975) *CIA Diary: Inside the company*. Harmondsworth: Penguin.

Aguayo Quezada, S. (1998) *Los archivos de la violencia*. Mexico City: Grijalbo.

—— (2001) *La Charola: Una historia de los servicios de inteligencia en México*. Mexico City: Grijalbo.

Aguilar, R. and J. G. Castañeda (2009) *El narco: la guerra fallida*. México: Punto de lectura.

Akers, J. (2001) 'Operation Gatekeeper: militarising the border', *International Socialist Review*, 18 (June–July).

Albarran de Alba, G. (2010) 'El narco es ya un poder politico y un desafio abierto', *Revista Proceso*, 24 October.

Alvarado Álvarez, I. (2009) 'Vulnerable, "blindaje" lectoral', *El Universal*, 16 February.

Amnesty International (2010) *Invisible Victims: Migrants on the move in Mexico*. London: Amnesty International.

—— (2011) *Annual Report on Mexico*. London: Amnesty International.

Aspe, P. (1993) *Economic Transformation: The Mexican way*. Cambridge, MA: MIT Press.

Astorga, L. (1999) 'Drug trafficking in Mexico: a first general assessment', Discussion Paper 36, UNESCO.

—— (2003) *Drogas sin fronteras*. Mexico City: Grijalbo.

—— (2005) *El siglo de las drogas*. Mexico City: Plaza and Janes.

Athey, L. E. (1984) 'Democracy in Latin America: promise and problems', *Latin American Research Review*, 19, 3.

Bacon, D. (2006) 'Oaxaca's dangerous teachers', *Dollars and Sense*, September/ October.

Bakan, J. (2004) *The Corporation*. New York, NY: Simon and Schuster.

Ballinas, V. and A. Becerril (2009) 'Infiltrados por el *narco*, 60% de los municipios', *La Jornada*, 28 May.

Banco de México (2007) *Las remesas familiares en México*. México: Banco de México.

—— (2009) http://www.banxico.org.mx/, consulted 15 November 2009.

Baranda, A. (2011) 'Matan, plagian . . . y estados se zafan', *Reforma*, 23 August.

Barkin, D. and E. Gustavo (1979) *Inflación y democracia: El caso de México*. Mexico City: Siglo XXI.

Baum, D. (1996) *Smoke and Mirrors: The war on drugs and the politics of failure.* New York, NY: Little, Brown and Company.

Becerril, A. (1996) 'Cayó 70% el poder adquisitivo durante 1996', *La Jornada*, 31 December.

Beith, M. (2010) *The Last Narco.* London: Penguin.

Benítez Manaut, R. (2011) 'El crimen organizado en México: amenaza a la democracia y la seguridad', *Mundo Nuevo*, 5: 31–45.

Blum, W. (2003) *Killing Hope: US military and CIA interventions since World War II.* London: Zed Books.

Bowden, C. (1998) *Juárez: The laboratory of our future,* New York, NY: Aperture.

—— (2010a) *Murder City: Ciudad Juárez and the global economy's new killing fields.* New York, NY: Nation Books.

—— (2010b) 'The war next door', *High Country News*, 1 March.

Brewster, C. (2005) 'The student movement of 1968 and the Mexican press: the cases of *Excélsior* and '*Siempre!*', *Bulletin of Latin American Research*, 21: 171–90.

Bricker, K. (2009) 'Mexican NGOs, Brigadier General, unite in letter against Plan Mexico', *The Narco News Bulletin*, www.narconews.com/Issue57/article3519. html, consulted 15 July 2009.

Broholm, S. (2010) 'Revisiting NAFTA: the gap between prediction and reality for Mexico's small corn farmers', *Journal of Politics and Society* (May).

Broz, J. L. and J. A. Frieden (2006) 'The political economy of exchange rates', in B. R. Weingast and W. Donald (eds), *The Oxford Handbook of Political Economy.* New York, NY: Oxford University Press, pp. 587–600.

Buendía, M. (1988) *La CIA en México.* Mexico City: Cal y Arena.

Bureau of International Narcotics and Law Enforcement Affairs (2009) 'The Mérida Initiative', 23 June, www.state.gov/p/inl/rls/fs/122397.htm, consulted March 2010.

Buscaglia, E. (2010) 'No sane Mexican would want to live in the US', *The European*, 15 October.

Buxton, J. (2006) *The Political Economy of Narcotics.* London: Zed Books.

Calderón, F. (2007) 'Primer informe de gobierno', www.presidencia.gob.mx, consulted 8 August 2011.

—— (2011) 'Quinto informe de gobierno', www.presidencia.gob.mx, consulted 8 September 2011.

Cameron, M. and V. Aggarwal (1996) 'Mexican meltdown: states, markets and post-NAFTA financial turmoil', *Third World Quarterly*, 17, 5: 975–87.

Camp, R. A. (1985) *Intellectuals and the State in Twentieth Century Mexico.* Austin, TX: University of Texas Press.

—— (1993) *Politics in Mexico.* Oxford: Oxford University Press.

—— (2007) *Politics in Mexico: the Democratic Consolidation.* Oxford: Oxford University Press.

Campbell, H. (2009) *Drug War Zone.* Austin, TX: University of Texas Press.

—— (2011) 'No end in sight: violence in Cuidad Juarez', *NACLA*, 44, 3 (May/June).

Campos, I. (2011) 'In search of real reform: lessons from Mexico's long history of drug prohibition', *NACLA*, 44, 3 (May/June).

Carrillo Prieto, I. (2006) *Informe Histórico a la Sociedad Mexicana – 2006.* Mexico City: Fiscalía Especial para Movimientos Sociales y Políticos del Pasado.

Carlsen, L. (2008) 'Armoring NAFTA: the battleground for Mexico's future', *NACLA Mexico Report* (September/October).

—— (2009) 'The perils of Plan Mexico'. *Counterpunch*, 24 November.

Castañeda, J. (1993) *Utopia Unarmed: The Latin American left after the cold war.* New York, NY: Vintage Books.

Castellanos, L. (2007) *México armado, 1943–1981.* Mexico City: Ediciones Era.

Castillo García, G. (2008) 'El narco ha feudalizado 60% de los municipios, alerta ONU', *La Jornada*, 26 June.

Centeno, M. A. (1994) *Democracy within Reason: Technocratic revolution in Mexico.* Philadelphia, PA: Pennsylvania State University Press.

Centro Prodh (2010) 'Sociedad amenazada. Violencia e impunidad, rostros del México actual', report, Centro Prodh, Mexico City.

CEPAL (2000) *Anuario estadístico de América Latina y el Caribe.* Santiago de Chile: CEPAL.

Chávez, M. F. and M. Huerta (2003) 'Tres modelos de política económica en México durante los últimos sesenta años', *Análisis Económico*, 18, 37: 55–80.

Chomsky, N. (1999) *Profit over People: Neoliberalism and the global order.* New York, NY: Seven Stories Press.

Cimet, A. (1997) 'Incomplete allowance: Jews as a minority in Mexico', *Estudios Interdisciplinarios de América Latina y el Caribe*, 8, 2 (July–December).

Cleary, E. L. (1997) *The Struggle for Human Rights in Latin America.* Westport, CT: Greenwood.

CNDH (Comisión Nacional de Derechos Humanos) (1998) *Informe anual de actividades mayo 1997–mayo 1998.* Mexico City: CNDH.

—— (2009) *Informe de Actividades 2008.* Mexico City: CNDH.

—— (2011) Press release 078/11, 'Más de cinco mil personas extraviadas', 2 April, www.cndh.org.mx, consulted 23 August 2011.

Cockburn, A. and St Clair, J. (1998) *Whiteout: The CIA, drugs and the press.* London: Verso.

Collier, R. B. (1992) *The Contradictory Alliance: State–Labor relations and regime change in Mexico.* Berkeley, CA: International and Area Studies, University of California.

CONAPO (Consejo Nacional de Población) (2008) www.conapo.gob.mx/, consulted 6 May 2008.

CONEVAL (2010) *Metodología para la medición multidimensional de la pobreza en México.* Consejo Nacional de Evaluacíon de la Política de Desarrolla Social. Available on line: www.coneval.gob.mx, consulted 18 August 2011.

Cook, M. L., K. Middlebrook and J. Horcasitas (1994) *The Politics of Economic Restructuring: State–Society relations and regime change in Mexico.* La Jolla, CA: Center for US–Mexican Studies, University of California, San Diego.

Cornelius, W. A. (2003) 'Politics in Mexico', in G. A. Almond *et al.* (eds), *Comparative Politics Today: A world view.* New York, NY and London: Longman, pp.469–520.

Coronado, R. (2011) 'Sócrates Rizzo admite narcopactos durante gobiernos priistas', *Milenio*, 24 February.

Cothran, D. (1991) 'Introduction', in S. Schmidt, *The Deterioration of the Mexican Presidency: The years of Luis Echeverría*. Tucson, AZ: University of Arizona Press.

Craig, R. (1980) 'Operation Condor: Mexico's anti-drug campaign enters a new era', *Journal of Interamerican Studies and World Affairs*, 22, 3.

Cuéllar Ramórez, N. (2011) 'Las bases argentinas del narco', *El Espectador*, 14 June.

Curzio, L. (2004) 'La integración en Norteamérica y la experiencia de Europa', in J. Roy and A. Chanona, *La Unión Europea y el TLCAN*. México: UNAM.

Davis, D. E. (1994) *Urban Leviathan: Mexico City in the twentieth century*. Philadelphia, PA: Temple University Press.

Davis, D. E. and V. Brachet-Márquez (1997) 'Rethinking democracy: Mexico in historical perspective', *Comparative Studies in Society and History*, 31: 86–119.

DEA (2000) 'Statement by William E. Ledwith, Chief of International Operations Drug Enforcement Administration, United States Department of Justice, before the Subcommittee on Criminal Justice, Drug Policy, and Human Resources', http://www.justice.gov/dea/pubs/cngrtest/ct022900.htm, consulted 8 September 2011.

Dean, M. (2010) 'El Banco Santander, salpicado por blanqueo de dinero de narcotráfico', *Diagonal*, 134 (30 September).

de la Fuente, J. R. (2009) 'La encrucijada Mexicana', *Foreign Affairs Latinoamérica*, 9, 4: 70–4.

de la Luz González, M. (2011) 'Delitos aumentan en el país, alertan', *El Universal*, 23 August.

de la Vega, M. (1997) 'Gutiérrez Rebollo insiste in relacionar con el narco la familia presidencial y a los titulares de la SEDENA y de la Judicial Federal', *Proceso*, 21 September.

Delgado de Cantú, G. M. (2003) *Historia de México*. Mexico City: Pearson.

Delgado-Wise, R. (2004) 'Critical dimensions of Mexico–US migration under the aegis of neoliberalism and NAFTA', *Canadian Journal of Development Studies*, 25, 4.

Demmers, J. (2001) 'Neoliberal reforms and populist politics: the PRI in Mexico', in J. Demmers *et al.* (eds), *Miraculous Metamorphoses: The neoliberalisation of Latin American populism*. London: Zed Books.

Democracy Now (2009) 'Obama reverses campaign pledge to renegotiate NAFTA', http://www.democracynow.org/2009/8/11/obama_reverses_campaign_pledge_to_renegotiate, consulted 18 August 2009.

Diaz-Cayaros, A., B. Magaloni and B. R. Weingast (2000) 'Democratisation and the economy in Mexico: equilibrium (PRI), hegemony and its demise', unpublished paper, Stanford University and UCLA, 2000.

Dillon, S. and J. Preston (2004) *Opening Mexico: The making of a democracy*. New York, NY: Farrar, Straus and Giroux.

Doyle, K. (2003a) 'La Operación Intercepción. Los peligros del unilateralismo', *Proceso*, 13 April.

—— (2003b) 'Nuestros años cínicos', *Proceso*, 6 July.

—— (2004) 'Rebellion in Chiapas and the Mexican military', National Security Archive Electronic Briefing Book No. 109, www.gwu.edu/~nsarchiv/NSAEBB/NSAEBB109/#article, consulted 8 September 2011.

Duménil, D. L. G. and D. Levy (2004) *Capital Resurgent*. Cambridge, MA: Harvard University Press.

DuRand, C. (2010) *Confronting Global Neoliberalism*, edited by R. Westra. Atlanta, GA: Clarity Press.

Economist, The (2010) 'Outsmarted by Sinaloa. Why the biggest drug gang has been least hit', 7 January.

Economista, El (2011) 'Delitos aumentan en el país, alertan', 23 August.

Edmonds-Poli, E. and D. A. Shirk (2009) *Contemporary Mexican Politics*. Lanham, MD: Rowman and Littlefield.

Ellingwood, K. (2008) 'Mexico traffickers bribed former anti-drug chief, officials say', *Los Angeles Times*, 22 November.

Esquivel, J. (2011) 'Una frontera llena de fosas', *Proceso*, 17 April.

Estevez, D. (1999) 'Los Hank, en la mira antidroga de EU; son un riesgo, advierten', *El Financiero*, 31 May.

Fabre, G. (2009) 'Prospering from crime: money laundering and financial crises', in E. Wilson (ed.), *Government of the Shadows: Parapolitics and criminal sovereignty*. London and New York, NY: Pluto Press.

Fazio, C. (1998) 'México: el caso del narco-general', in M. Jelsma (ed.), *Drogas, poder y derechos humanos en América Latina*. Quito: Ediciones Abya-Yala, pp. 75–104.

Feiling, T. (2009) *The Candy Machine: How cocaine took over the world*. London: Penguin.

Feinstein, D. (2011) 'Feinstein, Schumer, Whitehouse report calls for stronger US response to firearms trafficking to Mexico', press release, 13 June.

Forbes (2011) 'The World's Billionaires', www.forbes.com/wealth/billionaires/list, consulted 13 September 2011.

Foster, L. V. (2007) *A Brief History of Mexico*. New York, NY: Checkmark.

Fox, V. (2006) Presidencia de la república, Mexico, 'Sexto informe de gobierno', www.presidencia.gob.mx, consulted 15 February 2007.

Fukuyama, F. (1998) 'The end of history?' in G. Ó Tuathail, S. Dalby and P. Routledge (eds), *The Geopolitics Reader*. New York, NY: Routledge.

Gamble, A. (2001) 'Neo-liberalism', *Capital and Class*, 75: 127–34.

GAO (United States General Accounting Office) (1998) 'Raul Salinas, Citibank, and alleged money laundering', report to US Senate, Washington, October 1998, http://www.gao.gov/archive/1999/os99001.pdf, consulted September 2011.

Geier, J. (2000) 'Vietnam: The soldier's revolt', *International Socialist Review*, 9 (August/September).

Geneva Declaration on Armed Violence and Development (2004) 'Intentional homicide rates per 100,000 population, 2004', http://map.genevadeclaration.org/, consulted 10 August 2011.

Gibler, J. (2009a) *Mexico Unconquered: Chronicles of empire and revolt*, San Francisco, CA: City Heights.

—— (2009b) 'The hidden side of Mexico's drug war: an interview with ERPI guerrilla leader Commandante Ramiro', *Z Magazine*, October.

—— (2011a) 'Marketing violence in Mexico's drug war', *NACLA*, 44, 3 (May/ June).

—— (2011b) *To Die in Mexico: Dispatches from inside the drug war*. San Francisco, CA: City Lights.

Gil-Alana, L. and C. Pestana (2009) 'A historical perspective of inflation in Latin America: a new approach based on fractional integration with a structural break', *International Economic Journal* (Korean International Economic Association), 23, 2: 259–79.

Gilly, A. (2005) *The Mexican Revolution*. New York, NY: The New Press.

Giordano, A. (2000) '1994: the consolidation of narco-power', *The Narco News Bulletin*, 15 June, www.narconews.com/fraud1994.html, consulted 6 September 2011.

—— (2006) 'Mexico's presidential swindle', *New Left Review*, 41 (September/ October).

Global Commission on Drug Policy (2011) *Report of the Global Commission on Drug Policy*. Rio de Janeiro.

Golden, T. (1998a) 'In breakthrough, Mexican official testifies in Texas', *New York Times*, 15 July.

—— (1998b) 'US officials say Mexican military aids drug traffic', *New York Times*, 26 March.

—— (1999) 'Mexican, in US suicide note, blames Zedillo for his death', *New York Times*, 17 September.

Gómora, D. (2011) 'Narco mexicano supera a mafias de Italia y Colombia', *El Universal*, 28 July.

González, M. L. (2011) 'Delitos aumentan en el país, alertan', *El Universal*, 23 August.

González, R. (2011) 'Más 2.5 millones de mexicanos no laboraron ni una hora a la semana', *La Jornada*, 13 August.

González Amador, R. (1998) 'Los salarios, en el menor nivel de 38 años, revelan cifras oficiales', *La Jornada*, 22 November.

González Casanova, P. (1970) *Democracy in Mexico*. Oxford: Oxford University Press.

Grande, J. (2011) 'Matan a 174 funcionarios en el sexenio; 83 eran jefes policiacos', *Excélsior*, 11 September.

Grayson, G. (2010) *Mexico: Narcoviolence and a failed state?* Piscataway, NJ: Transaction Publishers.

Grugel, J. (2002) *Democratisation: A critical introduction*. Basingstoke: Palgrave.

Gutmann, M. C. (2002) *Romance of Democracy: Compliant defiance in contemporary Mexico*. Berkeley, CA: University of California Press.

Hagopian, F. and S. Mainwaring (eds) (2005) *The Third Wave of Democratisation in Latin America: Advances and setbacks*. Cambridge: Cambridge University Press.

Hamnett, B. R. (2006) *A Concise History of Mexico*, second edition. Cambridge: Cambridge University Press.

Hanson, R. D. (1971) *The Politics of Mexican Development.* Baltimore, MD: Johns Hopkins University Press.

Hanson, S. (2008) 'Mexico's drug war', report, Council on Foreign Relations, 20 November.

Harvey, D. (2005) *A Brief History of Neoliberalism.* Oxford: Oxford University Press.

Harvey, N. (1998) *The Chiapas Rebellion: The struggle for land and democracy.* Durham, NC: Duke University Press.

Heraldo de Chihuahua, El (2006) 'Dejó Fox en manos de Luis Echeverría los mandos de las policías "federales"', 6 April.

Hernández, A. (2010a) *Los señores del narco.* Mexico City: Grijalbo.

— (2010b) 'Una historia de corrupción y fracaso', *Por Esto!* 14 August.

Herrera, C. and J. Aranda Enviados (2007) 'Asegura Calderón que cumplió con la tropa, al aumentarle 46% el salario', *La Jornada*, 20 February.

Heywood, A. (2003) *Political Ideologies: An introduction.* Basingstoke: Palgrave Macmillan.

Hodges, D. and R. Gandy (1983) *Mexico 1910–1982: Reform or revolution?* London: Zed Books.

— (2002) *Mexico: The end of the revolution.* Westport, CT: Praeger.

Holloway, J. and E. Peláez (eds) (1998) *Zapatista! Reinventing revolution in Mexico.* London: Pluto Press.

Hufbauer, G. C. and J. J. Schott (2005) *NAFTA Revisited: Achievements and challenges.* Washington, DC: Institute for International Economics.

Human Rights Watch (2009) *Uniform Impunity: Mexico's misuse of military justice to prosecute abuses in counternarcotics and public security operations.* New York, NY: Human Rights Watch.

— (2011) *Ni seguridad ni derechos: Ejecuciones, desapariciones y tortura en la 'guerra contra el narcotráfico' de México.* New York, NY: Human Rights Watch.

Huntington, S. P. (1991) *The Third Wave: Democratisation in the late twentieth century.* Norman, OK: University of Oklahoma Press.

IFE (Instituto Federal Electoral) (2009) www.ife.org.mx/, consulted July 2009.

INEGI (Instituto Nacional de Estadística, Geografía e Informática) (1999) *Estadísticas Históricas de Mexico.* México: INEGI.

— (2011) Banco de información económica, www.inegi.gob.mx, consulted August 2011.

INSP (2009) Encuesta Nacional de Adicciones 2008. Cuernavaca: Instituto Nacional de Salud Pública (INSP), Consejo Nacional contra las Adicciones (CONADIC), Instituto Nacional de Psiquiatría Ramón de la Fuente (INPRFM), Fundación González Río Arronte, IAP.

Jiménez, G. (2011) 'Hay 126 alcaldes bajo amenaza; 23 han sido asesinados durante el sexenio', *Excelsior*, 4 February.

Karam, T. (2000) 'Comunicación y democracia en México: una introducción general', *Razón y Palabra*, 18.

Kenworthy, E. (1995) *America/Américas: Myth in the making of US policy toward Latin America.* Philadelphia, PA: Pennsylvania State University Press.

Kose, M. A., G. M. Meredith and C. M. Towe (2004) 'How has NAFTA affected the Mexican economy? Review and evidence', *IMF Working Paper*, International

Monetary Foundation, Washington, DC.

La Botz, D. (1995) *Democracy in Mexico: Peasant rebellion and political reform.* Boston, MA: South End Press.

LaFeber, W. (1993) *Inevitable Revolutions: The United States in Central America.* New York, NY: W. W. Norton.

Landau, S. (2003) 'Bush's new butt-kisser: adios Minister Castañeda, hello Professor Jorge', *Counterpunch*, 1 February.

Lemus, H. (2009). 'Renuncian alcalde y regidores de Tancítaro por temor a amenazas del crimen organizado', *La Jornada Michoacán*, 5 December.

Levy, D. and K. Bruhn (2006) *Mexico: The struggle for democratic development.* Berkeley, CA: University of California Press.

Livingstone, G. (2009) *America's Backyard*. London: Zed Books.

Loaeza, S. (1994) 'Political liberalisation and uncertainty in Mexico', in M. L. Cook, K. Middlebrook and J. Molinar (eds), *The Politics of Economic Restructuring*. La Jolla, CA: Center for US–Mexican Studies, University of California, San Diego.

Lunhow, D. and J. De Córdoba (2009) 'The drug lord who got away', *Wall Street Journal*, 13 June.

Lustig, N. (1998) *The Remaking of an Economy*. Washington, DC: Brookings Institution Press.

—— (2001) 'Life is not easy: Mexico's quest for stability and growth', *Journal of Economic Perspectives*, 15, 1: 85–106.

Lyman, M. D. and G. Potter (2010) *Drugs in Society: Causes, concepts and control.* Burlington, MA: Elsevier.

MacLachlan, C. and W. Beezley (1999) *El Gran Pueblo: A history of Greater Mexico*. Upper Saddle River, NJ: Prentice Hall.

MacLeod, D. (2005) 'Privatization and the limits of state autonomy in Mexico: rethinking the orthodox paradox', *Latin American Perspectives*, 32, 4: 36–64.

Malkin, V. (2001) 'Narcotrafficking, migration, and modernity in rural Mexico', *Latin American Perspectives*, 28, 4.

Martínez Elorriaga, E. (2009) 'Analizan diputados desaparecer poderes en Tancítaro, Michoacán', *La Jornada*, 6 December.

Méndez, E. (2007) 'Las drogas destruyen al . . . maíz', *Excélsior*, 29 October.

Meyer, M. and W. Sherman (2006) *The Course of Mexican History*. New York, NY: Oxford University Press.

Milberg, W. (2004) *Labor and the Globalization of Production: Causes and consequences of industrial upgrading*. Houndmills: Palgrave Macmillan.

Milenio (2002) 'Los protectores del narco, según El Chapo Guzmán', 2 July.

Miller, T. (2009) 'Mexico's emerging narco-state', *NACLA* report, 1 July.

Montemayor, C. (1991) *Guerra en el paraíso*. Barcelona: Seix Barral.

Morales, A. and S. Otero (2011) 'Le hallaron 88 armas a Jorge Hank Rhon', *El Universal*, 4 June.

Morley, J. (2006) 'LITEMPO: The CIA's eyes on Tlatelolco. CIA spy operations in Mexico', National Security Archive Electronic Briefing Book No. 204, 18 October, www.gwu.edu/~nsarchiv/NSAEBB/NSAEBB204/index.htm, consulted 22 August 2011.

Morton, A. D. (2003) 'Structural change and neoliberalism in Mexico: passive revolution in the global economy', *Third World Quarterly*, 24, 4: 631–53.

Muñoz, S. (2006) 'Mexico between the Left and the North', *Los Angeles Times*, 11 June.

Muñoz Ledo, P. (2010) 'El control de México lo tiene el narco, no el gobierno', *Periódico Bien Informado*, 4 May.

Murray, K. (2003) 'Mexico disbands anti-drugs force in drive against corruption', *The Independent*, 18 January.

Musto, D. F. (1991) 'Opium, cocaine and marijuana in American history', *Scientific American*, 24–27 July.

Needler, M. C. (1994) 'The consent of the governed? Coercion, co-optation, and compromise in Mexican politics', *Mexican Studies/Estudios Mexicanos*, 10, 2.

Newell, R., and L. Rubio (1984) *Mexico's Dilemma: The political origins of economic crisis*. Boulder, CO: Westview Press.

New York Times (1997) 'The Mexican drug scandal', editorial, 23 February.

Notimex (2011a) 'Crecen delitos de alto impacto: México evalúa', *El Economista*, 23 August.

—— (2011b) 'Denuncian incremento de feminicidios en México', *Excelsior*, 23 August.

Olivares Alonso, E. (2011) 'Llama la UNAM a signar un pacto para reorientar las instituciones de seguridad', *La Jornada*, 9 August.

O'Neil, S. (2009) 'The real war in Mexico: how democracy can defeat the drug cartels', *Foreign Affairs* 88, 4: 63–77.

Oppenheimer, A. (1996) 'The Banquet', excerpted from *Bordering on Chaos: Guerrillas, stockbrokers, politicians and Mexico's road to prosperity*, www.pbs. org/wgbh/pages/frontline/shows/mexico/readings/banquet.html, consulted 7 September 2011.

Organisation for Economic Co-operation and Development (2008) *International Migration Outlook*. Paris, OECD, pp. 262–3.

O'Shaughnessy, H. (2010) 'US waves white flag in war on drugs', *The Independent*, 17 January.

O'Shaughnessy, H., and S. Branford (2005) *Chemical Warfare in Colombia: The costs of coca fumigation*. London: Latin America Bureau (LAB) Short Books.

Osorno, D. (2009) *El cartel de Sinaloa: Una historia del uso politico del narco*. Mexico City: Random House Mondadori.

O'Toole, G. (2007) *Politics: Latin America*. Harlow: Pearson Longman.

Pastor, M. and C. Wise (2005) 'The lost sexenio: Vicente Fox and the new politics of economic reform in Mexico', *Latin American Politics and Society*, 47, 4: 135–60.

Paternostro, S. (1995) 'Mexico as a narco-democracy', *World Policy Journal*, Spring.

Philip, G. (2003) *Democracy in Latin America: Surviving conflict and crisis?* Cambridge: Polity Press.

Pimentel, S. (2007) 'Mexico's legacy of corruption', in R. Godson (ed.), *Menace to Society: Political criminal collaboration around the world*. Piscataway, NJ: Transaction Publishers.

Polaski, S. (2004) 'NAFTA's promise and reality: lessons from Mexico for the hemisphere', in J. Audley (ed.), *NAFTA's Promise and Reality: Lessons from Mexico for the hemisphere*. Washington, DC: Carnegie Endowment for International Peace, pp. 11–37.

Poppa, T. E. (1998) *Drug Lord : The life and death of a Mexican kingpin*. Seattle, WA: Demand.

Pozas Horcasitas, R. (1993) *La democracia en blanco: el movimiento médico en México, 1964–1965*. Mexico City: Siglo XXI.

Quezada, A. (1971) 'Vuelta a la confianza', *Excélsior*, 17 June.

Rachman, G. (2010) 'Why Mexico is the missing Bric', *Financial Times*, 15 February.

Ramírez, C. (2006) 'Intelectuales, "perros guardianes" del sistema', *Diario Transición*, 18 June.

Ramírez Cuevas, J. (2004) 'Liga Comunista 23 de Septiembre: historia del exterminio', *La Jornada*, 4 March.

—— (2005) 'Una huelga de hambre que hizo historia', *La Jornada*, 28 August.

Ramírez de la O, R. (2002) 'Mexico: NAFTA and the prospects for North American integration', *C. D. Howe Institute Commentary*, 172: 1–25.

Ramos Pérez, J. (2010) 'Cisen: 28 mil muertos por guerra a narco', *El Universal*, 3 August.

Ravelo, R. (2006) *Los Capos: Las narco-rutas de Mexico*. Mexico City: Debolsillo.

—— (2008) 'Vínculos García Luna – "El Mayo"', *Proceso*, 16 November.

—— (2010) 'Los narcos imponen su ley', *Proceso*, 1773, October.

Reding A. (1995) 'Political corruption and drug trafficking in Mexico: impunity for high-level officials spurs lawlessness and growth of drug cartels', opening statement before the Senate Committee on Foreign Relations, 8 August.

Reuter, P. (2009) 'Systemic violence in drug markets', *Crime, Law and Social Change*, 52, 3: 275–84.

Reyez, J. (2009) 'Mercenarios en el Ejército Mexicano', *Revista Contralínea*, 139 (12 July).

Richmond, D. (1997) 'Nationalism and class conflict in Mexico, 1910–1920', *The Americas*, January.

Ríos, V. (2007) 'Evaluating the economic impact of drug traffic in Mexico', www.gov.harvard.edu/files/MexicanDrugMarket_Riosv2-14.pdf, consulted 10 September 2011.

Rivera Ríos, M. A. (1986) *Crisis y reorganización del capitalismo mexicano: 1960–1985*. Mexico City: Ediciones Era.

Rockwell, R. (2002) 'The Fox factor', in E. Fox and S. Waisbord (eds), *Latin Politics, Global Media*. Austin, TX: University of Texas Press.

Rodríguez Munguía, J. (2003) 'Los muertos tienen nombre', *El Universal*, 2 October.

—— (2007) *La otra guerra secreta*. Mexico City: Random House Mondadori.

Ross, J. (2007) 'New massacres loom in Mexico', *Counterpunch*, 22 December, www.counterpunch.org/2007/12/21/new-massacres-loom-in-mexico/, consulted 8 September 2011.

Rubio, L. (2004) 'Democratic politics in Mexico: new complexities', in L. Rubio and S. K. Purcell (eds), *Mexico under Fox*. Boulder, CO: Lynne Rienner.

Saad Filho, A. and G. L. Yalman (eds) (2009) *Economic Transitions to Neo-liberalism in Middle-Income Countries: Policy dilemmas, economic crises, forms of resistance*. London: Routledge.

Sachs, J. (2001) 'New approaches to international donor assistance', speech delivered at International Development Research Centre, 19 June, www.idrc.ca/, consulted 31 August 2011.

Salas, C. and E. Zepeda (2003) 'Employment and wages: enduring the costs of liberalization and economic reform', in K. Middlebrook and E. Zepeda (eds), *Confronting Development: Assessing Mexico's economic and social policy challenges*. Palo Alto, CA: Stanford University Press.

Saxe-Fernández, J. (2004) *Tercera vía y neoliberalismo*. Mexico City: Siglo XXI.

Scherer García, J. and C. Monsiváis (1999) *Parte de guerra, Tlatelolco 1968: Documentos del general Marcelino García Barragán: los hechos y la historia*. Mexico City: Nuevo Siglo/Aguilar, 1999.

—— (2003) *Tiempo de saber: Prensa y poder en México*. Mexico City: Aguilar.

—— (2004) *Los patriotas: De Tlatelolco a la guerra sucia*. Mexico City: Aguilar.

Schlefer, J. (2008) *Palace Politics: How the ruling party brought crisis to Mexico*. Austin, TX: University of Texas Press.

Schmidt, S. (1991) *The Deterioration of the Mexican Presidency: The years of Luis Echeverría*. Tucson, AZ: University of Arizona Press.

Scott, P. D. (2009) 'Drugs, anti-Communism and extra-legal repression in Mexico', in E. Wilson (ed.), *Government of the Shadows*. London: Pluto, pp. 173–94.

Scott, P. D. and J. Marshall (1991) *Cocaine Politics*. Berkeley, CA: University of California Press.

Secretaría Ejecutiva del Sistema Nacional de Seguridad Pública (2010) http://www.secretariadoejecutivosnsp.gob.mx/, consulted 19 August 2011.

Shannon, E. (1988) *Desperados: Latin drug lords, US lawmen and the war America can't win*. New York, NY: Viking.

Shapira, Y. (1977) 'Mexico: the impact of the 1968 student protest on Echeverría's reformism', *Journal of Interamerican Studies and World Affairs*, 19, 4.

Siddique, H. (2011) 'Mexico drug wars have killed 35,000 people in four years', *The Guardian*, 13 January.

Skidmore, T. E. and P. H. Smith (2005) *Modern Latin America*. New York, NY and Oxford: Oxford University Press.

Solomon, J. (1999) *Systemic Injustice: Torture, 'disappearance', and extrajudicial execution in Mexico*. New York, NY: Human Rights Watch.

SPP (Security and Prosperity Partnership) (2010) 'Myths vs facts', www.spp.gov/myths_vs_facts.asp, consulted March 2010.

Stanford, J. (2003) 'The North American Free Trade Agreement: context, structure and performance', in J. Michie, *The Handbook of Globalisation*, Cheltenham: Edward Elgar Publishing.

Steger, M. B. and R. K. Roy (2010) *Neoliberalism: a very short introduction*. Oxford: Oxford University Press.

Stiglitz, J. (2002) *Globalization and Its Discontents*. New York, NY: W. W. Norton.

Stratfor (2008) 'Mexican drug cartels: government progress and growing violence', *Stratfor Global Intelligence* report, 11 December.

Streatfeild, D. (2001) *Cocaine: A definitive history*. London: Virgin Books.

STyPS (2008) 'Personal occupado en la industria manufactura por división de actividad económica'. *Secretaría del Trabajo y Prevision Social*. Available on line www.stps.gob.mx, consulted 5 November 2008.

Taibo, P. I. (2004) *68*. New York, NY: Seven Stories Press.

—— (2011) 'Narco violencia en México: ocho tesis y muchas preguntas', *La Jornada*, 15 January.

Toledo, A. (2004) 'Echeverría o el fascismo', *Milenio*, 20 June.

Toro, M. C. (1995) *Mexico's 'War' on Drugs: Causes and consequences*. Boulder, CO: Lynne Rienner.

Tremlett, G. and J. Tuckman (2001) 'Mexican police exposed as killers', *The Guardian*, 11 December.

Tuckman, J. (2011) 'Mexican President under fire after tycoon's release', *The Guardian*, 14 June.

UNCTAD (2009) *Handbook of Statistics, 2008*. New York, NY and Geneva: United Nations Conference on Trade and Development.

UNDP (United Nations Development Programme) (2004) *Democracy in Latin America: Towards a citizens' democracy*, Volume 2. Madrid: Alfaguara.

UN ECLAC (2010) *Statistical Yearbook for Latin America and the Caribbean*. Santiago, Chile: United Nations Economic Commission for Latin America and the Caribbean.

Universal, El (2011) 'El mapa de las fosas clandestinas', 28 April.

UNODC (2010) *World Drug Report 2010*. Vienna: United Nations Office on Drugs and Crime.

US Embassy in Mexico (2008) http://mexico.usembassy.gov/eng/eataglance_trade.pdf, consulted May 2008.

—— (2010) 'The Merida Initiative', http://mexico.usembassy.gov/eng/eataglance_Merida_Initiative.pdf, consulted 18 August 2011.

USGAO (2007) 'US assistance has helped Mexican counternarcotics efforts, but the flow of illicit drugs into the United States remains high', report, United States Government Accountability Office, 25 October.

US State Department (2009) 'Mexico – Mérida Initiative Report'.

Vanguardia (2010) 'Genaro García Luna: Afortunado e impune', 8 May.

Villalpando, R. and Castillo García (2011) 'Registra Juárez en 2010 la cifra más alta de feminicidios en 18 años', *La Jornada*, 2 January.

Vulliamy, E. (2010) *Amexica: War along the borderline*. London: Bodley Head.

—— (2011) 'How a big US bank laundered billions from Mexico's murderous drug gangs', *The Observer*, 3 April 2011.

Watt, P. (2010) 'Saving history from oblivion in Guerrero', *Monthly Review*, March.

Webb, G. (1998) *Dark Alliance: The CIA, the Contras and the crack cocaine explosion*. New York, NY: Seven Stories Press.

Weinberg, B. (2000) *Homage to Chiapas*. London: Verso.

Weiss, J. (1996) 'Economic policy reform in Mexico: the liberalism experiment', in R. Aitken *et al.* (eds) *Dismantling the Mexican State*. Basingstoke: Macmillan.

White House (2009) Office of National Drug Control Policy, www.whitehouse drugpolicy.gov/international/mexico.html, consulted July 2009.

—— (2010) 'Fact Sheet: US-Mexico discuss new approach to bilateral relationship', White House Website, www.whitehouse.gov/the_press_office/Fact-Sheet-US-Mexico-Discuss-New-Approach-to-Bilateral-Relationship/, consulted 21 February 2010.

Woldenberg, J. (2002) *La Construcción de la Democracia*. México: Plaza y Janés.

Womack, J. Jr (1999) *Rebellion in Chiapas: An historical reader*. New York, NY: The New Press.

Wood, D. (2002) 'La conexión de EU con la guerra sucia', *La Jornada*, 2 November.

Wood, T. (2011) 'Silver and lead', *New Left Review*, 70 (July/August).

World Bank (2007) 'Migration and Development Brief 3', report, Development Prospects Group, Migration and Remittances Team, World Bank, Washington, DC.

Yutzil González, I. (2011) 'Hogares, con ingreso más bajo en 10 años', *El Universal*, 16 July.

Zaid, G. (1990) 'Intelectuales', *Vuelta* 14 (November).

Zapata, F. (1995) *El sindicalismo mexicano frente a la restructuracion*. México: El Colegio de México.

Zermeño, J. (2011a) 'A diferencia de los tres últimos sexenios, actualmente México carece de un Programa Nacional para el Control de Drogas', *Reforma*, 26 June.

—— (2011b) 'Arroja guerra magros resultados', *Reforma*, 26 June.

Zeta (2011) 'Quinto Año de Gobierno: 60 mil 420 Ejecuciones', *Semanario Zeta*, December, www.zetatijuana.com/2011/12/12/quinto-ano-de-gobierno-60-mil-420-ejecuciones.

Index